The Four Quarters of the Night
The Life-Journey of an Emigrant Sikh

Tara Singh Bains is one of those rare people who sees the hand of God in every facet of his life. A man of strong convictions, he has consistently refused to compromise his own truth. *The Four Quarters of the Night* is as much the story of his faith as of his life.

Identifying himself as both an Indian and a Canadian but first and foremost a Sikh, Tara Singh has shuttled back and forth between Canada and India, finding personal harmony while incorporating two very different countries and cultures into his life. He was raised within an amritdhari, or baptised, Sikh tradition in a small village in Punjab, India; his values and identity are firmly rooted in Punjab Sikh culture.

Sponsored by his sister, Tara Singh emigrated to Canada in the early 1950s and settled in British Columbia. He came alone, without his wife and children, as most Punjabis did. His greatest initial shock in Canada was his experience with racism, and its impact on his relatives, who tried to persuade him to shave his beard and abandon his turban – two sacred symbols of the Sikh. Refusing to betray his beliefs, he resisted his family, just as he later fought against the exploitation of immigrants in the saw mills where he worked. Throughout the years he has been active in fighting for immigrant rights and speaking out for the Sikh faith in Canada.

The Four Quarters of the Night is more than one man's life story: his single voice reveals much about the collective experience of immigrants. Tara Singh's compelling narrative presents an evocative picture of a newcomer's experiences in a land of foreign customs, culture, and religious beliefs. Hugh Johnston, to whom Tara Singh told his story, has created a unique and invaluable document on immigration and ethnic history.

TARA SINGH BAINS is an Indian army veteran and a retired lumber worker and farmer who lives part of the year in Richmond, BC, and part in Punjab, India.
HUGH JOHNSTON is professor of history, Simon Fraser University.

D0223563

McGill-Queen's Studies in Ethnic History
Donald Harman Akenson, Editor

The Four Quarters of the Night

The Life-Journey
of an Emigrant Sikh

TARA SINGH BAINS AND
HUGH JOHNSTON

McGill-Queen's University Press
Montreal & Kingston • London • Buffalo

© McGill-Queen's University Press 1995
ISBN 0-7735-1265-9 (cloth)
ISBN 0-7735-1266-7 (paper)
Legal deposit second quarter 1995
Bibliothèque nationale du Québec

Printed in Canada on acid-free paper

Funding for this publication has been received from
the Department of Canadian Heritage, Multicultur-
alism Programs. Publication has also been supported
by the Canada Council through its block grant program.

The cassette tape recordings and notes from the in-
terviews for this book have been deposited with the
Simon Fraser University Archives, Burnaby, British
Columbia V5A 1S6, Canada.

Canadian Cataloguing in Publication Data

Bains, Tara Singh, 1923-
    The four quarters of the night: the life-journey of an
    emigrant Sikh
    (McGill-Queen's studies in ethnic history; 21)
    Includes bibliographical references.
    ISBN 0-7735-1265-9 (bnd)
    ISBN 0-7735-1266-7 (pbk)
    1. Bains, Tara Singh, 1923-   . 2. Sikhs – British
    Columbia – Biography. 3. Immigrants – British
    Columbia – Biography. 4. Immigrants – India –
    Punjab – Biography. 5. Sikhs – Ethnic identity.
    I. Johnston, H. J. M. (Hugh J. M.), 1939-   .
    II. Title. III. Series.
    FC3849.R53Z49 1995   971.1'00882946
    C94-900875-3   F1089.5.R53B35 1995

This book was typeset by Typo Litho Composition Inc.
in 10.5/13 Palatino.

*To the memory of my parents
Stafford and Jean Johnston*

Contents

PAHREI (THE QUARTERS)

In the first quarter of the night, my merchant friend, God cast you in the womb,
And you found comfort in His Name, recalling it with each beat of your heart.
You remembered Him and were saved by Him in the fire of the womb.
Then you were born into this life and your parents both rejoiced.
Remember who created you; with the Guru's help, reflect.
Says Nanak,
In the first quarter of the night, accept his Grace and think of Him.

In the second quarter of the night, my merchant friend, your thought began to stray.
As your parents fondly held you tight while boasting, "This child belongs to us."
They thought that you would care for them when they were old of age.
The fools were clinging to the gift while the Giver they forgot.
The being is rare who steadfast keeps both heart and thought with God.
Says Nanak,
In the second quarter of the night, a being like that will not know death.

In the third quarter of the night, my merchant friend, your mind was on your home;
You acquired riches and dreamed of wealth, but you lived a life that had no room for God;
You had no room within yourself for the Name of your final friend.
Yet worldly goods are all a sham. They pass and leave remorse.
We find the truth, by the Grace of God, along the Guru's path.
Says Nanak,
In the third quarter of the night, the mind through prayer will find the Lord.

In the fourth quarter of the night, my merchant friend, your time to leave is near;
You must make haste to serve the Lord, at once, before the night is gone.
Be His servant every moment, and dare not wait, for life eternal calls.
Annul the pain of death and birth: enjoy your bliss with God.
Conceive the Lord in the Guru's touch, which makes all worship sweet.
Says Nanak,
In the fourth quarter of the night, may your devotion bring forth fruit.

Guru Ram Das

Translated from Sri Rag Pahrei, composition of Guru Ram Das,
Sri Guru Granth Sahib, pp. 76–7

Foreword

I want to clear any misimpression from the hearts of people who are mentioned in this book. I have mentioned them to make a truthful and realistic story, and not with any prejudice or malice at my heart. For example, about my father, I am totally convinced that it was no fault of his that he treated me quite harshly. It was all predestined. As a matter of fact, I now feel that my life could have been otherwise if that treatment had not been part of it. It made me a better man. Similarly, for all other people mentioned, I have no ill feelings against anyone, whether in family or public life. If any pain, even unknowingly, occurs to anyone, I apologize, and I feel I will be forgiven.

In my mind it was the design and plan of Almighty Mother/Father to raise me in Punjab, India, as a Sikh and to transport me to Canada for the best part of my life. I respect and love Canada and India equally, and people to me are all brothers and sisters, no matter who they are or where they are from. I have learned, in my life, that Almighty is always helpful, and if I could attune my consciousness to Him, He created circumstances and resources to bail me out of difficulties. And I have also learned that if I started to think that it was my individuality that performed in different avenues and directions, then I deprived myself of His help. I am nothing at all. It is all Him. If the effort to present my experience can mould the thoughtfulness of even some individuals, then I feel it has been worthwhile.

Tara Singh Bains
Richmond, BC, 5 August 1991

A Word from the Amanuensis

Tara Singh Bains has lived between two cultures for most of his adult life. In the years since he first emigrated from India, at the age of thirty-one, he has shifted his residence from his native to his adopted country and back again many times. Now that he has retired, he is once again in India, but he returns to Canada nearly every year to see his children and grandchildren. Recently there have been many weddings in the family, and he and his wife have come for them. The pattern of his life, with its repeated shuttling between two homes, is one of his own choosing, but it has grown out of the general situation of his community, which has adopted one country without yet completely abandoning another. Among Tara Singh's people are many families that hold village property in their homeland, although they have been residents of Canada for several generations. Nearly ninety years after their grandfathers or great-grandfathers first emigrated, these families retain fields and buildings halfway around the globe. Some of their ancestral homes are falling into disrepair; some have been improved and are well maintained; but in either case the owners keep them because their identities spring from this land.

Tara Singh's life illustrates a collective experience, and putting his recollections down on paper has been a small exercise in immigration and ethnic history. His father came to North America early in this century and stayed ten years before returning home. Tara Singh's elder sister arrived in Canada as a young bride in the

1920s. Thirty years later she sponsored Tara Singh, and together they brought out five more siblings and their families and other relatives. Tara Singh's own wife and children stayed in India for many years while he worked in Canada, but eventually they all immigrated, along with a daughter-in-law and a son-in-law. Most of his near and distant relatives immigrated after 1967. Among Sikhs in Canada, particularly those who have settled in British Columbia, this history is common. More would have come earlier if it had been easier for them to enter the country. When it did become easier, people seized the opportunity, and what happened in Tara Singh's family happened many times over within his community.

I met Tara Singh for the first time in 1983 and saw him infrequently over the next four years. By then I knew a good many Sikhs. A casual interest in an exotic culture at my doorstep ten years before had deepened after I had written a book about the early history of Sikhs in Canada and, as a direct consequence, received many invitations to attend and speak at Sikh functions. That led to a research fellowship in India in 1983-84 and a struggle to learn to read and speak Punjabi. Over the years my sense of the human dimensions of the Sikh community had grown. But when the idea of presenting the life history of one of these people came to me, of all my acquaintances I thought first of Tara Singh. I knew that he had been active in Sikh organizations and that he was a man of strong convictions, which he expressed with eloquence – a compelling speaker in English and Punjabi. He is an amritdhari Sikh with full hair and beard, and I wanted that perspective. In September 1987 I asked him if he would be willing to record his life, and he immediately said, "God has brought us together to do this." He told me that this was something he had wanted to do, but when he finally had the time, he had too much pain in his back and shoulder to hold a pen or pencil except to write a brief note in a trembling hand. In his view it was no accident that I appeared at his door. What he wanted to share were the lessons of his life. He would not say that he was an important man or that what he had done should be given special notice, but he believed that what had happened to him could guide others if they knew about it and thought about it.

I came to Tara Singh with this book in mind because he was a practising Sikh whom Sikhs respected. A friend of mine, Sarj

Singh Jagpal, told me that when he heard people of an older generation mention Tara Singh Bains, he imagined a very big man, just by the way they referred to him. When he finally met him he was surprised to see someone so slight. What Tara Singh projected had nothing to do with his physical size. Even so, I did not appreciate how deep and authentic and absolutely central to his life his Sikhism was until he began to talk at length. What unfolded in this narrative of an immigrant was the story of his faith. This was what he wanted to tell, but with a detail that has made it social history as well. In his view family life, working life, community life, and spiritual life are all so interconnected that it makes no sense to describe one in isolation. His purpose is didactic. As a consequence, I have done my best to let his words stand on their own. The book would not have much value in his eyes if it included a contextual analysis that in any way detracted from what he said. None the less, I expect readers will engage in their own silent dialogue with him, frequently seeing events in a different light and often surprised by his rationale. The text in fact is incomplete without the side of the discourse that the reader provides.

This book is the result of a collaboration. Tara Singh has told his story and I have put it on paper, but I have been more than a recorder because, looking at me as he spoke, he was constantly reminded that he needed to explain and amplify for someone who did not know his culture well. If I had been a Punjabi, it would have come out differently. We arrived at the shape and content of this final version through a mutual exploration. I did not know what he had to say. He did not know how much I wanted to hear. In the beginning he thought that we would be finished in a few sessions. After I came back for the tenth or twelfth time, he knew that I had a large interest, and before we finished we spent a good part of sixty or seventy days together. We had most of our sessions in the living-room of his son Tarsem's home in Richmond, BC, and I did not leave that home once without eating. During our interviews he would lie on the floor to ease the pain in his back, or sit straight up on a hard chair, and late in the morning or in the evening the tape recorder would pick up the sound of Mrs Bains in the kitchen, kneading chapatis. On one occasion I told Tara Singh that I had an appointment downtown and would go as soon as we finished our work. He said, "It would bring pain to our hearts if, for the first time, you left our house hungry." So I stayed.

Over lunch or supper, when the tape recorder was not running, our discussion would often lead to another story, and when I asked if we could have that for the book, he might express surprise, but he was always willing and would repeat it, word for word, without missing a beat. These were stories that he had told before to his family and others, and they had a well-developed structure and purpose. Bringing them all to the surface, however, took time.

By the summer of 1988 we thought we were finished, and the Bains family invited my wife and me to dinner to celebrate. During that dinner Tara Singh described a dream in which he went to Mars on a spaceship and landed in a country that looked like Punjab, where he met Guru Nanak, the First Sikh Guru. I realized that we had not talked about dreams and that they were important to him. The next week I went back, and that subject led to others that involved another fifteen or twenty sessions. Some stories that he told me contained elaborations he did not give me at first but that emerged later on in other connections. We frequently returned to episodes of his life long after we thought we had completed them because a different aspect came up inadvertently in our conversation. Anyone who has tackled a similar project will know the process. We were following the pathways of memory, and the order that we achieved did not come immediately or automatically. When I finally produced a typescript, Tara Singh went over it carefully to make a number of corrections. He particularly wanted to add material to chapter seventeen, and we had two more sessions in the summer of 1991 to do that. The final text has been drawn from his memory. We did look in an old passport to confirm the dates of one or two flights; we used a brief diary in which he had listed the names of groups that toured the Vancouver Sikh temple in 1974; he showed me a couple of old letters; and a few times he checked with his wife to confirm the dates of births or marriages. Otherwise, his memory has been our only source.

This is his story as he recalls it and tells it. He has given it openly, and that for me is one of its great attractions. But he has not given it rashly. On a few occasions we shut off the tape recorder so he could speak about something that he did not want included, and there were intimate subjects that we did not tackle because I did not ask and he did not volunteer. He was conscious that what he said could have an impact on others, and he explained to me that, when elaboration served no good end, then it was best to cut the story short. At one point he told me that books make the best companions: when you associate with people, you see the worst of their behaviour; when you associate with people through the books they write, you see their virtuous side, and that motivates you to develop the higher aspects of your own nature. The reasoning was not what I had expected, but I could understand what he meant, especially when I looked at the kind of material he chose to read. I could also see that he was as honest as possible about himself. As he said, he had to describe his own faults and failings to give a complete picture. There was no merit in distortion.

Tara Singh's memory is much better than most. Part of the difference is that he is a story-teller, and it has been his nature and his role to share with others the lessons of his life. He has always found meaning in what happened to him and given that meaning dramatic expression. His recollections are connected and structured. They have a coherence that one would not find in a scattered mind. They have also been shaped by his own perceptions and understanding. One might stress the disadvantages of an autobiography based on memory, but I am more aware of the advantages. This one should be read for its subjectivity. Tara Singh has given significance to the events of his life. His understanding is the real subject-matter of this book.

A few of my colleagues have asked me why I thought his story had any value. What could one man's narrative tell us? Why should someone wishing to learn about Sikh religion or Sikh culture or about the immigrant experience pay any attention to it? My answer is that this book does not stand on its own. It is suggestive, not definitive. It might be a starting-place or something tackled later on, but it should be placed within the context of wider reading and experience. A personal document like this is rare. The same themes appear as in larger and more objective studies – particularly those concerning family, minority politics, immigrant–host-society relationships, and the confrontation of modern and traditional values. In this story, however, they appear within a context and with surprises that again and again remind us of the subtleties that a more abstract and broader study can not so easily capture.

Those who come to this book looking for material on Khalistan will be disappointed. Tara Singh's active role in his community ended shortly after Khalistan became an issue, and he doesn't

have much to say on the subject. I did not ask him for more because I thought that what he gave me truly reflected his own outlook and focus of attention.

Acknowledgments

The research for this book was assisted by a grant from the Social Sciences and Humanities Research Council of Canada, and it was supported and encouraged in a number of small but important ways by the Department of History at Simon Fraser University during the chairmanship of my colleague William Cleveland. I was able to make a side-trip to Punjab in the summer of 1991 thanks to the Shastri-Indo Canadian Institute, which invited me to give a paper at a conference in Shimla and paid my return airfare from Vancouver to Delhi. A number of people read the manuscript before it was submitted for publication, and I particularly want to thank Angali Bhelande, Michael Fellman, Harjot Oberoi, and Stephanie Walker for their thoughtful comments and suggestions.

During my interviews with Tara Singh I spent many hours in the home of Tarsem Singh and his wife Rajvinder Kaur and their children, Harleen, Mandip, and Keerat. Prakash Kaur was also living there at the time, and, of course, Bibi Karam Kaur. I shall always remember the warm hospitality extended to me by every member of that family, from the most senior to the youngest. I had the same experience at the home of Kuldip Kaur and her husband Balbir, where their daughter Ravinder Kaur was also living. Through this project I came to know many members of Tara Singh's extended family, and it has been a great privilege. My ultimate thanks go to Tara Singh for sharing his recollections so generously.

H.J.

Above, Tara Singh at the age of five in a formal family portrait taken in 1928 with his father, Basant Singh, centre, his father's mother, Kishen Kaur, on the left, and his stepmother, Swaran Kaur, on the right.

Right, formal portrait of Tara Singh and Bibi Karam Kaur taken in Rawalpindi in June 1947, six months before the birth of their first child, Kuldip Kaur.

Left, Tara Singh in Nanaimo, 1954.

Below, Hyde Park, London, 1976:
Tara Singh, Bibi Karam Kaur, and
Parkash with a cousin.

Above, Tara Singh and Bibi Karam
Kaur in 1986 with their daughter
Parkash on the right and their
grandchildren Ravinder, Keerat,
Harleen, and Mandip from left to
right.

Right, Tara Singh speaking at
Manjit's wedding in 1986.

Formal portrait of Tara Singh and Bibi Karam Kaur taken in Los Angeles in November 1988, during a visit with their son Manjit.

On the road from Kultham to Mandhali, with the village of Kultham in the distance, June 1991.

The Shahidan gurdwara, Kultham, June 1991.

The shrine of Kultham Abdullah Shah, June 1991.

Guard at the shrine of Kultham Abdullah Shah, June 1991.

Tara Singh's youngest brother, Santok Singh, at the entrance to the former family home in Sirhala Khurd, June 1991.

Entrance to the village of Sirhala Khurd, June 1991.

Havaldar Khem Singh School, June 1991.

PART ONE

A Punjabi

1 In Father's House

No roads led from Sarhala Khurd, the village where I was born, only cart tracks. My family has been there, right in the heart of the Hoshiarpur District, from the time of Maharaja Ranjit Singh, when the Sikhs ruled all Punjab. Father was putting up a pakka (brick) house at the time of my birth, and when it was finished it could be seen from afar, towering over the mud-walled homes around it. No other house compared. We even had our own well inside. People called father *pakkainwalla* on account of his three-storey brick house. They also called him Canadian because he had been abroad. In those days, returnees from America advertised their success by building big houses. Father had gone to Canada in 1908, and from Canada he had gone to California. Before he emigrated, he and mother had two children. The son died as an infant, but the daughter was nearly ten years old when father came back to Punjab in 1919. I was born four years after that on the sixteenth of February 1923.

My sister was married to a Sikh in Canada when I was four, so I don't remember her from my childhood. My mother died when I was a breasting infant, and I was raised by my grandmothers. First I would stay with nani in mother's village and then with dadi in father's village. When I was four, father remarried, and I got a stepmother to care for me. I was lucky to be born in a village with a primary school, even though a voluntary school without government funding. Havaldar (Sergeant) Khem Singh ran it. He was a villager born and raised, and a very patriotic Sikh who had served in the army and been discharged without a pension after he had protested because he had been insulted by an officer. Havaldar Khem Singh provided the school premises where he taught children from our village and from adjoining villages. In a big courtyard under a blue sky a couple of hundred children sat cross-legged on jute mats in lines of fifteen or twenty, with girls on one side and boys on the other. When it was too hot we moved to the shade of a veranda or into the school building or under a tree. There was a jaman tree in the courtyard and a neem tree and another fruit tree, and they provided enough shade for at least three classes.

When we started, we wrote with our fingers on mother earth. Later, to learn the alphabet, we used reed pens dipped in small pots of black ink, and we wrote on wooden slates. For mathematics we used stone pens on stone slates or, when I was older, black enamelled tin, but for beautiful handwriting in Urdu we needed wooden slates smoothly coated with gajani, a yellowish clay. A hundred feet from the school was the village well, where water ran continuously with the turning of a Persian water-wheel. When our slates were full we ran over to the well, wiped them clean, and recoated them with clay.

The elders of Sarhala Khurd provided some money to pay the salary of a second teacher who came from a neighbouring village by bike, but the school belonged to Havaldar Khem Singh. He was a majestic six-foot-three or six-foot-four inches tall, with a flowing beard and a striking way of speaking and teaching. I was aware of his self-discipline, his punctuality, and his strong Sikh faith, and his life impressed me, his dedication and service – how he gave his time, his effort, his buildings, and even, on occasion, his money. He had a deep sense of psychology. Havaldar Khem Singh was the greatest positive influence in my life. He used to explain my father's behaviour to me, and he was such a strong personality that my father would never contradict him in person, although he would disagree afterwards. I liked to go to school because it was a place of openness and appreciation for what you did. In those days teachers were respected by their students. I remember some of them and my heart glows with love.

The bronze bell for school rang three times in the morning before the start of classes, for a minute or two at a stretch. It rang for midday break and for the commencement of afternoon classes, and it rang at quitting time. It could be heard all over the village and for a good distance beyond. We could also hear the bell at Nangal Kalan, which was a mile and a half away. The school bell is associated in my mind with one of the beatings father gave me. He was a big man and had a violent temper. You could not even raise your eyes when he shouted orders. A little hesitation would bring heavy blows. If something small broke, he would strike you. The only reason I tell this about father is to explain what I learned at an early age – that children should be guided, supervised, advised, accommodated by their parents, not suppressed and jeopardized physically and psychologically.

One morning when I was seven I could hear the bronze bell ringing for the start of school. At the same time I felt the need to move my bowels. It was a cold winter morning, and there was a frosty crust on the village ponds. I ran out of the house, and after my motion I cleaned my bottom with some dirty pond water after breaking the ice. Father saw me, and when I was coming back he grabbed me and pulled me into the cattle enclosure. He had prepared a green stick, and he beat me like an animal. His wrath didn't cool as fast as it rose. He took the large crown of my long hair, divided it, tied a knot, and hung me over a peg and went on beating me. Only when some nearby men jumped the wall and released me did he stop. That was the kind of punishment he used to give.

At that age we were let out of school early, and in the evening we had time to play. The elders used to sponsor games – wrestling, soccer, and kabaddi, a team game in which one took a deep breath and ran to tag an opponent and then get back to the safety line without being caught and without taking a second breath. There was a playground in the village that was an acre and a half or maybe more. For grades five and six I walked a mile and a half each way to the adjoining village of Nangal Kalan. For grades seven and eight I walked three miles each way to Barian Kalan. The school day was long, so I generally went at sunrise and came back at sunset, but I used to enjoy the walk.

Ours was a small- to medium-sized village with seven hundred or eight hundred people, or about two hundred families. Half of them were farmers, members of the Jat caste. There were three Brahman families, but we did not employ Brahmans for ritual purposes because our village was mostly Sikh. One Brahman was the village doctor, who practiced ayurvedic, herbal, medicine. Another two were farmers. Aside from the farmers and the Brahman families, most of the villagers were lower caste or outcaste, some weavers, some carpenters, some blacksmiths, some spinners and sweepers. There were quite a few Muslims, and many of their men had worked abroad in Malaya, Sumatra, or Java and were living on their savings. Some poorer Muslims were leasing orchards from farmers and selling fruit. Some were street hawkers. When I was a boy the hired sweeper kept the village streets very clean, much cleaner than today. Since independence things have deteriorated.

Father did not always live in his own village. For a time, when I was in grade six, he stayed in my stepmother's village, Barian Kalan, where he had a house, and I walked from there to school in Nangal Kalan. One day my stone slate was broken by another boy. Someone was chasing him; he was running, and he accidentally stepped on it and broke it. I told teacher that it would be hard to go to father for a new one because he would beat me. Teacher said that the other boy should bring me a slate, but that boy's family did not agree, and the slate did not come for a month or so. I let my stepmother know about it, but she could do nothing. Father was too strong for her. After a while teacher became impatient waiting for me to bring a slate and started to give me some punishment every day, light punishment but upsetting for a small boy.

For a few days I stayed away from school. Someone told father, and he decided to put me straight in his own fashion. My stepmother tried to talk him out of it, but he was resolved. He took me into the room where the utensils were cleaned, shut the door from the inside, and beat me so hard with a stiff cane that I could not go to school the next day and the day after that. When I could go, he went with me, and lifted my shirt to show all the welts and cuts and blood. He wanted the teacher to see the kind of exemplary punishment he had given. Teacher was shocked and said, "Had I thought you were such a devil, I would have bought a slate for the boy myself."

I learned more from father's negative side than from his positive. It became imbedded in my mind that when I grew up I should control such excesses. Almighty had given me that gift of distinction. I saw in father what one should not emulate. He was a good hard worker, but he used to drive people too hard, and oxen. One side of him was religious, and he took part in the gurdwara liberation movement in the early 1920s, in the years of renaissance for the Sikh nation. In those days the British rulers were not popular among Sikhs because they supported the corrupt management of Sikh shrines and gurdwaras (temples) across Punjab. Sikhs travelling to North America learned to feel strongly about freedom in society, and they had only to look to their own religion for the right lessons. So Sikhs started movements against Britain. One was Ghadr Lahar and the other was Akali Lahar, or the gurdwara liberation movement. Father took part in the independence movement and the gurdwara movement. He joined in many marches, and he received beatings and went to jail several times. Once he escaped jail but was recaptured. All this happened before I was three years old, and I don't remember it except as stories, but after independence in 1947 father was given a freedom fighter's pension.

Father told me to memorize the morning prayer, the Japji Sahib, composed by Guru Nanak, our First Guru. It has thirty-eight verses and takes twenty minutes to recite. It was the only verse from the holy scriptures that I learned by heart before I became an independent person. Father made me do it; he ordered it; but it was a good thing. Sikhism was all around me. I came from a staunch Sikh family. My education began with Havaldar Khem Singh in a private Sikh school. I went to a Khalsa (Sikh) high school. In those days when we had the Akali Lahar and the anti-British movement, the renaissance of the Sikh faith was at a high level. Preaching, teaching, practising were the order of the day. There were big sessions at the village gurdwara. That influenced me quite a bit. Sikhism entered my mind, became established, and carried on, progressing, shaping, and becoming the fixed point, the axle of my life's vehicle.

Father said don't tell lies; be honest; yet I saw instances in which he defied his own rule. He said he wanted truthfulness, yet when you told him the truth he would hit you. He was harsh with my stepmother. He beat her for little things that were not her fault, and she could not do anything of her own will; she could not move a single step as an individual. He was manipulative, domineering, dictatorial, and suppressive, and he was abusive verbally as well as physically. He would call terrible names that hurt and that taught me that name-calling was as wrong as stealing and telling lies.

I used to get comfort from my stepmother. There was no girl in the house, so I helped with household chores, washing utensils, sweeping the floor, milking the buffaloes, and at an early age I even learned to cook. My stepmother's father and her grandfather stayed with us when I was a youth, and they offered help and kindness. Father's mother, my dadi, lived independently and kept her own milk buffalo and a goat, and looked after them herself. Grandmother died at the age of eighty-five when I was fourteen. Until then she had good health and a strong physique; she could chew dried corn, anything hard, until the end of her days. She also had a sharp personality, and she would defend me against father's cruelty.

Father had ten acres of land, which is a good property in Punjab. When I was small and when father was involved in the gurdwara movement, he did not farm his own land but rented it. In 1935, a couple of years before I entered high school, land consolidation came to our village, and we received a single block in place of our many small parcels. Father now took up farming. Because father had been in America and had worked with farmers there, his ideas of agriculture were more advanced than those of his neighbours. Our farm was designated a model farm quite a few times by the agricultural department. We came to spend most of our time there, waking and sleeping, and not in the big house in the village. On the farm father had to build shelters for the oxen and milk buffaloes, and quarters for farm workers. We could stay there, and for convenience we did. When I was in my teens, we planted a sizeable orchard of an acre and a half. We had oranges, lemons, pears, twenty-eight guava, about fifteen malta bushes, bananas, half a dozen fig trees, a dozen lokats, and plums. We also grew vegetables commercially, and we grew sugar cane. For father the farm came first. He was uneducated himself, and he saw no value in schooling beyond learning to read and write. I was the eldest son, and he wanted to use most of my time in the fields.

After I passed out of vernacular middle school at Barian Kalan (my third school), I entered Khalsa High School at Mahalpur, which was a police station and a town of five thousand or six thousand people on the highway five miles east of our village. As long as I went to middle school, I went by foot, although bicycles were becoming common. There were no buses, and I walked to high school too, until father finally bought a bike. Then I rode over the cart tracks with my brother on the crossbar or the back wheel. Khalsa High School was an English medium school. At the vernacular schools I had studied in Urdu. (At home I spoke Punjabi, but my Punjabi schooling ended in grade four.) To learn English I had to do two years extra. When I had completed that, I was ready to enter grade nine, but father threw up an obstacle. The school fees were only two or two and a half rupees a month, but he told me he would rather take me out than pay. I went to the principal with tears in my eyes and said, "My father won't pay my school fees." The principal, Harbhajan Singh, was a great personality, but his face was serious. He knew that father had land; he knew his financial situation; and he said that the rules of the education department made no exemption for a boy like me from a well-to-do family. I asked, "Does that mean the end of my education?" The tears were running down my face. That touched his heart and he said, okay, he would have to go out of his way to do something. And he did. He found an excuse in some corner of the regulations to charge just one brother when two were attending, and he gave the exemption to me because he knew that if he gave it to my younger brother, I would be withdrawn. The next year he exempted half of my fees and half of my brother's.

When I entered high school, I felt elevated. For me it was quite an occasion, and it opened up avenues of competition and achievement. There was the goal of high marks, and there was soccer. And high school gave me access to the surrounding world. I joined the scout band and went on a few service projects to fairs like the one at Anandpur Sahib, where at least a million people, mostly Sikhs, gathered together from all over India. That was exciting. Our high school was very famous in education and in sports, a top school in Punjab. I remember the visit of the director of education, Mr Armstrong, and I remember something our principal said. Mr Armstrong wrote in the log book of the school: "A visit to a school with spacious grounds and very nice buildings and courtyards, sturdy boys, a very nice staff, being headed by a very sensitive principal." (The last part I don't remember exactly, but most of it I do.) Immediately afterwards, our principal made the comment that Mr Armstrong, the director of education, had not used a verb.

In grade nine the optional subjects included sciences and physiology. I wanted to take those subjects, but there was an additional laboratory fee of half a rupee eight annas, and father would never agree to that. I had to go back to Urdu and Persian. It was also a punishment to be a good soccer player and not be allowed to play. I was a favourite with my principal for my sharpness, my hardworking nature, and my truthfulness. But I did not get extra hours of study at home. My principal once told my father, "Your son is very intelligent. He can rise very high in education. But he sleeps on the desk quite a bit. You don't let him sleep at nighttime." I would do my homework late at night, and father used to wake me up too early, generally at four or four-thirty in the morning, while it was still dark, and we would work for him for two hours before the sun rose. Then I would ride five miles to school with my brother on the crossbar. On Sundays, when we had a day off from school, he would have all kinds of hard labour lined up.

Even when I wrote my matriculation exams in March of 1941, a few weeks after my eighteenth birthday, it was the same. I had to get up at four in the morning, work for two hours processing the newly harvested sugar cane, ride with my brother to school, write my exam papers, generally two papers a day, each for three hours or more, ride back, help on the farm another two hours, have supper, sit down with my books for a couple of hours, and have four or five hours of sleep at the most. These matriculation exams were set by Punjab University in Lahore, the only university in all Punjab. There was a fee of forty rupees for students appearing for the exams. Father wouldn't pay, and, although I was eventually allowed to write, I felt great frustration beforehand.

Once I graduated, I was with father twenty-four hours a day, and that was worse than anything that had gone before. It was hard work, hard work, and say nothing. My principal was a recruiting agent for the military, and he told father that I could become a pilot officer in the air force because my marks were high (633 out of 750) and my English was very good (better than graduates of today). Father said no, and he told me he would dismiss all my inheritance rights if I defied him and left the house to enrol. His threat was a great blow because I had seen nothing of the outside world; I hadn't faced it, and couldn't imagine surviving in it alone. What I knew was from school, and that was theory, not practical experience.

One day, about two months later, father told me to yoke the oxen to the flour mill. There was one oxen-driven mill for the whole village, and he wanted me to get up at 1:00 a.m. so that no one else could get there first. He slept at the village house, and when he came out to the farm at 2:00 a.m. he found me still asleep and he was infuriated. My stepmother's old grandfather was still asleep too. This was after a hard day's work and without the benefit of an alarm clock. Father lashed out at great-grandfather with his tongue, but to me he said, "Okay, I'll finish you off." I couldn't see if he had the dagger with him because it was too dark. There was no moon at all. He may have had a stick, but he talked about the dagger. Knowing him, I was afraid. So I ran out of the house, and he chased a distance and threw something at me. On the other side of the orchard, in the real darkness of the night, I walked away from the farm towards the village. Father thought I would come back. Where could I go? He never thought I could do anything but come home.

At daybreak I walked to a relative's house in a village ten or twelve miles away. The name of the village was Domeli. Those relatives had once mentioned to father that they could use my help for a few weeks so they could go to West Punjab, where they owned some land. When I arrived at their door, I pretended that father had sent me. They were happy because I could milk the cows and buffalo and cook and manage the household. But it was the rainy season. Their village was on low land, and I caught malaria. It was a severe attack. One day I was lying on my charpoi by the cart track that ran past the fieldhouse where they kept the animals. A lady who was married in an adjoining village passed by on her way to her birth village, which was my birth village as well. She recognized me and talked to me, and she told my relatives that father didn't know where I was. They sent word to him, and he replied that I was dead to him and that he wouldn't let me in the house.

Years before, when I was eleven or twelve, father had engaged me to a girl in a village fifteen or sixteen miles away. Then he had a falling out with the mediator who arranged the engagement, a man from our village, and it was called off. When I was fifteen, I was engaged to my wife, who was born in the village of Kultham in Jullundur, also about fifteen miles away. My mother-in-law had died earlier. Father-in-law was a simple man, completely illiterate, who had lived in the United States for thirty-three or thirty-four years, until he was deported. He had also spent a few months in jail after the Indian government discovered that he had donated funds to the Ghadr (Mutiny) Party when he was in America. It happened, luckily for me, that there were two or three girls from my wife's village who were married into Domeli, the village where I was staying. Father-in-law found out that I was there, and he came. By that time the malaria fever had gone, and I was convalescing.

Father-in-law was so polite and so insistent, and he tried so hard to offer his help, I could only say to him, "Father, why do you want to push me back into a slave camp, and why do you want your daughter to go there too? My life is on a bed of thorns. Why do you want the same for your daughter? Nothing will be easy in my father's house." He was totally convinced that I was the only match; "Don't you see any moon in the rest of the world better than me?" He assured me that all would be okay, although I was certain that father would not let me back in the house without punishment.

Father-in-law visited the mediator who had arranged the engagement. (This man was related both to father and to father-in-law.) Together they went to father and persuaded him to let me come home. After a couple of weeks father-in-law came to Domeli and took me to his village and kept me there overnight, secretly. According to custom, I was not to see my wife before we were married, and neither she nor anyone else could know that I was in the village. Early the next morning he took me to the village of Mazaari. Our relative, the mediator, was the village collector, and I spent about ten days with him recuperating while negotiations continued with father to make sure that everything was all right. I had told a few horror stories about father, so people were concerned.

All went well. My marriage was arranged for that winter, and after my marriage I felt more manly and more independent. Father's threatening presence hung over me all the time, but I no longer had to fear physical beatings. The abuse came in verbal form. In those days the elderly people in our home, stepmother's father and her grandfather, were sympathetic allies. Father used to call them names, but he never dared to go too far because their age demanded some respect, and they were a great help on the farm.

Not long after I was married, the principal of Khalsa High School spoke again to father about enlisting me in the armed services. This time he said there was still a good chance, with my marks, of entry into the army medical corps. High-school graduates were being enrolled directly as junior commissioned officers, second lieutenants or jamedars, as they were called by the British Indian Army, with one star as their rank badge. If I enrolled in the medical corps as a jamedar, I would immediately receive thirty months of instruction on medical science. Father agreed, and I was full of anticipation and prayed and prayed. All the arrangements were made. We were supposed to catch the bus to the recruiting centre in the morning. I rose early, feeling that the moment of my emancipation had come, and I did the house chores, starting the fire, churning the buttermilk. When mother got up I asked why father did not come. She said, "He has cancelled his plans." He had told her that the day before, when he had been coming back from the tahsil (subdistrict) court in Ghar Shankar, he had met my wife's cousin. (Father was constantly in court with property disputes and financial disputes; he was fond of litigation.) According to father, this cousin said that my wife's family wanted to send her in a few months for the muklawa ceremony – which was a married couple's introduction to living together – and they didn't want me to join the army. Later, I realized that father had never intended to let me go, and this story of a conversation with my wife's cousin was a total fabrication. The only reason I can think of for what he did was that I was his main worker, although I had three younger brothers, and he did not want to lose my labour. That morning, when mother told me he had cancelled his plans, the words fell on me like death.

None the less, the day came when I went to my wife's village and got her. The muklawa ceremony was a wise system for helping a couple to adjust at the start of married life. It could fall within a year or three years or more of a marriage, depending on the age of the bride and the groom, and it had this value, that the bride and groom, when separate, burned with desire to see each other. My wife stayed about three weeks. For the first few days I could not meet her because she had to be baptized. Then we were together until she went back. She was such a nice person, and the affection that was so abundant in my mind had an outlet at last, and I had a measure of it, for life, to live for. She was what I would call an old-fashioned girl, but she had a primary-school education, which was rare in those days, and we could communicate our love in letters.

A few classmates from my village were working in the Bata shoe factory near Lahore. That was good work. So I asked them, "If I leave my house, can I stay with you till I get employment?" We made a plan, and I slipped from the house. I knew where father kept money, but the eternal soul guided me not to take it. One youth who was a little older and in the army was on vacation. I told him my story and he offered clothing, but it did not fit. Then I went to a merchant in an adjoining village where father used to buy whatever cloth he needed on credit, and I got enough for a couple of shirts, trousers, and a turban. Later on father said so much about that – that it was a kind of theft. But I didn't get too much, only bare clothing. I gave the cloth to the village tailor, who was sympathetic. He made shirts and trousers and did not charge anything.

After getting these clothes sewn up, I went to my wife's village and said that I could not take it any more with father and wanted to go to the army. My father-in-law and the uncles of my wife and my wife did not want me to do that. They were afraid because there was a war going on, and my wife wept. So I went to Jallo, which is a station on the grand trunk railway line of India fifteen or twenty miles east of Lahore. In Lahore I got work at Bata Shoes in the children's shoe section on a stapling machine. I was earning ten or twelve rupees a week and staying in company quarters, where six or seven of us were batching together, cooking our meals in turn. I was taken on to the company soccer eleven and once was made captain. That was the first glow of independent life. But there were too many mosquitoes in our quarters, and I got malaria again. I tried to treat the malaria, but my means were too scant, and I had to quit. I wrote to my wife, and her family asked me to come to their village.

My wife's cousin approached father and again negotiations, counselling, and shuttling back and forth created a situation in which I was to go back to father – this time with a more liberated mind. The two families decided that I should bring my wife to my father's home for two or three months. This was for trauja, the third ceremony in a marriage, coming a year or so after the muklawa ceremony. As with the muklawa ceremony, the bride comes with gifts from her parents. We were surrounded by caution in our married life in those three months. Father ordered me to stay in the farmhouse while my wife slept at the house in the village. That carried on for a few weeks until some good relatives spoke to father and I was allowed to come home at night. But there was enough time together, those couple of months, and I drew up the map of my life. I said, "Don't worry. God will not forsake us. We have been tied together in this wedlock not by coincidence but He imposed this wedlock, so it is His plan."

After a time she had to go back, according to the custom. A few months of working brought wheat-threshing time in the pitch of summer. Father would not spend money for my medicine, and for lack of treatment the malaria entered my spleen. An attack of fever came at noontime, when my labour was needed for threshing. Father had gone to district court. My brother and grandfather were working at the threshing, but I did not join them. It was around 4:00 p.m. when father came home. The Persian water-wheel was turning for irrigation, and I was washing my hair with buttermilk at the edge of the well. When father learned from my brother that I had not worked, he thought I must have pretended to be ill. He had a strong lathi in his hands, and without argument or speaking to me he gave me a full blow with that rod. With divine help it scratched my ear only. I didn't know he had come and didn't see him. I jumped to my feet and ran. "What a lucky fellow," father said. "He didn't fall in the well." Had he hit me squarely, I would have gone in.

I ran through the orchard, but father knew I couldn't go anywhere. I was naked and my hair was smeared with buttermilk. The problem was to get a shirt. Then I remembered I had one. At that time of year the oxen and other animals were tied in the fields for fertilizing, so we had beds in the field and I had a shirt under my pillow. I sneaked through the orchard and picked up my shirt and came back to a distance of sixty or seventy yards from the well. With full blast of voice I shouted, "I am going – leaving the house." Father ran after me. He shouted crudities at me and threw lumps of earth. Younger brother also called names, and the two of them were running after me. This was the first time I had revolted openly, and while I did not use any crudities, I shouted back stern words. I called him "slave-driver" and things like that.

The wheat had been harvested and the fields were all open. I ran through the fields until I came to the perimeter of the village, a race of two hundred or three hundred yards. At the perimeter of the village four of my cousins and two of my uncles were standing by a Persian water-wheel. They had seen the whole drama, and when I reached them they said, "Don't go any further. We will protect you." Father yelled at them to stop me. He said he just wanted to talk. My two uncles, one older than father and one younger, took an oath from him that he would use no force, no stick, only fair language. Then the argument started. By that time I was quite liberated, and what I said infuriated father so much that his anger superseded his pledge. He was leaning on his lathi with one hand against on his hip, but I noticed the other hand was moving. All of a sudden he blew the trigger and swung the lathi with full force. I jumped like a frog, and the stick grazed the knee of a cousin. He called father names, and my uncles and other cousins told him how shameful he was. "What a man. He is a religious man and he went against his pledge."

I said, "There is no way I can be with him," and I stayed openly with my cousins in the village. This was the summer of 1944. I borrowed ten rupees and told my cousin, "I will return this if I live." With the ten rupees I purchased from the same shopkeeper as before enough cloth for new clothing, and then I walked to my wife's village. There I had a discussion with my father-in-law and with my wife's uncles and told them that there was no alternative but to enrol in the army. Finally they agreed.

My high-school principal gave me the date when the army recruiters would be coming to our district. They had a touring program and they used to fix a time and place in each district and announce it. The night before I enrolled, I slept in the village where my wife's cousin was married. I got up about 2:00 or 3:00 a.m. and walked in the early morning darkness for seven miles through foothills country with wild animals on either side. God gave me courage and protection. A group of us gathered on the main road at 6:00 a.m., and one of the teachers went with us to the recruitment centre. I was enrolled as a havaldar clerk (a sergeant with three stripes) in the ordnance corps. I couldn't get a junior commission at this time because only quality BAs were being taken in for commissioned ranks. A year before I could have had one, but I missed due to father's decision, suppression, and control.

From the transient depot I was transferred about a thousand miles away from my home to Jabalpur in central India, where there was a big Ordnance and IEME (Indian Electrical and Mechanical Engineers) training centre. There I learned that I was transferred to the IEME side. Freedom of life, total glow of life, started with my army career. It was total relief and total happiness and relaxation too. I was by nature a hard worker, god-gifted to perform my duty honestly and to the maximum of my strength. At the same time, I was impregnated with religious orientation. Even when I was a little child I was attuned that way. I carried on my religious life very regularly, although not perfectly. I tried to get up before the others, take my bath, complete my prayers, all before sunrise. Morning physical parades, obstacle races, rifle training, lmg (light machine gun), training, everything went on like that for months. This was a nine-month training period. And during the day there were theory classes that lasted pretty near five hours a day.

For the first three months of our training, before our exams, office-side clerks and stores-side clerks were together. After that, the top half of the class were diverted towards office training while the lower half went to stores – stores accounting, receiving, maintaining, issuing, and so on. With His gift of brains, I was number one, with marks close to 95 per cent, and I was the first one in my class to go for my classification session with Major Oates. He was a First World War veteran who had lost his left arm up to the elbow in the war. Prior to my classification I had gone to him because I had a burning desire to become a technician, an artisan, whichever way I could. I was willing to give up my stripes and take a cut in pay to transfer into mechanical training. He was a very nice gentleman, but he said that it was not in his jurisdiction. The commanding officer was Lt-Col. R.N.G. Scott. I appeared before him and he said, "No. We need you where you are now."

At classification time I asked for Mr Oates to put me into technical stores instead of office training. He laughed and said, "Well, it is a problem for me because students with top grades are needed on office side for mapping, correspondence, and this and that." I wanted to be in stores to be in touch with technicians to learn the technical side. I can't remember the words I used politely to argue with him. But I convinced him after more than five minutes. He said, "I don't know why I am convinced. You are the first and perhaps the only one from the top of the class that I am converting to the technical side."

After the training I had two months' leave, and I took it without knowing what my posting would be when I came back – whether it would be to an operational theatre or not. I went to my wife's village because I had mutinied against father when I left the house. My time in Jabulpur had been a free exercise in writing letters to my wife. This chain of letters deepened us in love and understanding. The gap in distance deepened the desire to see each other. Too much closeness sometimes creates quick trouble. It doesn't give time for adjustment.

After I came back to my wife's village on leave, my father-in-law and my wife's eldest cousin shuttled around to father with some elder relatives. I told them I would go back to father only if I had a separate place. Finally father gave in. My father's younger brother was not married, and he lived in Malaya. I have only vague memories of him, but his nature was cool while father's was fiery. They were totally different personalities. Father once broke his brother's arm and did not say a word. Father had bought a couple of good oxen, and uncle fed them with green corn, which can make an animal bloat, so father struck him with a stick. After that uncle left for Malaya, and he never returned and never made a claim on the inheritance. By rights he was half owner of the property of ten acres. He still had a house in another corner of the village, well away from father. It was empty, so my wife and I went there with all we got from the dowry – a bed and bed coverings. The rest went to father. We cleaned and repaired uncle's house and happily lived in it for a few weeks.

When my leave was over, my wife's cousin, my brother-in-law, came to Sirhala Khurd and put our possessions in father's custody, although I had not agreed to do that. I had a hunch father would not give those things back once he had them, and I was right. Brother-in-law said they would be under lock and key. But father emptied the storage bin and used all my belongings and kept them. After that, when I was on leave, I stayed at my wife's place. My younger brother served as mediator whenever I went to father's house. Every time I came, father demanded money, and I would give him all my savings. He was greedy for the gifts and money I brought and for the work I did on the farm.

2 Army Service

After my first leave I joined the Fourteenth Indian Division at Chhindwara, right in the heart of central India in real hilly country where the summer climate is hot and humid. There were huge chunks of forest with teakwood and bamboo and lots of monkeys and langurs, and the odd time we would see a tiger. It was ideal for training to withstand the tropical exposures of the Burma front. That is why this far-flung place was chosen for the Fourteenth Indian Division.

We used to call it the nanga, or, in English, the naked division, because, in preparation for Burma, everyone, with the exception of the mechanics, had to take off his shirt and undershirt as soon as the morning cool went off the land. Everyone in the division had to do it, regardless of rank, except for technical personnel who had to handle chemicals or hazardous objects. As a technical storekeeper I was exempt and could wear coveralls during office hours, but for morning parade and in the late afternoon no shirts were allowed, just shorts.

Here was a funny game because, at Chhindwara, I had the privilege of working and living side by side with the British. Where our workshop was located we had a complete anti-aircraft regiment that was 90 per cent British; their mess was very close to our quarters, and in our workshop we had British officers. We saw the British having a very rough time without their shirts in the hot sun in this mountainous plateau area with its rocky soil, which held the temperature and bounced it back into the environment. The broken soil of a farming area does not react that way. The British personnel were used to a cold climate, and their skin would burn quickly and they would get boils on the body, sometimes up to two inches long. It happened particularly to the new arrivals. I remember a second lieutenant named K.F. Roberts, a young boy in his early twenties, around the same age as myself, whose body looked like a big lump of swollen boils even though he was in our workship unit and his duties kept him in the shade. We were near the parades and practices of the anti-aircraft regiment, and quite a few of those men had the same problem, and they envied our skin then.

The commanding officer, Major-General A.C. Curtis, had been a cobbler. So the slogan of the camp was "Fucking cobbler." It was an order of the day; you could hear it everywhere the British went, and it amused us. When they were not on duty, walking two or three together, that was language that should have been recorded. Then, in the evening, as a precaution against malaria, everyone had to wear complete uniform, including pants and socks and full sleeved-shirts. For evening roll-call we had to be in proper dress. And again the British had a problem with skin that had been cooked in the sun all day, and you could hear their complaints. They used to talk to us, and we knew how they felt.

The total strength of the division was eighteen thousand to nineteen thousand men in three brigades. We were training under field conditions, and the whole division was in tents. The kitchens were under temporary abutments, and lavatories were just dug out of the ground. My superior in the stores, Gurbuchan Singh Dahab, and I had a tent under a banyan tree. In the tent behind us was a junior commissioned officer, a Sikh jamedar, who was responsible for discipline. Behind his tent was a serpentine khadi or ravine about six or eight feet deep.

The jungle wilderness had all kinds of wild life. The monkeys were very naughty, and we had to save ourselves from them all the time. They would steal from us in open daylight, while wolves and jackals would come by at night to get food and garbage. And one time a tiger came up through that ravine looking for a meal. Generally we used to get our rations of meat on the hoof. The British were supplied with frozen or dehydrated beef, so there was no fresh meat for them, but we butchered our animals ourselves. And as we were a combined unit, the Hindus and Sikhs used to do the butchering together and the Moslems separately. A goat of our rations was tied to a tree until it could be killed on the weekend. Only a few days before we had heard that, in a camp twenty miles away, a tiger took their goat. We rose in the morning and ours was gone. When goats are attacked, fear stops their voices and they don't call out. The tiger had dragged our goat about a hundred yards into the ravine before eating it, and the balance was still there.

That evening we had a soccer game, and I was well exercised and had a good sleep. Now it happened that I slept straight flat on my back and the hands got interlocked over the heart. If that does happen, it is a dangerous thing. A heart attack can come, and it usually comes with a dream. I had read a few books of Indian research, so I knew it. When the pressure on your heart happens, before the pumping system stops, at that time you generally have a dreadful dream. In India, particularly among the superstitious, there are cult people who claim to control bad dreams through occult powers. Most of them are pretenders, because in front of the ordinary person it is easy to play the juggler. It is better that a person should not sleep on the back. Now, even when I lie down for reading, I try to keep the hands at the side.

When I was sleeping on my back with my hands clutched over my heart, a dream of a deeply impressed thought came in direct form into my mind. This happened within seconds. A tiger grabbed my complete head in its wide-open mouth. I started to moan, and from my tongue came the very sound I would have made if I had been caught in a tiger's mouth. It was so loud that it woke up people in the adjoining tents. That became the story the next morning. My companion, Gurbuchan Singh Dahab, understood what was happening, and he got up quickly from under his mosquito net to pull my hands apart. It took a lot of force, although I could hear his voice, "Wah Khalsa! Wah Khalsa! What's happening?" My heart was pumping in a way I had never experienced in any physical exertion, and I was on the verge of extinction. The superstitious would say that an evil spirit had attacked me, but it was just the pressure on my heart.

I used to call Gurbachan Singh "Bhai Ji" (brother) because he was older and also senior to me at the stores. He used to call me Khalsa, which is a good name for a strong Sikh. I was a revolutionary type, not an irritated type, but I would get into situations where I would correct things, and that is why he called me Khalsa. Each brigade in the division had its own electrical-mechanical engineers' workshop and supply and transport units. Of course there was the big central workshop of the division, generally called the infantry workshop, and this would have three hundred to four hundred mechanics. I was with the 109 Light Aid Detachment LAD Type E, which used to maintain the transport for one brigade. This unit had about one hundred personnel with a British captain or major in command and three or four British sergeant-technicians. One of these sergeants was an electrician, and another was a warrant officer. The electrician, Sergeant Clelland, was extremely short-tempered and would blow up over minor things. All the Indian tradesmen, including myself, were upset with his remarks all the time.

My counter faced the main workshop so that all the technicians could get parts directly from my lorry. It was a mobile camp, so all stores were in lorries. One day, after I had watched Sergeant Clelland abusing two Indian NCO's, one of then a havaldar with three stripes like himself, he came over to my counter and showed me a headlight bulb, but from the filament side, not the contact side. I happened to bring him the wrong type, a single contact instead of a double. I was standing on the tailgate of my lorry, and he jumped to his feet. "You bloody bastard Indian," he called me, and so many more names; "you're all chips off the same block." Without a thought, I hit him with the glass bulb right in the face. It caught him on the right cheek and opened up a gash. He was bleeding and the blood was flowing profusely, but I wasn't afraid of that.

Naturally, this was a serious matter according to army law. After Sergeant Clelland had been given first aid and been bandaged up at the hospital, the two of us were taken before Captain Williamson, the commanding officer, who gave us a lecture for five or ten minutes about how they were trained in England to take responsibility and keep their cool and this and that, and how the same was carried to the Indian Army. When a man is brought before an officer in such circumstances, he should stand at attention, but Sergeant Clelland was standing at ease, and he lit a cigarette. Now here the secret help came to me. When the captain finished, I said, "Thank you, Sir. I agree with your lecture and I abide by that. But I have a request." The captain said, "Yes, go ahead?" Then I asked how it was that Sergeant Clelland was not observing the type of military discipline he learned in England. "He is standing at ease and he is smoking a cigarette." My words made their point. Captain Williamson hit his table hard with his fist, and Sergeant Clelland leapt to attention and dropped the cigarette. Then I explained the whole situation, and witnesses whom Clelland scolded every day came forward and gave their statements. Finally Captain Williamson made peace between Sergeant Clelland and me by telling us to shake hands.

At that time, when we were in front of Captain Williamson, Lieutenant K.F. Roberts was there and he listened to the whole thing. Roberts had been a second lieutenant when he was first attached to our unit, but now he was a lieutenant. He was a good soccer player and he loved my play, but he was too temperamental, unlike Williamson, who was a well-tried, well-balanced officer. Soon Williamson became a major and was posted somewhere else, and Roberts became a captain and took command of our unit. He used to try to test me to find flaws in my office work, and I later learned that he put some red entries in my documentation. I don't know what jealousy he had, because he liked me on one side, yet he had a hidden motivation. One day he asked for some good Indian striped cloth for his pyjamas, from our Indian canteen. I brought it, and there was a party in his tent. Although he invited me, I did not join the party because a couple of times he had bullied me about some other things. Then he came to my tent and tried to convince me. I said, "I have nothing against you. Can we compromise?" and he said, "Let's have a friendly game today."

So we had a soccer game. He wanted me to be on his side, but I said, "No. I'll be on your opposite side." He was playing fullback, and every time I took the ball he came after me, and I knew he was in a full-fledged contest with me. When he came with a rush one more time, I side-stepped cunningly, and he rolled over three or four times on his bare back and received some severe lacerations. He couldn't say anything because it was his fault. I think it bothered him that I was not inferior in any field, either in office work or on the playing fields or in discipline. That must have been the reason. Otherwise he was friendly on the surface.

Perhaps he thought I was a revolutionary. Once my kit was searched and nothing objectionable popped up. Then I was posted to another unit in the same division that wanted me for my soccer game. K.F. Roberts was promoted to major, and he was posted to another unit. One day he came to my unit. I was putting newly received stores into the proper bins in my lorries. All of a sudden here was Major Roberts in front of me. He used to call me Gorgeous all the time. That was my nickname in his books. That day also he called out, "Hello, Gorgeous." I tried to stand up, but he said, "No, no. I didn't come as Major Roberts. I have come as Mr Roberts, as a friend of Tara Singh." He owed me four rupees for the cloth I had brought to his tent some time before, and he used the excuse of the four rupees to come to meet me. His face was friendly, and he was apologetic. Then I said, "You have made some red entries into my documents." He said, "Well, it's too bad. I was given some wrong impressions in England about Indians. I was told to suppress them, particularly the sharp Indians."

Although there were not many red-band Indian officers (officers over the rank of lieutenant-colonel), our brigade was commanded by a Sikh, Brigadier Jogindra Singh, a real royal Sikh from Patiala and a real disciplinarian. British officers hated to salute him, and he was keen to discipline them. I remember a captain and a major he kept standing at attention for a long time, and then he told them to come to his office. The British would try to look in another direction, as if they did not see him, and he would set them right.

A few months after Major Roberts returned the four rupees, I was posted to Taj Mahal City – to Agra Cantonment – and attached to the command workshop of the largest communications command in India. Lt-Col. Jones, the commanding officer, assigned me to training under a quartermaster in charge of rations and clothing for the personnel of the command workshop and the cantonment's station workshop – about five hundred people, or half a battalion. So my duties were those of a quartermaster instead of a technical storekeeper. The training was easy because a quartermaster handles only a few items, and I was well trained to keep account of thousands of items of technical stores.

After a week I told Lt-Col. Jones, "I know the ins and outs of all this handling." He said, "Well, you take over. This quartermaster is going on leave." Later on I found out that this quartermaster was selling supplies. It was hard to catch him, and Col. Jones wanted to remove him from the quartermaster stores. Col. Jones told me there were discrepancies in the accounts. "You will have to make up sugar deficiencies." The fish were surplus because the unit did not have many fish eaters. Because it was a command workshop, we had a garden of three or four acres with a gardener, a couple of bullocks, and an irrigation well. I organized the garden, took labour from the unit, and produced a lot of vegetables for the unit, which pleased the colonel. I told the colonel that something was happening under the table to our rations. "If you stand behind me, then I can eliminate that." We used to draw fresh rations twice a week and dry rations monthly. When I went to the Indian Army Service Corps depot for our monthly rations of rice and butter, I could see it was very nice rice, but each sack of one quintal (one hundredweight) looked light. In the same way the cans of butter, which we called ghi, were also light, both the cans of natural ghi and those of vegetable ghi. I said, "Would you kindly weigh these for me to make sure they are all right." But the NCO in charge would not do it. Finally he told me, "You bring your own labour and get it done at your own effort."

I went to see the officer in command of the supply depot, Major Wadia, a south Indian, but his people would not allow me in. I phoned the colonel and said, "I am finding a problem." The colonel phoned the major and then the major called me in. He said, "What is the problem, Hawaldar?" I said, "This is the problem. These supplies should be weighed. If they turn out all right, I am not wrong. They must be weighed. At least I should know." He told his men to go ahead. Each sack of rice was underweight, some up to thirty pounds. It was a good grade of rice, and that is why so much was stolen. The cans of natural ghee were four to five pounds underweight. They had to give me full weight, and they did. The NCO in charge served me quickly, completely, and correctly, and with respect from then on. He would give me select fresh vegetables and fruits, like apples from Kashmir, which we generally did not get in the NCO's mess.

Of course, the colonel appreciated what I had done. The thought came to me that, because the trains were running directly from Agra to Jullundur and took only so many hours, I could get home and back on a weekend if I returned early on Monday morning. I went to the colonel and asked him for an out-pass. "I am a young fellow, and there is no arrangement for my wife to be brought here yet. I can go to Punjab on a weekend if you will allow me." He said, "Okay. At your risk, but I will issue an out-pass." I stayed at Agra for eight months or more, and it was a good life. I travelled twice a month on out-passes. When I was in military dress, no one would ask me for a fare and I would go for free, although I should have paid. My wife had come to Sarhala Khurd again to live in father's house because I was contributing a lot, and his behaviour had improved. During the weekends I would work a couple of mornings on the farm to appease him. I could manage that, and the sleeplessness, just to be with my wife.

While I was at Agra, I received my sixty days' annual leave. In preparation I had some canisters made up at Agra workshops – kerosene cans fixed with latches – and I filled them with surplus items from the stores, sugar, cans of fish, and other cans of food, tea leaves, extra clothing, mosquito netting, and a gross of matches. (I bought the matches from the canteen, but it was illegal to carry them because they were a controlled item.) When I added my own clothing and bedding, what I carried on the train from Agra looked like enough for several people. By the time I reached the interchange at Phagwara Junction, it was too late to catch the train home, so I had to stay overnight in the second-class waiting-room. I was the only one there that night, and to prevent any theft I put my baggage in the small washroom and pushed a chesterfield across the doorway and slept on it. The door to the waiting-room could not be locked because trains came all night and it had to be available for other passengers.

In the morning I was up long before the appearance of the sweeper who cleaned the washroom, but he saw my arrangement and told the Phagwara ticket inspector. When my train was imminent, I put my baggage on a four-wheeled cart and got some coolies to bring it on to the platform. The ticket inspector came up with two railway policemen and wanted to search what I had. I told him, "This is family baggage and I am a military person, and that is why it looks more than it should." The inspector persisted, and I became stronger in my attitude. When you have the right intent in your life, Almighty, with a hidden hand, will save you from the wrongs you do.

Many people gathered around. Some elders asked what was going on and I explained to them respectfully. I offered one of them the keys to the cannisters. I said, "If nothing comes out, what compensation will this fellow give me?" All the people joined in. "Go ahead," they said to the Phagwara ticket inspector, "now you say something." But he said nothing. The train came and I was saved. A God-conscious person would say that God put those words in my mouth to protect me because I was not taking those things for myself. I was trying to please my greedy father.

I wanted to get a posting close to home, so I went to my colonel. He thought I should stay where I was. "You are pretty well off. You are going on out-passes. Later on you can bring your wife here." But I had a deep craving for a home posting in Punjab, so Col. Jones circulated my application through Western Command. This was in the early spring of 1947, and the question of India's independence and partition was in full swing. On 2, 3 and 4 March, for three days, Muslims were murdering Hindus and Sikhs in West Punjab. The colonel told me, "If you are going there, you should be careful."

I wanted a posting at Jullundur Cantonment or Ferozepur Cantonment not far from home, but that was not my destiny. At Western Command headquarters at Rawalpindi (now Islamabad, the capital of Pakistan) a Sikh officer had a vacancy. Because I was a Sikh, he pulled me to his unit. Instead of getting Jullundur or Ferozepur, I received a posting that was nearly as far from my home as Agra. When I reached there, I demanded quarters for my wife. I wrote to my wife and to my family to get her ready, and I went home on a short leave and brought her back. I first reached my new unit at Rawalpindi on 7 March 1947. By Independence Day, on 15 August 1947, Punjab was complete bloodshed from east to west, from the side that was in India to the side where I was posted now in Pakistan.

Our workshop was attached to an all-Sikh company of sappers and miners – 250 in strength – which had specialty vehicles for roadwork and bridging. Because it was maintaining just this one unit, our workshop was small, with about thirty personnel. Our ordnance depot was in Chaklala, which was like a twin city to Rawalpindi. We would collect the stores there ourselves instead of receiving them by dispatch. Whatever I ordered on Friday, we would collect on the following Monday. When I took a lorry to go to Chaklala, I used to stop for groceries at a small shop that was owned by a Muslim. I could find more evidence of God-consciousness in that man than among my co-religionists.

During the strife of independence and partition in August 1947 even military people could not move around easily or freely. Snipers would shoot at them. I had a Sten gun and my driver had a Sten gun, and when I stopped at that shop every Monday I used to buy groceries for my neighbours and friends as well as for my wife and myself. Muslim fanatics who were murdering Hindus and Sikhs came to the grocer and told him, "Don't let that Sikh come around here; otherwise, we will finish him off." The next time I came, he spoke to me with tears in his eyes. "These people don't know what is humanity. Kindly don't come again."

I saw decomposed bodies quite a few times in Rawalpindi, in dung carts and trailers and elsewhere. Our unit was put on duty guarding the trains carrying refugees from Pakistan to India and from India to Pakistan. On these trains one batch of guards would be Muslim and another Sikh. I had a complete view of the situation. I was right in the heart of what was happening. One day a tank regiment commanded by a Sikh came through Rawalpindi from the west, from Peshawar or some other cantonment. They had a couple of days' stay in Rawalpindi, and that major was bold enough and compassionate enough to load his tanks with Hindu and Sikh refugees. That story came by hearsay to my unit, and it created in my mind a desire to do something for those people.

I told my driver to go to the main Sikh gurdwara (temple), where refugees had gathered from the surrounding areas. The gurdwara was enclosed by walls and had been fortified after the bloodshed had started in March. When we went in, the people greeted us with affection. They said that they had a lot of material gathered from neighbouring gurdwaras. "You can help us take it to India." They asked if I could take some refugees. "Well," I said, "this is not within my jurisdiction, but I'll load this truck with the materials." I took cookware the first time and brought it to my stores and told my unit commander.

He was happy with what I was doing, but there was some reluctance from the company to which we were attached. A senior officer, a subedar (major), called me in and asked me why I was going about without permission. I said, "I am doing something good. I'm not getting anything out of it. What's the difficulty?" In the end he had to agree. The other officers told him, "You are thinking the wrong way. We should give whatever help we can." In my trips to the gurdwara I brought back big and small kitchen utensils, which I used to distribute among the men of the company so they could carry them whenever they reached India and donate them to needy gurdwaras or needy people. Finally, I brought back three hundred volumes of Sri Guru Granth Sahib, the holy book of our Guru. Those volumes were kept with full respect in my stores and were later taken to India by train with full respect and distributed wherever they were needed.

My wife was pregnant when I took her to Rawalpindi. By the end of September she was close to eight months. We had a neighbour in the family quarters whose wife was also pregnant. A chance came to get back to India. The specialty vehicles belonging to our company and our unit were being transferred to India ahead of most of the personnel, who were being retained for transfer-of-population duties. My technical stores were being loaded on transport vehicles, and I was to accompany them. I fixed up a bed for my wife in one of the lorries, and I told my friend and neighbour that his wife could go too. He said, "Okay. I will stay here and my wife can go with your wife." We made our decision by praying before the Guru Granth Sahib. "Help us. We are taking your refuge. Kindly deliver them safely because they are in a condition of approaching delivery."

At this time heavy rains in East Punjab created the greatest natural havoc of the century, washing away refugee camps and villages and breaking up all the roads. We got up around 1:00 a.m. When we got up my neighbour said, "During the night we changed our minds. There will be so many jolts and jerks on the road that there will be a danger of miscarriage and no medical aid available." I told him, "We both prayed to Almighty. He should be with us. Don't be afraid. Don't turn around on your decision. Have faith in the Guru and God." He would not take any risk. "Well this is not turning around," he said. "It is a measure of safety."

We started out. On the first night we stayed in Lahore, and we could smell the stink of bodies. When we came into Amritsar, it was daytime, and we could see as well as smell. Hindus and Sikhs had been murdered by Muslims and Muslims by Hindus and Sikhs. Refugee camps and villages had been attacked, and the floods had killed so many people and animals. Along our route we could see the bodies and carcasses, the decomposed skeletons, and vultures, kites, and crows were flying and settling over the remains.

When we reached close to our village, it was evening. The convoy had an overnight stay at Jullundur, and I was allowed to take a lorry and driver to my wife's village and to rejoin the convoy at

Phagwara early the next morning. Because the road was broken and pitted, we drove slowly. It was a moonlit night. Our village of Kultham was a mile off the road, and when we came to the turn-off point, I looked across the fields from the road to the village. I could see the reflection of the moon on water all the way. Old people, men in their eighties and nineties, later told me that in all their years they had never seen the land in flood like that.

I called at a house in a village on the road, a neighbouring village, to get a guide to help us reach home. The people in the house saw the guns hanging over our shoulders, and the old man said to his son, who was talking to the driver and myself, "Hey, son, don't go. They have guns. They might kill you." Earlier on a Baluch regiment (a Muslim regiment) had passed through, shooting people without provocation. The old man and his son did not know whether we were Sikhs or Muslims, and they were afraid. I asked my wife to speak to them to tell them who we were and who our relatives were. Then they were satisfied, and the young man took us by the best passage.

I had a four-wheel-drive stores lorry, and it went through mud and water axle-deep, and even engine-deep, without a stop. We reached home around midnight. The next morning we got up early, and the driver and I set off on the return journey to meet the convoy at Phagwara. Here was the miracle. The night before, with my wife aboard, the vehicle went through without a stop. But in the morning it got stuck right near the village and would not go. People came running to help. They cut sugar cane in a nearby field and pushed it into the mud and water in front of the wheels, and they stood in knee-deep water and shoved, and with a great effort we made it. We were late at Phagwara, but the convoy was still coming, vehicle by vehicle. I was questioned by the commanding officer, but I explained, "We got stuck." At length we arrived at our training centre at Roorki near Hardwar in Uttar Pradesh, about one hundred miles east of the Punjab border.

After a few weeks the balance of the unit came by train. My friend, who had changed his mind on the morning that we left Rawalpindi, arrived by train with his wife. She was soon admitted to the hospital at Roorki, where she gave birth to a dead boy, and she was in danger herself for some time after. Within a week or so my wife, who had travelled by rough roads for 250 miles from

Rawalpindi to Kultham, also gave birth. I got a letter saying that we had a healthy girl and that my wife was doing fine. Can you believe that here also was the secret hand?

3 A Disabling Illness

The caste system among the Sikhs is a violation of the Guru's teachings. I weigh it on the same scale as cutting the hair. In Kultham, my wife's village, it was more serious than in Sirhala Khurd because so many of the people were illiterate and innocent. I saw it when I visited Kultham during my annual leaves. One summer afternoon, around 1:00 or 1:30 p.m., I went to a Persian water-wheel near the village boundary to take a bath. An old man was sitting behind the oxen as they circled to turn the driving gear, pulley, chain, and spindle system, with large rotating galvanized pots that drew water from the well. The water emptied on to an iron tray, spilled into a concrete trough, and poured out of the trough into an irrigation channel. People would bathe in the trough because there was a constant flow of water.

While I was bathing, a Chuhra lady (a sweeper) approached with a water pitcher on her head and started to wash the pitcher in the water that fell from the trough into the channel. I watched and saw that she was going to fill her pitcher with the same water. Because I knew her, I called her by name. "I am bathing in that water and you are taking it for drinking? Why not take the fresh water from the well?"

She said, "We are untouchables. We can't do that."

"That is a great injustice," I said. "All right, if you are afraid, give me your pitcher and I will fill it for you." I took the pitcher and held it under the flow of fresh water. The old man, who was watching, stopped the oxen and spoke in surprise. "Oh, respected son-in-law of the village, you are such an intelligent educated man. Don't you know what wrong you have done?"

"Well, dear father," I said, because that is the way we address our elders, "I don't understand what it is. Kindly explain to me." I was pretending not to know.

He said, "They are untouchables. If they touch that water, it is all defiled." In a field about fifty yards away some Chuhra men were cleaning grain by shaking it in baskets over their heads. I asked, "Does that grain belong to you?" He said, "Yes." I asked if he washed it before grinding it for cooking, and he said "No." Then I asked how it was that a Chuhra lady could not take clean water, yet Chuhra men could work at the threshing with their feet in the grain lying on the ground around them.

"Well," he said, "that is dry stuff, so it is not maligned, but water gets maligned because it is wet." In a careful way and in a very nice way I told him that these ideas were all hypocritical. He could see what I meant, but in the end he replied, "Well, it's tradition. That's why we follow it."

After partition and our transfer from Rawalpindi my unit stayed at Roorki for only a few months. Then we were posted to Jullundur Cantonment along with the Forty-first Field Park Company, to which we had been attached in Rawalpindi. Although the Forty-first Field Park Company was an all-Sikh company, our unit was mixed, with personnel from all over India. Jullundur Cantonment was only twenty miles by road and rail from my wife's village. We were in kachcha (temporary) and not pakka (permanent) barracks, and we were close to the railway station. I used to take a weekend out-pass to my wife's village, stay there, and be back to report for duty on Monday.

The Sikh major who was our commanding officer was a rich man. In civilian life he ran a truck transport outfit and he owned a Ford v8 car. This car needed a new dynamo or generator. The major wanted to exchange the old dynamo for a good one from the stores, and he wanted to do it for free, without any record. He sent his transport NCOs to see me. (He would not ask me himself.) I said, "Too bad. People of that calibre want to loot India right away." And I insisted on entering the exchange in the relevant vehicle log-book. It was not a lot of money for him, 150 or 200 rupees, but he became very hostile towards me.

The company command restricted the issue of out-passes to those who required them on compassionate grounds. Somehow my out-pass was cancelled and not reissued. My workshop officer was understanding, and my relations with the other personnel were good, so I would sneak out without a pass, catch an evening train, and nobody would know. One Saturday, late in the evening, all of a sudden orders came from division headquarters for a special roll-call to announce a division parade on Sunday. So I was found absent, and when I came back I was ushered in to the major, who deducted twenty-eight days' pay, which was the maximum he could confiscate. A simple warning would have been enough. All the workshops in the division were under the command of Lt-Col. Khanna. I went to see the staff captain, and then I went directly to Lt-Col. Khanna and told him the whole story about the dynamo and the punishment I had received. He asked what would be the best thing for me. I said, "Well, you had better take me out of the unit." He could see that I was an honest and patriotic young man and posted me to 1309 Transport workshop section, also stationed in Jullundur, where I was needed.

He sent me there because, during the time of partition, this workshop had been looted by the workshop personnel. Tires, batteries, minor assemblies, and so on had been sold on the open market. The technical storekeeper who had been around when all this happened was a man from Maharashtra, a senior person around fifty years of age who (I later found out) had been a court reader before he enlisted. His name was Parkhee. He was quiet, but a tricky fellow. His chance had come when the subedar in command of the workshop abandoned his post for several weeks at the time of partition. This subedar was a Hindu from West Pakistan, and he went to evacuate his family. While he was gone, the stores were pillaged, and when he came back he was afraid to report his own NCOs, who were responsible, because he had been absent without leave. He had been in the army for twenty years, and his life's career and pension were at stake. So he covered up for his NCOs while they falsified the records and bought used parts in the local market to fill out the store.

When I arrived, all the parts and tools were mixed up and lying on the floor, and nobody knew how many items of this or that we had. The workshop had a new commanding officer, a lieutenant recently promoted to captain, but he was not a well-educated man and had no background in technical stores. So he depended on me, and we carried on the work of investigating and assessing what was missing. Soon after we started this work, we received orders to transfer to Ambala, which is more than 120 miles south and east of Jullundur and a long way from my wife's village. It seemed as if two major-generals were in a tug of war over our unit, the commander of No. Four Division at Ambala and the commander of the East Punjab area, with headquarters in Jullundur. We had four transfers in one year, twice to Ambala and twice to Jullundur, and we were never long in one place before we were shuttled to the other. During this time we prepared a typed document of eighty-four legal-sized pages itemizing all of the items – "batteries, 6 volts," etc. – that had been looted in a three- or four-week period at the time of partition.

One day at Ambala Cantonment a carpenter NCO came to me on behalf of the Hindu subedar who had formerly commanded the workshop unit. He told me the subedar's story. He hadn't taken anything from the stores himself, but he had co-operated in concealing the losses, and he had even been induced to make some false entries in the ledger-book himself. He was worried about those entries. His messenger asked if I would destroy them for a reward.

I told the carpenter NCO "I am sympathetic, but I won't do it myself, and I won't accept any fees or favours whatsoever." There was a station workshop nearby with a civilian storekeeper who was the subedar's friend. After twenty-two years of service the subedar had many friends. This civilian storekeeper agreed to recopy the entries, and so I pulled out twenty pages. And I got them the special sheets of paper used in the ledger volume so they could recopy the entries.

They destroyed the originals and brought back copied sheets and I inserted them in the ledger, but when I did that, I discovered another page in the subedar's hand. Compassion came to my mind. I said "Okay," and I copied it myself with my left hand as cunningly as I could, so it wouldn't look like my writing. Mr Parkhee had kept the ledger before I did, and he kept checking it even after I started a new one. Those entries were like eggs under his hatch because they made the subedar look like the main thief. When Mr Parkhee discovered that twenty-one pages were gone, he reported it to the company commander, who reported it to the division commander, and the ledger was sealed and taken into custody. When the company commander asked me what had happened, I told a lie. I said, "I don't know."

While the matter was under investigation, the commander of the East Punjab area succeeded in bringing our unit back to Jullundur, where I was allocated family quarters. There was a junior commissioned officer on the mechanical side, a jamedar (lieutenant) who was always at a fuss with the artisans and technicians. A cold war set in between him and me. At that time India and Pakistan were fighting in Kashmir. One hot summer day a special convoy prepared to leave for Kashmir with four hundred vehicles. I had to go to the Jullundur Cantonment railway station to collect a rush order of spare parts for the vehicles in the convoy. My parcels were at three different military delivery offices, and because of the conflict in Kashmir there was a big rush at the station. So it took me three hours. While I was there, I encountered a civilian relative of one of our officers, and I gave him a ride to Sadar Bazaar, which was our cantonment bazaar, and dropped him off at the intersection in the military area. As I dropped him off, the jamedar rushed up. "Why are you late? You are holding up the convoy." He was furious. Later we met in the repair-yard, and he yelled at me and showered me with names. The blood in my body built up, and I grabbed him by the arm and pushed him back to the wall. He struck his head against it and fell down. This was during afternoon break, so people were watching, and when they saw him fall they laughed.

The jamedar reported me to the captain. I was opening parcels in the stores when I was called into the captain's office. The captain took away my belt, which meant that I was under open arrest for attacking a commissioned officer. The unit had a new adjutant, a subedar, and while the matter was referred to him, the captain sent me back to my office and told me to go on opening parcels. I later learned that a person under open arrest cannot be put to work, but I did not know that then, nor did the captain. When the subedar came to me, I told him that the jamedar had insulted me, and when it happened a second time, I lost my cool. The subedar said, "You did a wrong thing," but he decided that a compromise would be best, and he brought the jamedar and me together and we shook hands. On that day, when my belt was taken away, my wife, my father-in-law, and my one-year-old daughter came to Jullundur to live in the family quarters. I told friends, "Don't let them know I am under arrest." Finally it was settled, and I was able to go home.

The ledger books were under investigation, and all the personnel who had made entries had to have their handwriting tested. Dr Goyal, the all-India expert, came to give his opinion, and I was the first to see him. They took my belt away, brought me to Philaur Fort, a police training centre and educational college, and ushered me in to Dr Goyal. He made me write this way and that way. The next day he wanted to see all the other personnel connected with the stores. This time the testing was done at his residence. I had my belt back, but I was taken along with the others and seated outside.

Here was another miracle. If you are doing what is right and what is compassionate, God will help. Dr Goyal identified the handwriting on the pages that had been recopied by the civilian friend of the old subedar as Mr Parkhee's handwriting. When he came to the twenty-first page, Dr Goyal said, "This page seems to have been written by Tara Singh." But he was not sure, and because he was not sure, I was put with the witnesses in the case and not with the criminals. I was so thankful because it could have meant a long prison sentence. One day later on Dr Goyal came to Jullundur Camp to take my statement under oath, and he asked me about that page. I said, "It looks as if someone tried to write it as if it were my handwriting."

All this happened in 1948. In the spring of 1949 our whole division stationed at Jullundur was ordered out on a one-day march of about twenty-nine miles with full equipment and then back again the next morning. As an office worker I did not have any preparation to sustain that kind of effort, and my determination, which took me to the last step, caused extreme exhaustion of the body. Within two weeks the effects were pronounced. The lymphatic glands on the right side of my neck became enlarged. On examination, the medical specialists classified my condition as tubercular.

At first I was depressed. I was admitted to the military hospital and X-rays were taken. The radiologist, a Sikh major, asked me, "Do you want to stay in the army, or do you want a disability pension?" I said, "Sir, first you let me know the state of my disease. Is it curable or not?" He said it was very curable, but he could give me a larger per centage of disability to qualify me for a larger pension. It was in his hands.

Why did he say that? I think it was because we were Sikhs, and he believed that there was prejudice against Sikhs in the Indian Army. When the Kashmir war ended in January 1949, twenty-one lieutenant-colonels from Western Command were court-martialled. Nineteen of them were Sikhs, and only two were Hindus. Up to this stage my thinking was unprejudiced, as a Sikh's should be, but this kind of action started to affect me, not as a reactionary but as a cautious man. The intelligence officer of 109 Brigade was a Sikh and a friend of mine. He had access to more information than I did, and he was alienated by what he knew. We used to discuss these things, and we were hurt by them.

This intelligence officer knew the background to the courts martial, and he was suspicious about the death of one of our Sikh generals, Major-General Atma Singh. Atma Singh was the youngest major-general in the Indian Army. He was a simple man, sympathetic to his soldiers, who used to go in disguise to check their conditions and to see how they were treated by their officers. He might have become commander-in-chief of the Indian Army if he had lived long enough. He was driving back to Srinagar after attending a conference of army officers and politicians at Jammu during the Kashmir war. The Srinagar highway was a one-lane highway with passing pockets. A jeep from a side-pocket struck his vehicle, and although his injuries did not seem that serious, he died in the Srinagar hospital that night. I was born a patriot and grew up admiring Nehru and Gandhi, and I resisted the suggestion that they were prejudiced against minorities or that there was a conspiracy against the Sikhs. As a young man I was proud of Nehru and India. But the evidence of discrimination was gradually alienating the minds of Sikhs.

I think that is why the radiologist asked if I wanted to stay in the army. I told him about my situation at home and that army service was better for me. He agreed and gave me a 30 per cent disability, which was realistic. Then in the evenings I used to put on civilian clothes and slip out of the hospital into the Sadar bazaar, and there I saw a few physicians. I got the impression from them that my disease was a disease of the rich. Only the rich could afford treatment. One physician was an exception. It was late evening, and I kept sitting there until all the patients were gone. Then I explained my family situation and my economic ability, and I asked if I could pay for the whole amount of the treatment gradually later on. "If I die, I promise to pay you in the next life."

That fatherly doctor, who happened to be a Sikh, grabbed me into his arms with a very warm feeling and said, "My son, you are all money. If you get healthy, which you will, that is all the payment I need." He asked for nothing, and he must have given me two hundred or three hundred injections. All I had to spend was for the drugs I got from the druggist, and even that he helped with by writing slips for a concession price.

In the medical hospital they would only give you ordinary medicine and not the kind of treatment I could get outside. My private treatment was unauthorized, but my commanding officer was sympathetic and let me go. Gradually I became healthy, and a medical review board looked at my case. A medical specialist had already recommended that I be sent home, and he stood his ground. "He is not fit for army service because his disease can develop at any time under stress." What he said was true because it happened later on.

I appealed that decision three times, but the answer was the same. A 30 per cent disability meant unfit for military service. A special directive to release me came from Western Command HQ, and towards the end of 1949 I was sent to the Records Office in Bangalore in South India for discharge. The commanding officer wanted to give me a personal letter to the commanding officer of the Records Office for reassessment, but I told him, "I don't want that letter because I am very confident now that my destiny is somewhere else – not in the army."

A son was born that year. My wife was pregnant when I first got sick, and she gave birth before my final discharge. In January 1950 I came home and gave father the major share of my discharge allowances, but I told him I was keeping four hundred rupees for my treatment. During the summer I had to work hard in the orchard and on the farm. His approach was still negative. He wanted all of my allowances, but I knew he would not pay for any treatment. And he expected me to do more than I could. The glands started to swell again, and in the house my wife was having a rough time. The family, particularly father, were not happy with us, and made pinching remarks. That was not important, but the disease was getting worse, and I could see that if I worked the way father wanted, there would be no health left.

Jullundur was too far away to get injections every day, and there was no physician near our village, so I was going without treatment. Occasionally father-in-law would visit us. I talked to my wife, and then we discussed everything with him. He said, "You come to my village." Finally we had to go. First I sent my wife and two children. Then one day I had a hot discussion with father. He wanted me to do things I could not do, so I left.

Four days later I went to Jullundur to see Dr Jiwa Singh, the same good doctor as before. (He was a retired civil surgeon from Burma.) With his letter I bought thirty vials of streptomycin. It was a new drug on the market in India, and I had to go to Kundan Pharmacy in Ludhiana to get it. In the fall of 1950 that was the only place it was available. I had a friend in Jullundur on active service with a family and a house, and I stayed with him and started getting my injections. After the third injection I began to feel pain in the bowel. The next day I had blood in the stools. On the fifth day it was very bad. Dr Jiva Singh said, "It is not fitting your system. Better stop it." He sold the remaining twenty-five vials to another patient and gave the money back to me.

Father-in-law was a nice, simple-minded man who never faced much responsibility. He had about four or five acres of land, which was enough to support him without working. He would rent his land and share the crop, half and half, with the cultivator. He was fond of drinking but never got drunk. That was his favourite hobby. At Kultham with father-in-law we at least had peace of mind and food. But we were lacking milk and other things we needed with two children. My disability pension did not start. I had to write letters, but because it was a 30 per cent disability, they tried to ignore it.

That fall my wife developed an ulcer in the throat. It became enlarged in a few days. An ulcer like that can block the passage, and with the pus going down into the stomach and into the body system, it can kill you. I knew what it was but never told my wife. There was one ayurvedic physician who had a shop in the village, although he did not belong to the village. I used to sit with him a lot, and I studied the medical magazines that he kept. He subscribed to a couple. This man tried to treat my wife with herbal medicines, but he knew and I knew that she needed penicillin, and I had no money for that. My money had gone on various treatments for my own disease following traditional methods that village physicians knew, and I had already sold my extra clothing, watch, tools, and other things at a cheap price.

When my wife was close to the danger-line, I had to ask her to go to father-in-law for money. I intended never to be a burden on him and never to ask him for money for my own treatment. He went to two or three people close to him, but he found no money available anywhere. One morning her throat became so swollen that she could not drink. It was a cold morning, and the fog was thick. I knew that she might not last more than a few days. So I went into the back room and I cried before Him in a prayer. "I admit this punishment may be due to my sin, but two things fall on your side. One is that I have no means to feed her. The other is that you are the one that can excuse. If she dies, with this disease how would I be able to bring these children up. I'm not saying that you are doing injustice to me, but I do protest that you can show clemency to me."

With this I left the house, carrying the son and leading the daughter with my finger, walking to the outskirts of the village, where we had a milk cow in a cattle-house. All the way I was praying to Him and waiting for the worst. Within an hour the mail delivery boy came to me. "Uncle Ji," he said, "there is a telegram money order for you." We had a commission-type post office in a shop in the village, and the delivery boy came from there. I did not believe him because no one would send a telegram money order except in an emergency, and who could know about our emergency? I asked where it was from, and he said it was from Africa. "It is definitely not mine," I said. "Maybe a namesake."

After half an hour or so he came back with a message from the grocer and postmaster, Harbans Lal, a Brahman. Whenever we had no money, Harbans Lal would help us by lending groceries, and he knew the situation of my life to some extent. The boy said, "Harbans Lal says, 'Ask Tara Singh to come to me.'" Finally I agreed to go. By the time I reached his shop it was ten or ten-thirty in the morning and the fog was thinning here and there and the sun was breaking through. Harbans Lal was sitting on a platform outside his shop to catch the warmth of the sun. I had the two children with me. I gave my greeting to him and he to me.

His first question was, "Have you any relative in Malaya?" I said, "Yes. My uncle, Bachint Singh." He said, "There is a telegram money order for you for one hundred rupees." At this tears began to flow. He looked at me. "Why are you weeping so copiously?" I said, "Pandit Ji, please don't ask me this question. Let me lighten my heart." Here was the Super Father. Through Him, help came at the right time. I had complained to Him, and I was repenting. Until I lifted this burden from my heart, I could not speak.

Right away I took my wife to Banga, a town of ten or fifteen thousand, to a very good physician, Dr Kartar Singh, well known for his successful practice. He started the treatment with an injection and gave her some mixtures to nullify the infection of the stomach and throat. She was not well enough to travel back, so we went to the village of Mazaari, a mile from Banga, and we stayed in the house of my wife's cousin, her uncle's daughter. After a week of penicillin treatment Dr Kartar Singh said there was no need for more. He gave us some mixtures and sent us home. It cost us around twenty-five rupees.

Even when it came, I could not understand why uncle sent the hundred rupees. It should have been several hundred to make it worthwhile to wire it from Malaya. There was a reason, and I finally learned it ten years later from a cousin, Mit Singh. I had returned from Canada and happened to be in Sirhala Khurd when he came to visit. This cousin lived in Malaya and had a rubber garden near Taiping. My uncle lived in Bagan Serai, which, according to Mit Singh, was some distance away. Mit Singh said that uncle relied on him to read his letters and look after money matters. Uncle could not read and would not show his papers to anyone else.

I had written to uncle soon after I was discharged from the army. He had gone to Malaya when I was four or five and he had never come back, but I acquired his address and wrote to him, explaining my situation and asking for help. No reply came, and after seven or eight months I had lost all hope of getting one, if I ever had any. All this time Mit Singh had not visited uncle. One weekend he felt an extreme urge from within to go. When he arrived, uncle showed him my letter, and Mit Singh read it to him. Then uncle learned about my situation, and he felt so sorry and so repentant he wanted to send money the fastest way possible, because it was already too late. At that time he did not have enough cash on hand, but insisted on sending whatever was available. The best they could do was one hundred rupees. Anyone with a little thoughtfulness can see who caused that delay and who created that urgency. Had the money come before it did, what would have happened when I needed it most?

Father-in-law did not have any sons of his own, and he loved my brother-in-law, Bakhshi, who was the only son of father-in-law's deceased elder brother. Bakhshi had been raised with great care, with the idea that he could become an excellent wrestler. He was six-foot-four or six-foot-six and about two hundred pounds. It was an unusual thing for me to live in my wife's village with father-in-law, and in his own mind Bakhshi did not like it. There was some evil inside Bakhshi, and eventually father-in-law came to understand that. From then onwards he never trusted him as he had before. The turning-point came after father-in-law decided to emigrate.

At that time British foundries needed good labour. The British knew how well the Sikhs worked, and they encouraged them to migrate. There was a big rush of Punjabis from the farming class to the United Kingdom. Almost all of them worked in foundries, and they were willing to work seven days a week. Bakhshi persuaded father-in-law to go to England, and he promised to take good care of us. Secretly they sold some land for travel money, and within a few days they secured some kind of passport. Bakhshi got father-in-law to sign a power-of-attorney in Bakhshi's name and sent him to Bombay with some other person.

Overnight we learned that father-in-law had gone. Bakhshi asked my wife, "Why do you keep that sick man here?" One morning, about the third day, I had a hot quarrel with him, and I warned him: "All right, once you touch me you will be behind the bars. I am an ex-soldier, and you are a known scoundrel." So he assaulted me only with his bad language. Neighbours and other villagers learned what was going on and advised him not to interfere with our lives, and one of the village elders assured me that the half-share of the produce from father-in-law's land would come to us despite the power-of-attorney in Bakhshi's name.

There are some ascetics living in the hills, isolated from the world, who know herbal medicines. With father-in-law gone and Bakhshi there, I made up my mind to go to the hills in the garb of a sadhu. I told my wife and asked her to get a garment made for me out of khadar, or homespun cotton. Every evening I asked her, and I could read in her eyes what she was saying, although she would not speak. This continued for four or five days. All of a sudden a voice came from within. "Look here, man, you were married in this house to this lady before Guru Granth Sahib. You gave a pledge to live together through thick and thin. Wouldn't it be a disaster for her if you went away sick and in despair and left her behind? Be a true husband and stand up to your promise and pledge."

I told my wife, "I don't need that garment any more." And that took the pressure from her mind. Within two weeks, silently, father-in-law and his companion came back. They had gone to Bombay, but they had not managed to get a flight. How could father-in-law have gone, when Almighty did not want him to go?

4 Going to Canada

My mind was full of prayer to the Guru and to Almighty, even when I thought I would not survive. When I could not treat my disease because I had no money, I accepted my responsibility for the wrongs of a previous life that I could not remember. At the same time, I knew that prayer was the only remedy. That thought kept carving its impression on my internal tape, that memory film that never stops, and one night I saw Guru Nanak in my dream. What I saw was his face and beard as far as the breast, although the picture we had in the house showed him full length. He was life-sized and radiant, and his right hand was raised, although he did not move.

When I got up from that dream I was so happy and felt such release and calm that, after that, the fear of death left my mind. My attitude changed and I faced my situation in high spirits with confidence, as if the Guru were with me. "Why worry? Let it be his will. Continue with your prayer. Whatever happens, it is totally right." Within a year I had another dream in which I found myself before Guru Gobind Singh as he is pictured in the prime of his life. In the way of dreams, I could see his face, even though my forehead was touching his feet. He patted me on the shoulder-blades and spoke words that meant "God will bring good. All will be well." The first dream was static, but this dream had action, words, and movement.

In the summer of 1951 a retired havaldar, a Sikh, came to me with a plan for a co-operative cottage-industry project. There was an ashram in Kultham, built by Swami Purna Nand, and the pandit at the ashram was a partner in the project. (This pandit was also the district secretary for the Socialist Party.) A Muslim fellow from a village three miles from Kultham had joined as well, and each had put in one thousand rupees.

They were going to set up a small poultry business at the ashram, along with an ox-driven mill to extract oil and a manually driven machine for manufacturing the twine used in making cots or manjas. The Muslim fellow was a professional oil extractor and had been working for the ashram before this, making good-quality mustard oil, linseed oil, and mustard cake. When I said that I did not have the money for this project, this ex-havaldar said, "Don't worry. I'll put the money and you work for me and our share will be fifty-fifty." It was a boon for me, so I said, "Sure, I'll do my best."

I took my bed to the ashram and started working there. We built pens for fifty or a hundred pullets and bought two twine-manufacturing machines and twine grass from the Shivalak Hills, the foothills of the Himalayas. And we got four milk buffaloes and a milk cow. The business went well, but the Muslim fellow and I were the only work-horses. The pandit was away most of the time with his politics, and when he was there he did no manual work. The Muslim fellow and I were at a big disadvantage because the pandit kept the books. There was no pay, only a share of the profits, and we did not know what the profits were.

After two or three months we called a meeting and said that a person should have some return for his work. It took some hot words, but we made our point and started getting a little remuneration. Then we asked the pandit to hand over the accounts because he was absent most of the time, but he did not like the idea, and the rift became wider. We carried on for another month or so, but he started to talk about disbanding the project. Finally we split everything three ways. I took the ex-havaldar's full share and promised to repay him whenever I could. The pandit kept all the chickens we had hatched and the two twine machines and the twine grass. He kept the best buffalo and made us take the cheaper animals. My share was a bicycle, a buffalo, a cow, and four or five laying hens. My father-in-law already had a cow, so that gave us a buffalo and two cows. By selling a few eggs and milk we had a start, and I had a bicycle to go around.

I had taken a pledge in my mind to remain celibate for a year for the sake of my health. While I was working at the ashram, my health improved. After eight or ten months, all of a sudden the sexual urge became so adamant it was almost unbearable. Being a religious man, I did not want to break my pledge. One day a Sikh priest, a devout man, took me to a holy gathering. On the way, while riding our bikes, I mentioned this problem of mine. He said, "Look here, gentleman, you are not going to do anything wrong if you fulfil your desire, because she is your wife. But if you don't do it, you may be committing a far more serious sin. A being may be destined to enter your family through this urge and its time of conception has come." He quoted a verse from Guru Granth Sahib, "Bind guai ta(n) nark adhikar" (When the moment is lost, then hell is earned).

This conversation resulted in the conception of our third child. After that I was satisfied, and the urge was gone. Every individual is predestined. Some have brighter destinies than others. This fellow was four or five months in his mother's womb when a letter came from Canada. From then on things started to change for the better. I was in the fields at the irrigation well taking my nap under a tree in the peak of the midday heat of summer. My niece came running out to the fields, in that heat, with a letter from my eldest sister in Canada. If she had not held the letter in her hand, I would not have believed it, because there had been no communication before that. How could my sister know my wife's address? How could she know I was married?

My sister was born years before me and was married to a Canadian Sikh who took her to Canada when I was only three or four. After that we hardly heard from her. When I was in high school, she wrote to father about the death of her husband and the difficulties she had now that she was a widow with four children. I stole the address from that letter and sent her a letter describing my life with father. I asked her to write me at my school address, but an answer never came.

The years had gone by. Early in 1952 a young lady who was related to my sister came to Canada. She was my sister's second husband's elder brother's sister-in-law. She also had a maternal aunt in Kultham, my wife's village, and at one time she had lived in Kultham and had been friendly with my wife. This young lady reached Canada on the first instalment of quota immigrants under the quota that the government of Canada gave to Mr Nehru in 1951. My sister invited her to dinner, and during the talk my sister learned about me, not the whole story, but some of it. That is when God created a deeper sympathy in her mind. That is why she sent that letter and addressed it to my wife. She had been told I was still in the army and did not know where I was posted.

In my first reply I gave her the whole story, and told her that God had strengthened me to face further calamities. And it was true; my strength had returned. When she got my letter, she sent a money order for four hundred Indian rupees and a reply. So we made a connection and started the process for my quota application to go to Canada. Here again, one can see that it was the Destiny Maker who performed this play to help me.

My doctor told me, "You won't be able to go to Canada, because you won't pass the physical examination." I told him, "Dr Ji, I have a very good feeling which is with me all the time, and I feel that the Guru is directing me and I will reach Canada."

I started treatment again with streptomycin, the new drug that had caused such pain and bleeding in my bowel in 1950. This time it cured me almost completely within thirty days. A drug can only do good with the help of some secret hand. My weight returned at the rate of two pounds a week. I used to weigh myself at the railway station at Kultham or on the doctor's scales.

Every day I would go to Jullundur Cantonment to Dr Jiwa Singh for injections. At that time my first son's ear became infected, so I would take him with me for penicillin. He was then three years old. The doctor told me to eat fruit during the treatment, and after the injections I would buy some in the market near the cantonment railway station. One particular day I got enough for the two of us but not for the whole family. I used to be a little selfish to conserve funds, although I never liked to do it. By the time we reached the railway station we had eaten most of the fruit I had bought. As I peeled the last orange, my son questioned me: "Dad, aren't you going to save some for mom and sister?" My mind was ripe with the recitation of His name, and when I heard that reprimand, I burst into tears and stepped two or three yards to lean against the wall of the signal cabin and a true prayer came to me: "Give me health and livelihood to serve these children and this wife, even if it is not my destiny. You are the One who can excuse me for now and give the balance of punishment later."

In Kultham people respected me for two reasons, because I was
a religious man and because I was a son-in-law of the village. During those years I spent much of my time in prayer or in reciting
His name. I used to go to the gurdwara to give morning respects
to the Guru, after my ablutions, and I used to go there to recite
Guru Granth Sahib instead of reciting at home, because we were a
one-room family. Kultham was a big village and had several gurdwaras. The Jats (the farmers) had two; the Chamars or Ramdasias (leatherworkers) had one; and the Julahas (weavers) had
another. The Shahidan (martyrs) gurdwara on the edge of the village was a common gurdwara; but I used to go to one of the Jat
gurdwaras because it was nearer.

In the early morning about a dozen religious people would
come to this gurdwara for their prayers. One morning the priest,
who was a sincere, practical person but not very knowledgeable,
expressed a desire to celebrate the birthday of Guru Gobind
Singh. I said, "You do your best and we will try it." A few days
later he told us that the people who could help the most, the gentry of the village, were not going to take any initiative. I said,
"Bhai Ji, what must we have to celebrate?" And he said, "An akhand path (a reading of the Guru Granth Sahib from beginning to
end) and karah prasad (an offering of holy food)." I said, "I will
give some ghi (butter)," and another said he would give in kind as
well. So the plan was fixed right in front of the priest. A few days
later, he said, "Now, once this plan is out, the ones who did not
want to do anything are in the front row." People took collections
all through the village, and it became a big ceremony.

We did a sahaj path (a reading of the entire Guru Granth Sahib
at a natural pace) and an akhand path, which is faster and is completed in forty-eight hours without a break. At the end of the
paths came the bhog ceremony. For the karah prasad offering, we
had two kinds of ghi. Some people, particularly some weaver
families, had given pure ghi. Others had given money, and we had
used that money to buy vegetable ghi.

In the morning some weavers brought tea, and a few people refused to take it. That warned me that we could have trouble with
the offering. I knew that the priest was weak and easily influenced, so I took the ceremonial dagger and stood up with him
when the time came to cross the offering with the dagger, which
we do to show that the Guru is taking it. In a small two-kilogram

pot we had the offering prepared with pure ghi from the homes of weavers, and in a large fifty-kilogram pot we had the offering prepared from vegetable ghi. I crossed the offering on the small pot first, and then, with the same dagger, I crossed the main offering. An old lady and a couple of others stood up and said, "Goodness, what are you doing!" They did not want any particle of the ghi that had come from the weavers to go into the offering that they were going to share. When I heard that, I said, "I have done the right thing," and I picked up the small pot and mixed it with the large. "This is the real offering," I told them. "We don't have any superstition in Sikhism."

When we distributed it, this old lady was one of the ones who would not take it, although a Sikh should not leave the gurdwara without eating some. After the ceremony and the distribution of the offering we had langar, which is what we call food from the Guru's kitchen. At the closing time, when we were cleaning up, people were taking away what was left over. This lady had several pots, but we put nothing in them. She was an old widow, and her husband's younger brother was living with her. Two or three of us carried her empty pots back to her house. In many courtyards girls would sit with their spinning-wheels to work in the sun, protected from the wind by the outer walls. Ten or twelve girls would work in her courtyard. When we opened the door, we saw that old lady with some of the offering of karah prasad that she had been unwilling to take at the gurdwara. She had carried it home on her own and was sharing it with the girls and tasting it herself. She was the kind of person who made a show of observing untouchability in public but didn't bother at home. "Oh mother," I said, "now I understand why you refused at the gurdwara. You wanted more than you could have there."

During my sickness I was always praying for a chance to meet some holy person, but it did not happen. Then, one day in the summer of 1952, in the scorching heat, I was riding home from Phagwara City, a distance of six miles, carrying groceries for the family on my bike, and feed for the milk animals. I had come some two-thirds of the way and was pedalling in the shade of the big sissoo trees alongside the road when I met a majestic elderly man with a flowing white beard like the picture of Guru Nanak. He was dressed in a loose cloth over the shoulder and tied at the hip, and he wore a turban. I later learned that he had fitted out his bicycle to accommodate all the necessities of life, a string and a pot to pull water from a well, a stove, rations, and utensils. When I came up beside him, our eyes met. He was full of health and smiling.

I could not carry on, and I stopped and greeted him. He greeted me, and then he said, "Gentleman, is there any good drinking water here?" I said, "Yes, it is only a few hundred yards ahead." So we rode to a Persian water-wheel where the oxen turned to draw water for the summer crops, sugar cane and fodder crops, and we sat beside the cement trough that carried water from the well. He washed his face and was just going to drink when a young fellow came running out from the cattle-shed behind us, saying, "Please stop. I have fresh buttermilk inside, so kindly accept that."

This young fellow brought some buttermilk, and we sat with the smiling personality I had met on the road, and we drank it. My heart said, "Here is the person you are looking for." We talked about this and that for fifteen minutes, and he told us that he was assistant foreman at the Motor Vehicle Command military workshop in Meerut. He was going to spend his two-month leave in the Shivalak Hills around Anandpur Sahib, the place where Guru Gobind Singh first baptized the Khalsa. "You can concentrate better and benefit more," he said, "by worshipping in the footprints of the great prophets in those great surroundings."

We got on our bicycles and rode another mile and a half until we came to the side-road to my village. There he wanted to say goodbye, but with clasped hands I asked him to spend the hottest hours of the day in my home. He said, "I am very strong and can withstand the heat. Everything is loaded on the bike, and I need nothing." The second time I asked him, I was more humble, but he was more than humble in reply. When I asked a third time, he said, "All right. My pilgrimage may not turn to disaster. Fine."

We were living in a little room, twelve feet by twelve, with an eight-by-eight extension for cooking. Six of us shared that room, including father-in-law and the three children. My second son was a toddler by then, crawling on the ground. In Punjab we have a sweet cold drink made with almonds we call shardai. I wanted to serve some to my guest, but I was cautious and asked him what he would like. We had good, home-made brown sugar and nothing else, so when he said yes, I bought the almonds and dry seeds from the village grocer. We made the paste in a clay pot with a wooden grinder made from neem wood, four feet long and three inches thick. When the paste was ready, I asked him how much water I should add. "Look here, my dear Sikh," he said, "When a langar [food from the Guru's kitchen] is prepared, then everyone present partakes."

I could not deny it, so we filled the bowl, and I asked him to perform the ardas (prayer), and he performed an impressive ardas and added a couple of words at the end, a request to the Almighty and to the Guru. Then he took his baptismal dagger from his sheath and touched the drink with it, as is the custom in the Sikh faith, and I saw for the first time that he was a baptized Sikh. His loose cloth had been wrapped in such a way that it hid the dagger.

We gave him the drink and everyone took a portion, and we had a good talk. His name was Foreman Khidmat Singh, and he was from Sansarpur village adjacent to Jullundur Cantonment. During my army service I had lived in that village with my family but had not heard of him. Such people do not publicize themselves. An ex-havaldar from my village who had been stationed at Meerut later told me many stories about his holiness and his spiritual nature. He would rise at 1:00 a.m. to go to the East Jumna irrigation canal for his bath. He would recite the name of Almighty with deep concentration until 4:00 a.m., and then after he returned home, his wife would join him and they would recite the Guru's verses, the gurbani, for two more hours. At 6:30 or 7:00 he would go to a nearby canteen or tea-stall, where twelve cups of tea would be ready for him in a thermos bottle and twelve bhaturas or buns made from fermented flour. He would ride his bike until he had fed twelve disabled beggars each a cup of tea and a bun. Then he would take his morning breakfast. Of course he was exempt from morning military parade.

At the end, when he was about to leave, I told him about our situation and humbly explained that we could not give the hospitality that we wanted to. He said, "Dear Sikh, don't say that. The people who live in this house are very lucky. This is a fortunate place and it will flourish."

After that I met him a few more times and discussed problems with him and took his guidance. I got my entry permit to go to Canada, and my sister sent me money. In March 1953 my travel ticket arrived. I already had my passport, so I went to Delhi for my visa. Foreman Khidmat Singh had advised me to perform a sahaj path before going to Delhi and an akhand path on return. He said I should find missionary-minded priests for these ceremonies, not the kind of priests who only look for money.

On my way to Delhi I stayed overnight at his residence in Meerut Cantonment. I told this holy man, "I don't have that much money to stay in hotels," but he said, "Don't worry. The first thing you do is to go to the Guru's house." So I took a night train and arrived in Delhi early on Thursday morning. I went straight from the railway station to Sisganj Gurdwara in Chandni Chowk in Old Delhi, where the Ninth Guru was martyred by Emperor Aurangzeb. There they have a counter where you can buy karah prasad (holy food) to offer at the altar. I performed my prayer and asked for help. And a prayer from a sincere heart results in success.

From Chandni Chowk I took a bus to the Canadian embassy and arrived there just before the immigration office closed its door for the afternoon. Then I learned that this was the week of Good Friday and the embassy would be closed from noon Friday until Tuesday morning. In those days the immigration attaché employed only two people, a secretary, who was a Punjabi lady, and a guard. I don't know what sat in the mind of that Punjabi lady when I spoke to her, but she told me that if I completed my tests in time, she would do the rest. "Sahib comes at noon," she said. (That is what she called the attaché.) If I could get an X-ray done before noon Friday and a stools test, which meant going to two places, she would get all the papers ready for the attaché to sign. Then I would have to get my visa stamped by 1:00 p.m. So she made all the appointments for me by phone, including one with Dr F.E. Buckler, who had the visa stamp.

That night I stayed with a fellow from my birthplace village. He was a senior driver for the American embassy, which was close by. On Friday morning I took his bike and got my tests done by 11:30 or 12:00 and came to the attaché's office. The medical results were all good. The attaché was there, and the Punjabi lady got his signature on all the papers she had prepared. She phoned Dr Buckler to tell him I was just leaving, and I drove my bike very fast. When I reached his office, he was looking at the clock on the wall, and it was a few minutes past 1:00 p.m. He could speak Punjabi, and he said, "Aa gya, late ho gya" (You have come but you are late). I gave him the sealed envelope, and he opened it and went over the papers. When he picked up the visa stamp, I was close to communion with thanks to Almighty. I asked him to take four rupees. "I'm happy I'm going to a wonderful country and will see my sister for the first time, so I want to give this for sweets for your employees." He called in his peon and told him to distribute sweets to everyone. I was a man who was known to nobody. I had no special approach, and yet within half a day, on an important holiday, I had completed all four steps and obtained my visa. Here was the hand of Almighty.

A fortunate being is welcome everywhere. All was changing for us. My wife was expecting our fourth child. My health had improved. Our worries were behind us, and we received special attention and regard from our relatives and from all the people we met or saw. My brothers often used to visit me in Kultham, and they brought messages from father. I went to see him. He was happy that I was going to Canada and dropped his prejudice or shoved it behind a door somewhere.

I left India around 15 April 1953. From Delhi I flew in an Indian National Airways Dakota to Karachi in Pakistan. At Karachi I spent a night in a hotel where the Muslim chefs treated me very well. The next day I took a BOAC flight to London, stopping at Beirut, Zurich, and Frankfurt. At a customs-free shop in Zurich I bought a watch for seven pounds British. (It was a good watch and lasted me for nearly twenty years.) After buying that watch, I had only three or four pounds in my pocket. From Zurich and Frankfurt we went on to London, where we landed in the evening. From the airport a bus took us to the central London terminal. There they told me that I had to wait three days for my TCA (Trans Canada Airlines) flight to Canada. I had thought I was going straight on. And because the stopover was for more than twenty-four hours, my ticket did not cover any hotel or food. At the desk they tried to find out how much a hotel would cost me. I was not worried, and I said, "If you can tell me how to get to Birmingham, I can manage." They called a taxi for me, and I took it to Euston railway station.

Chilly rain was falling in London at the time, but I was warmly dressed in a greatcoat. On the train to Birmingham an English gentleman shared my compartment. He was curious about me, and we talked all the way. When we reached Birmingham, he came to the bus stop with me and stood in the heavy rain until the bus came so that he could tell the driver to drop me at 209 Oldbury Road. Seven or eight men from Kultham lived together in that house. They had come to Britain during the previous two years and were working in the foundries. The bus driver stopped at the right spot and pointed to the house a few doors away. It was past midnight when I knocked on the door and got them out of bed. They were amazed to see a person from so far away at such a time in such weather.

They made me a welcome guest until it was time for me to leave. I was a son-in-law of the village and educated and able to be helpful, so they respected me, and I enjoyed their hospitality. Before my return to London each of them gave me a pound or two, and they may have bought my ticket. I didn't have any difficulty going back. Travelling was a kind of hobby for me after my long journeys from Punjab to Jabalpur, Chhindwara, and Bangalore, and I had money in my pocket.

I arrived at the London airport terminal and asked for TCA, and I found a counter with two wickets and a single clerk. She looked at my luggage on the scales and said that it was overweight and I would have to pay an extra ninety-eight dollars. Most of my luggage was full of things my sister had asked me to bring – saris, ornaments, and various gifts. At that time only one store in Vancouver carried anything from India. It was located on Water Street and sold curry powder, black beans, and kidney beans and nothing else that was Indian, not even lentils, and people were homesick for Indian goods.

I was just thinking what to do when a big sturdy fellow came in for the same flight. The same clerk weighed his luggage and approved his ticket. When he turned away, I asked, very innocently, "Is that fellow going on the same flight with his luggage?" She said he was. Then, with the help of Almighty, I said, "My weight and luggage combined will be far less than the combined weight of that gentleman and his luggage." She burst into laughter. It was my way of saying it, although I am not normally a comical person. "All right, Mr Singh," she said, "we will take you."

My flight reached Gander airport in Newfoundland in the early morning of 19 April. Because the next flight from Gander to Vancouver was quite a few hours away, they took me to Montreal and put me in a hotel, where I developed some stomach pain. The next day my flight left for Vancouver, and I arrived in the early evening. All this time, in London and in the hotel in Montreal, I felt comfortable in my surroundings and not at all strange. My past experience and reading had prepared me well. I knew what kind of culture and what kind of people I was going among. I knew what kind of country Canada was.

5 Keeping My Faith

My sister and brother-in-law were at the airport when I landed in Vancouver. This was the first time I had ever seen my sister, and our meeting was very enthusiastic. That night my stomach pain developed more and more. In the morning my brother-in-law gave me some whisky, but it did not help. They tried to use some home medicines, but the pain got worse. They phoned their family doctor, and he may have suggested some medication over the phone, but nothing could treat me. My situation was a problem because I was a new immigrant without any medical coverage. The doctor's name was Rose. He was a very good human being and ran a private hospital on No. 10 Highway on Langley side, over the hill past Cloverdale. When Dr Rose came to the house and saw my plight, he said, "All the laws of service go to save a life. I'll admit him right away. It doesn't matter about insurance."

By then I was nearly unconscious. My stools were full of blood, and the pain was running at full throttle. In the hospital I was unconscious for one or two days with intravenous food and medication. On the fourth day in the hospital I felt relieved, but really down. My sister told me how they had been feeling. "What will happen? Will it be a tragedy?" Finally, after a few days, I came home, and my health gradually improved with the weather. At one point my weight was 135 pounds, which was the maximum I ever had in the army. After a month or so I started to work on their farm.

During this month we went to so many parties at the homes of their friends and family. My niece, my sister's eldest, was living in her own home in Ladner, south of Vancouver, where her husband farmed a big chunk of land with frontage on the Fraser River. My five nephews all lived with my sister. The oldest was only five or six years younger than myself, and the youngest was a child of eight. They were all Canadian-born. The older ones were from my sister's deceased husband and the younger from her second husband, but they were all living together as one family without distinction.

These nephews thought that if I shaved, I could make better progress in Canada. Gradually they brought up the subject of my hair and beard, and then more and more, and it was very painful to me. They talked about Indian culture, how backward it was and so on, without thinking that I could be well informed about cultures and affairs around the world. In fact they were generally well behind me. They came to acknowledge that, but all their talk was aimed at inducing and seducing me to shave. They wished me to change my outer form, which was my God-given form. Quite a few times I reminded them, "Look here, fellows, faith is faith. I don't feel inferior being an Indian or being a Sikh, and I never thought it would be my own people who would hate my hair. No white man has done that to me so far."

In the beginning these discussions were friendly. Then they became more combative. They frustrated me so much that at one point I told my brother-in-law, with tears in my eyes, "I did not know that my hair would be an obstacle, and I am greatly grieved." He must have admonished them, and their tone became less aggressive, but the discussions continued. One evening I was reading the paper on the chesterfield, and my brother-in-law and sister were preparing to go out to see a cinema show in a moviehouse. My sister said, "We would be glad to take you, but they don't allow turbaned people in." That remark hit me hard because it showed what she was thinking. I didn't want to see a cinema picture. The thought had not entered my mind. And there probably would have been no problem if I had gone. I never heard anyone else say that turbaned people could not go.

That was the first indication that my sister agreed with my nephews, and I understood then why she had never tried to intercept their remarks. When I went with the family to parties with friends and relatives, then somehow the question of my hair would be taken up by our hosts. I found it hard to stay in the house when this subject kept coming up. I wanted to get away from it without causing any disturbance. About twenty-five or thirty yards from the house, adjoining the barn, they had a bunkhouse for their employees. It had a good vacant room on the side facing the main house, so I spoke to my brother-in-law and sister. "I enjoy my early morning prayer when I sing it loudly. I can't do that in the house because the children are sleeping. Let me move into that room in the bunkhouse." That was my excuse, and it was a truthful one, so they fixed up that room, and I moved into it.

From then on I was spared a lot of those discussions because at break times, after eating, I could go into that room to rest or read something. The Chinaman in the other room was an experienced person but knew just enough English to get along. I could still feel the force of their campaign to get me to shave. Communications were restrained, and that weighed heavily on my mind. If I had not been as well educated as I was, I could not have resisted as I did. All the time I was bothered by the thought that I was a source of displeasure to my elder sister and benefactor. This began to affect my health. My mind kept going back and forth: "If I do submit, would I be the same again, or could I recuperate from my weakness?" Finally, my human wit conquered my faith.

One evening, at supper break, as I was washing my hands and face in the laundry room in the house, Mac Singh came in from his farm. He was my sister's eldest son, an intelligent, hard-working person who later married a Dutch girl and eventually became land commissioner for Surrey. At that time he was renting a farm of his own but living at home. All of a sudden I said to him, "How about if I cut my hair? It should be a matter of pleasure to you people." I stayed back to let him break the news to everyone inside. Then all the restrained behaviour disappeared. All was happiness. I told my sister and brother-in-law that I wanted two large, good-quality photographs, one before and one after I shaved. My brother-in-law asked why, and I told him that I wanted to keep them on my bedside table to remind myself what I was and what I had become. He understood from that that I had not made a willing choice. But my sister was so happy she went out to the bunkhouse for the first time in weeks and made up my bed and changed the sheets.

The next day I wrote a letter to Piara Singh, my younger brother, who was working as a machinist for Indian Railways at Bina Junction in central India on the Great India Peninsula Railway. When I left India, Piara Singh saw me off at Delhi and said, "I would like to see my brother come back in the same form." At that time I believed it would be easy to keep my Sikh form, and the opposition of my relatives in Canada came totally out of the blue. In my letter I told Piara Singh how I had been defeated for the time being but that I would recover. A wound may leave a scar, but it will heal. I could go clean-shaven while it was necessary, but I could regain my Sikh form.

The postal services in those days were very efficient. A reply would come from India within a fortnight or, at the most, sixteen or seventeen days. Generally my wife and I exchanged two letters a month. With the help of Almighty, my brother-in-law was slow to arrange for my photograph, so I had not cut my hair or shaved when a touching reply came from Piara Singh. He promised to pay my return airfare if things did not turn around, even if he had to sell his wife's jewelry. I got the letter at noon during lunch break, and after taking my lunch I went to my room and read it. It troubled me so much that I started to weep aloud. I tried to keep my voice low, but my tears were flowing, and I lay on my bed, determined to keep my faith, and decided that I would leave the house right away if it had to be.

My sister's third eldest son, Udham Singh Gill, or Jack, as he was called, came to my door. My nephews and I were nearly the same age, so they called me by my name. He said, "Tara, let us go. Time is up." He saw my wet face and said, "What happened? Is there any sad news in the letter?" I said, "Now listen, Udham, I am going to bury this matter once and for all. Would you be kind enough to go into the house and tell them if this matter is raised again, no matter how slightly, I will leave and that person will be my opponent totally." Of course he did what I asked, and from then on things started to stabilize. Better days followed. My form was accepted in the family, and although outside the family from time to time people would ask how long I could carry on, I felt no pressure.

During my first summer and fall in Canada we went to gurdwaras (Sikh temples) three or four times. We were busy and attended only the important functions, like Guru Nanak's birthday, when they were hosted by friends and we were invited. Generally my sister and brother-in-law would go, but not my nephews. We went to different gurdwaras, to Abbotsford, Vancouver, and New Westminster. At Abbotsford gurdwara on one occasion I spoke for fifteen minutes. I wanted to illustrate the attitude that Sikhs had towards their faith, and I spoke of the musk deer with the musk in its belly, button that roams around trying to find the source of the scent that is actually within itself. I had a spontaneous desire to express myself, and the Lord gave me the energy and skill to speak before an audience for the first time very successfully.

At the end of the summer I asked my sister and brother-in-law if I owed them anything, and they said no. They were paying me fifty cents an hour and deducting my airfare and whatever they had sent me. I had complete faith in my sister and never asked her how much I had owed. It would have been unfair to doubt such a good person. When I needed money, they would give me some, but that was not often, except for the money I sent regularly to my wife. Sometimes we worked fourteen hours a day. In the evening, when we had big lettuce orders to fill, we could cut and pack the lettuce with vehicle lights on. In farming, when the work is there, you have to do it, and a farmer can not afford to pay overtime or limit the hours of work.

In the fall, around October, the farm work stopped. After a few weeks my brother-in-law and sister found a sawmill job for me with a clean-shaven Punjabi contractor on Vancouver Island. This man had a contract to pull lumber from the green chain at the Parks Logging Company at Nanaimo. He employed four people per shift for two shifts a day, and he owned an old house in Nanaimo heated by a makeshift wood burner made from a forty gallon barrel that stood near the kitchen. This house had been built in the old mining days in Nanaimo, and it was not insulated, but he kept his shift workers there and charged them fifty dollars a month for rent, which would have been enough for an excellent house at the time.

When I arrived, six other Punjabis were living in that house and working on the green chain. The other worker was Chinese, and he lived somewhere else. Among the Punjabis, five were clean-shaven and one old fellow, Udham Singh, was bearded, so I was the second bearded Sikh. I started on Tuesday evening on the shift that went from 7:00 p.m. to 4:00 a.m., and I worked until Friday before I was told that I was not being paid for my first four shifts because they were considered a training period. That drove a wedge into my mind about the exploitative nature of the man we were working for, but I kept working. We were paid $1.45 an hour for eight hours, but when we did overtime, we worked for free. And it happened many times that we worked through our coffee and lunch breaks and for some time after our shift was over. If we did not work, the job would be on the line. At times we would have no chance to go to the washroom for an entire shift.

The mill had two gang saws, and each shift these saws would cut fifty thousand or sixty thousand board-feet of moisture-laden hemlock or fir, heavy wood, with none of the lighter cedar as relief. It was mostly two-inch lumber in widths from three inches to twelve and in lengths up to twenty-four feet. From the mill this lumber carried on to the green chain and down the green chain to the pull-off sections where we stood, two on each side, taking it as fast as it came and piling it according to size and order on wooden blocks, load by load, for removal by a carrier truck. The lumber rode down the green chain with the ends even on one side and showing various lengths on the other. That was the more difficult side to work on, especially because the platform was wider and the loading-blocks farther away, so that we had to carry each piece ten feet instead of four. That was the side my companions gave me to start with. The small lumber was hardest because we had to handle more pieces. Once in a while a few would go by, and when the mill stopped while the other workers took their coffee break, we would pick those pieces up. Every piece was counted, and if we couldn't keep up, there was no coffee break for us.

In our house the night-shift workers got up around noon or 1:00 p.m. after seven or eight hours of sleep and cooked vegetables and dal (cooked lentils) for everyone. In the system we followed the night-shift people did most of the cooking, but the day people made their own fresh rotis (Indian bread). We would prepare and eat our breakfast porridge of oats, milk, eggs, and sugar in the early morning after we finished our shift and before we went to bed. The day-shift people would also make their own breakfast. During the cold weather of winter the day shift would feed the fire with wood before they went to bed, and we would rekindle it when we came back in the early morning because it was usually out by then. On the weekends the mill stopped and we had common time, which we needed to visit and buy our groceries. This time was more important to me than the others after I started a lumber-grading course with classes twice a week.

Our routine continued like this for a couple of months until it was interrupted by a happening at the workplace. Each order of lumber called for an average length. If the lumber inspector felt that we were close to completing an order and needed more long pieces to finish it, he would start a new order and put a mark on it. Sometimes long pieces would keep coming for a couple of hours, which meant that we could not get the old order out of the way while we kept piling lumber for the new one. Then we would run out of spots to stack our loads. At that point we would ask the driver of the carrier truck to shift some loads to create some room. If we were too crowded on one side, he could move them to the other. He used to do it, but sometimes he was a little offensive.

One night shift, when he came to pull a full load and I asked him to move a couple of others to make room for us, he reacted with "Fuck you." His name was Dick, and he was a heavily built man. Because he was sitting at the controls of the carrier truck ten or twelve feet above the ground, I said, "Dick, would you kindly come down to listen to me?" And he said, "Do you want a fight?"

"Do you think I am a match for you?" I said. "You are twice as big as I am. How is it possible?" Finally he came down, and I told him, "You can move these loads with your machine, but we will suffer physically if we have to move them by hand." He said he would do it, but not too many times, so I asked him, "Don't you think we are human beings?" And he told me, "You are human beings all right, but you are working like slaves and you are setting a bad precedent." I knew he was right; but what could we do? "If we don't do it that way," I told him, "our jobs are at stake. Where would we go then? We are all batching people living in a rented house that belongs to the contractor, with families in the old country supported by our earnings."

We were members of the union, but we had no union strength. Our paycheques came directly from the company, not the contractor, with the union dues deducted, but we were being paid only eight hours a day. The major hurdle was the language barrier, and that was why no one had dared to disobey the contractor before I started working there. Dick said, "We will help you through the union, if you will stand up with the union." When I asked him if he was sure they would back us up, he said, "Well, I'll discuss it with the business manager, and someone will come back."

We were lying on the lunchroom benches on our midnight break a few nights later when the union business agent came in. His name was J.F. Colwell. He was a logger by trade and a nice, honest young man. Later on we became real friends, and I met his wife, who was an even better person than he was. He spoke to one of the young clean-shaven fellows, Bawa Singh, who just told him to speak to me, and I explained the whole situation. "There is too much work for four," I told him. "We need five on a shift." Among Punjabi mill-workers in Canada there were very few well-versed in English like me. We decided to stop pulling lumber until the matter was resolved. Mr Colwell pledged the full support of the union, but I asked for a few days to discuss it with the others.

At a joint meeting in the house on the weekend, we told the three people on the other shift. A couple were weaklings. One of them was a big fellow physically, but he was not too bold. So we threatened them and said that if they did not co-operate with us, we would not co-operate with them. That convinced them after a while, and we all took an oath of allegiance: "Whoever deserts or does not co-operate will be the bastard son of a scoundrel." On Monday we changed from night to day shift. During the day the contractor came around to haul sawdust with his truck. (He had a wood-hauling and sawdust business.) We asked him for an extra man because the union had already given him notice to provide one, but he said he didn't have one. So we stopped pulling lumber.

The mill kept going for another two hours until the two sections of the green chain were so overloaded the motors stopped. Mr Neal, the mill foreman, and Mr Moore, the mill manager, called the business agent for the union and arranged a meeting in Mr Moore's office with the contractor. I went as the representative of the four of us on the green chain. A long discussion seemed to solve nothing. Finally Mr Moore spoke to me, and I told him, "You are a nice gentleman and you are the manager, and you know we have been doing so much extra work for nothing and are the subject of jeering and hatred by our fellow union workers. I better leave it to your judgment." So he took the contractor into another room, and they came out with a proposal for an extra worker on shifts when the mill cut was above average.

For the next week we had an extra man, but on the weekend the contractor came to the house with his nephew, early in the morning before we had eaten, and started to disconnect the plumbing. I told my comrades, "Let us leave the house and buy groceries and inform the union about this." We were about half-way to the union office when he came up from behind and told Udham Singh, the old man we called Bhai, "You are very smart people. I know why you have left the house and I have reconnected it."

The mill paid the contractor by the board-foot, and because he made more money if he used fewer people, he gradually stopped supplying the extra man. We had some orders for a ship that was tied up at the mill's wharf, and the union people told us that the company had to load these orders right away. With the backing of the whole mill crew, we began to let some pieces go by, and they got buried in a big pile at the end of the green chain, where they were very hard to get out. The contractor tried to show the union that we were not doing a proper job, but the union president chose to come to see us when we were handling so many small pieces, two by threes and two by fours, that we really needed two extra men instead of one. The contractor used threats and intimidation, and he fired one newly hired man and got a white man in his place. In the beginning this white man acted a little offensively towards us, but he soon learned what was going on and began to cooperate. When the union president asked him, "Hello, Henry, how are you doing?" he gave a good answer. He said, "I am killing myself."

On the next night shift Mr Neely Moore, the mill manager, came to me about 9:30 p.m. to ask politely and in a friendly way how the situation could be solved. I reminded him that we had an agreement that had been broken, and I said, "I again leave it to you." For a few moments he paused, and then he said, "If a fifth man is given on each shift on a permanent basis, will there still be any trouble?" So I talked to the others and then promised an honest performance without any default. That settled it. Henry became the fifth worker on the other shift and another white man, a heavily built, slow worker named George, was added to ours. As charge hands for each shift, Henry and I got five cents extra.

On the weekend after we first went on strike, my brother-in-law phoned from Cloverdale. He wanted me to quit the job and get out of trouble, and he had arranged another job for me at a cedar mill on False Creek in Vancouver. I told him respectfully that we had all taken a pledge to stick together: "You would not like me to be the son of a scoundrel." He did not appreciate my answer because sister and he knew the contractor. That is how they got me the job. So he said, "Well, if you are so determined, we don't want any relations with you," and he put the receiver down. I used to go to Cloverdale with Bhai Udham Singh, the old man, but it took two years before brother-in-law and sister could be soothed and the differences forgotten.

During my discussion with Mr Moore, the mill manager, I asked if he would keep enough of us on the job to run a house economically if we bought one. He said he would. After some effort we found a good house a few doors from the one we were in, a little closer to the mill. Three of us bought it for five thousand dollars. We gave the contractor thirty days' notice and moved in during the summer of 1954 without any trouble or interference on the job. After this the work was easier. We could enjoy it, and the odd time, when pieces got by us, we would still pick them up during our lunch breaks and coffee breaks.

The executive of the union sublocal took me in as second vice-president and then as first vice-president, and they put me on some committees at the local level. Our pictures were printed in the union monthly paper, *The Barker*. At the same time I was attending the local grading classes, which were held two miles away. When I was on day shift, I went to the night classes and walked both ways in the dark. An acquaintance of the contractor came to me with a warning. "You are walking in the dark, which is not free from attack." I said, "I am a religious person and I don't worry about that. No bullet can be fired until my end comes." Then I told him, "Look here. You brought the message. You are threatening. Don't you know you are also liable?" And he said, "You are too smart."

Then the contractor found a way to harm my reputation and stop my progress in the union. He came from Ghar Shankar in the Hoshiarpur District, about fifteen miles from my village, and he knew something about my background. In our family we had an aunt who married an educated man from the village of Isspur, five miles away. This man went to the United States to study and got a PhD. His name was Dr Bhag Singh, and he was a dedicated member of the Communist Party of India. Dr Bhag Singh had two sons, and the elder, Pritam Singh Gill, was my class-fellow at high school. We had very different ideologies because he was a materialist from childhood and I was a spiritualist. This Pritam Singh came to British Columbia before I did and joined the university as a student. On his summer vacation he worked for the contractor on the same job that I later got. So the contractor knew him, and the contractor knew that Pritam Singh and his father were Communists. All the contractor had to do was tell the union that Pritam Singh and I were cousins.

I had been elected a delegate to the twelfth annual convention of the British Columbia Federation of Labour, which was held in Vancouver. During the two-and-a-half hour crossing on the ferry from Nanaimo to Vancouver, I drafted two resolutions. One concerned apartheid in South Africa, and the other concerned China. I wanted the union leadership and the Canadian public to create contacts with the common people of China to keep them closer to the free world. I thought my resolutions would receive good attention from the union brass, but it did not happen. They could not believe that I was capable of drafting them myself, and I think they assumed that some Communist cell had given them to me. For that reason they kept my resolutions off the main agenda, although the Communists and the CCF supported them very well. My picture was printed on the front page of the second section of the *Vancouver Sun*, along with Jack Moore from the Port Alberni local of the IWA, so I got a lot of publicity. But the top brass were cool, and I wondered why. On the closing day, when a picture was taken of all the delegates, the leaders of my own local (IWA 1-80 at Duncan) did not want to stand near me, and that deepened my doubts.

I asked Mr Colwell, the business agent of local 1-80, who was my closest friend in the union, if there was any problem, and he said there was something, but he would talk about it later. A few days after that an immigration agent phoned to make an appointment and then came to my house. He started asking about my birth and my life in India, but he had two names and he wanted information about them. The names were Pritam Singh and Bhag Singh, but, because he was unfamiliar with our names, he asked, "Who is Pritam Bhag Singh?" I had no idea why these names were coming up, and out of surprise and curiosity I tried to look at the paper he held in his hand. I was sitting on the kitchen chair and he was sitting on a sofa, and because I was higher, I was able to read it. Then I saw why the union brass at the local and district level didn't want to know me any more, and I knew who was responsible. I told the immigration officer, "Gentleman, I have read your paper and I understand what the story is, so let us talk very frankly. You don't know who these people are. You don't even understand that they are two different people." Then I told him about the strike, about the contractor, and about Pritam Singh and how we were related. The immigration officer was well convinced because I gave him the background of my life, my philosophy, and my daily routine, and he was impressed with the way I presented it – simple and factual and much more than he wanted to know.

Very quickly I contacted Mr Colwell and told him that it was now clear to me that I was considered a Communist. He admitted it, and he admitted that he did not want to tell me himself, but from then on he worked to clear my name. Over the next six months my movements, my contacts, and my way of living must have been screened without my knowing it. Mr Sonny Jones of the Nanaimo office later confirmed it. Finally, at a private meeting, Mr Colwell and Mr Jones told me that a top intelligence officer would come to my house one day and that I should give him the information he wanted. So it did happen, sometime in the summer of 1955. Seven of us had bought another house by then, bigger but older, with two storeys, on Nichols Street. The first house was on Irwin Street, near the waterfront close to the mill, and we had rented it and were living on Nichols when the intelligence officer came. He must have been well satisfied because everything was cleared with immigration and with the union. In their books I became a non-Communist once again.

The publicity about my union activity brought some Christian clergy to my door. At that time I did not know all the denominations, only Catholics and Protestants, and I took them to be Christians only. They spent a lot of time and effort on me, and I was very cordial to them and we had long discussions, but when they asked me to convert, that is when the competition started. Generally they would come two or three together. One time they brought a fourth, a fellow from New York, some doctor of divinity. These discussions lasted up to two hours at a time, and we met more than twenty times. But their arguments were just like beating around the bush. I took the first hymn of Japji Sahib and translated it into English, and they claimed it was from the Bible. Either they didn't know my capacity, or they didn't know what they were doing. I was polite, and of course they had to be polite, and for me it was a learning process.

Once they brought a long letter, a manuscript of seven sheets written on both sides, from a Sikh in Bombay who said that, ever since he had adopted Christianity and cut his hair, he had tapped into the realm of paradise. The language about Sikhism was sarcastic, and I didn't believe it was a real letter. A few sessions after that they said, "Okay, you can keep your hair and turban and still be a Christian." It didn't matter to me because I had started these discussions sincerely, but midway through I had become a pretender, and they didn't know my mind. One time they arranged for me to go to their church at Nanoose Bay, twenty miles north of Nanaimo. When they came with their car to pick me up, they had two girls in the back seat and they wanted me to sit with them. They could see I was a young man, and they thought I could be attracted to these girls, that sex would be a lure. I said, "I am a married man, and my body should not touch another woman." Still, they wanted me to get in with them, and we discussed the matter for five or ten minutes before two of the men moved to the back and I sat in the front with the driver.

At that time Nanoose Bay had only a dozen houses, a fuel station, and the church. Music was playing in the church, and the priest was drawing wonderful chalk drawings on the blackboard for the congregation. Then came preaching about healing, and people were bowing and kneeling on the floor. I didn't kneel with them because they didn't understand that no one can cleanse you of wrong thinking and wrong doing but yourself. If you repent and stop doing what wrong you were doing, then the healing is prayer, with help from the Secret Father. After that they quit coming, except for the odd visit. They had tried hard to convert me because I could speak English. If they could get me, then they could get the others in our house. But they found out that I was not much use to them.

When I went to work in the sawmill in Nanaimo, the fight for the rights of East Indians in Canada was going on. Late in the spring of 1954 the Canadian East Indian Welfare Society was organized at a meeting there. Nanaimo was a good place for meetings because Sikhs from Port Alberni, Duncan, Victoria, and other places on the island could gather there, and Sikhs from the mainland could come over on the ferry. The meeting started at noon and went on for five or six hours until dark, and it gave me a full knowledge of what was happening with the immigration quota, which was the main issue. I didn't have to do much reading to understand. Dr Durai Pal Pandia, who gave such a lot of service in the struggle to get the vote for East Indians, was at the helm, along with some well-to-do Sikhs. Working people didn't have much say. During the meeting I led the opposition. My experience in the union and my speaking ability gave me that role. We wanted representation on the executive for the working people, and we wanted to read and debate every paragraph of the constitution that the controlling group had written. This was on a weekend, perhaps Saturday. The next morning Dr Pandia, with some of his colleagues, came to my house for a cordial chat. He said, "You are worthwhile. We should try to get you involved in the struggle." So they took me on the advisory committee, and my community service began.

At that time the Sikhs had gurdwaras in Vancouver, New Westminister, and Abbotsford on the mainland and at Victoria, Paldi, and Hillcrest on the island. Each of these gurdwaras would host one annual function for the whole Sikh community, and the Christmas function was held at the Victoria gurdwara. To avoid further travel, the executive of the East Indian Welfare Society fixed the annual meeting for the same weekend. It was well attended. After the annual report from the stage came the elections for the next year. Without being asked, I was nominated for secretary-treasurer. I thought it a little more than I could manage with the travel and expenses, and I was afraid that if I took up this position, then someone might start up more false allegations against me, so I wasn't willing to accept. But people were pressing me and pushing me to do it, and when the time came to withdraw my name at the call from the stage, one fellow put his hand in front of my mouth.

The contractor from Nanaimo, with whom I had so much trouble the year before, had been the treasurer, and he was running for re-election. So we were the two candidates. The other positions on the executive were nearly all chosen unanimously. In the show of hands for treasurer the people on the stage counted a tie. The president, Mr Nand Singh Palahi, who was a labour contractor at Hillcrest Lumber Company, wouldn't cast the tie-breaking vote. He said, "One is my friend and the other is a good person, and I don't want my vote against either of them." The matter went to a recount, and the people on the stage still announced a tie. My supporters were alert, and after a good protest we added one person from the floor to count as well. In the end I had a victory by four votes.

This was Christmas 1955, and I was secretary-treasurer for 1956. That was the year that the government increased the immigration quota for India from 150 to 300 a year. Of course we were asking for equal rights with European immigrants, but it was a big success to get the 300 quota approved. We saw the leaders of all the political parties, the MLAs and MPs from British Columbia, and nearly all of them agreed with us. We sent a delegation to the minister in Ottawa, Mr Pickersgill, and finally he came up with the formula. He said, "It's a small community, so if we increase the quota to 300 and make it legal that should solve the problem." The president of the welfare society, my namesake Tara Singh Bains of Port Alberni, did a lot of the work, along with Dr Pandia and others, and the effort was supported by the whole community. We stipulated twenty-five dollars for each working man as a contribution for the campaign, and as secretary-treasurer I put out a financial report in 1956 that showed contributions of over $17,000. My work in the welfare society was good for my relationship with my sister and brother-in-law. It pleased them. My brother-in-law was there when I was elected, and the fellow who stopped my mouth so I couldn't withdraw was his close friend.

6 A Lumber Worker

In the spring of 1956 the Canadian Pacific Railway bought our mill-site to build a ferry terminal for the railway. The mill shut down in the late spring, and we had to look for work elsewhere. We could see it coming, but we stuck to our jobs to the final day. One of the partners in the Nichol Street house bought the rest of us out, but we had difficulty selling the house on Irwin Street. Finally, in the summer of 1956, with the help of my namesake Tara Singh Bains, I got a job in Port Alberni at the MacMillan Bloedel Somass Division sawmill. To begin with I worked on the green chain, and most of the time I was at the end of the chain, which is the toughest place to be. Each fellow is supposed to pull off his share, but what the others miss comes down to the last fellow, and he gets no slack. When the logs are bigger and the cut is greater, then the fellow at the end gets a disproportionate part of the load. And when the others don't work as hard as they should, he is the one that pays the price.

According to the union contract, I was on probation for thirty days and had to take the end position. It was heavy work for someone who weighed only 125 pounds. This mill was a big operation employing 1,800 people, with three green chains and four planer mills. After three weeks, when I was close to completing my probation period, I went to the personnel manager, Mr Moncur, a French fellow, very tall and very nice, and I told him that working all day like that, every day, was hurting my body, particularly my back. "I am a lightweight man. Is that going to be my work all the time?" This made him think that I had a back problem, and I had to tell him that my back was very solid, and I could get a doctor's certificate to show it. Then he said I could take three days off, but I didn't want that because I was on probation. So he said, "Wait until we get a chance to move you." He did not lay me off. That was his kindness.

Later on I was given an easier spot on the green chain, but only for a few days. Then I was taken to the planer mill, where eight men were taking lumber off the planer chain. Three pulled long lengths from one side while three pulled short lengths from the other and two pulled from the end. The long side was harder because you never got a break. When the machine was planing short pieces, there would be no long ones coming down, and we all had to pull from the short side. But when it was planing long pieces, there would still be some short ones – six-foot lengths trimmed from the ends of twenty-fours and so on. At least 80 or 90 per cent of the lumber would be coming off the long side, and the short-side men were supposed to help, but they also had to jump back to their own side to pull off the short pieces, and they could waste time without being noticed by the foreman. The long-side men had to keep pulling all the time, and unfortunately for me, I was given the long side.

One day, after two or three months, we had nothing but long lengths of two-by-six-inch hemlock to handle for nearly the whole shift. Hemlock was the heaviest – all water – then spruce and fir, and the lightest was western red cedar. The sun was warm, as it can be in late September or early October. After half a day I had drunk about two gallons of water. At one time I said to the people on the short side, "You come here. I am going for a drink." They couldn't keep up, so they hit the button to stop the machine. As soon as the machine stopped, the planer-mill foreman came over, and the pull-off crew told him I had gone to the tap. He was walking up to the tap as I was walking back. Naturally, he asked why I had gone, and I told him I was dry like a fish, and he told me I shouldn't leave my spot because it stopped production. "Well," I said, "you are the foreman and you should know what is going on. You should have a solution." He saw my argument, but he wouldn't say anything, so I said, "Why don't you put the men on rotation, either on a weekly basis or a daily basis? Or put me on the dry chain where the dehydrated lumber comes. I am a fast worker but a light-bodied man."

He put my idea of rotation into practice soon after that, and he kept my other suggestion in mind for two or three weeks before putting me on a lighter job, first a rip-saw and then the dry chain, where the lumber was mostly one-inch, kiln-dried clear wood. So finally I had a better spot, and I worked there very nicely for a year or so. During that year I took my grading and tallying exams and finished first in my mill, 1 or 2 per cent ahead of my inspector, Art Roe, and just a fraction less than I needed for an A certificate. The manager of that mill, Mr Pete DeMan, knew how the bearded Sikhs worked because he had grown up among the Sikhs in the forest industry on the island. He noticed my high marks and, as a reward, sent me a cheque.

The market situation improved a lot in 1957–58, and the mill opened up another planer machine, which meant they needed another three graders and trimmers, one for each shift, and they put me on the trim-saw job, which was a good promotion. In the first three or four days they had trouble with the grading. From my position on the trim-saw, looking down on the whole mill, I saw Mr DeMan talking to the head foreman, a Swede, and pointing at me. So I wasn't surprised later on when Almighty sent the foreman to ask if I could grade on that machine. I started the next morning. A senior grader was supposed to coach me for two or three days to help me gain speed and accuracy. During the first couple of hours he gave me a few chances to do it for a few minutes at a time on my own. We were working with one- and two-inch green lumber. After the ten-minute break he gave me longer intervals, with one-by-eight dressed shiplap. After the lunch break I was doing it myself nearly all the time, and he was just picking out the odd mistake.

The lumber was going by in random lengths of six to twenty-four feet at four hundred lineal feet per minute. Each piece had to be examined for wood or planing defects, then turned and marked and either sent on or sent back for trimming. The rest breaks came every two hours. At the end of the day the senior grader told the foreman that I could handle it on my own. From then on I was a lumber grader, a key position with better pay, and a job that East Indians usually didn't get. Perhaps only five of us were doing it in the whole province in those days.

That was nice work for a year or so until the market slackened and they cut back to two shifts on the planer machine. Naturally, I went back to my old place on the dry chain. We had a new head foreman at the planer mill because the old one had died. This man would never give me a chance at grading or trimming when one of the regular men was absent. Instead he would put two boys on those jobs, although I had seniority and at one point had coached one of them on the lumber grading for several days. One was the son of a foreman and the other the son of a lumber inspector, and he always used them instead of me. The only explanation I could think of was prejudice, so God gave me an idea and I began to prepare a case.

In the machine-room the machine-setter kept a chart each shift to record time lost in production. Sometimes the grader would get behind, or the trimmer, or the pull-off crew. If any of them was in trouble, he could push a button and the machine-setter would stop the machine. Every time that happened, he would record it, and his chart gave management a picture of what was happening. When one of those boys was on the job, I would look at the chart at the end of the shift and list the stoppages in a pocket notebook, and day by day I put all those entries on to a sheet that I kept in my bedroom.

This new foreman began to put me on a heavier job, working all day dumping cars loaded with rounds of kiln-dried lumber that were so big it took three men to move one of them, using special crowbars. When I had to do this job several times in one week, I spoke to the head foreman, but he wouldn't listen, so I went to the assistant manager. "I don't want to refuse to do the work," I told him, "but I am a lightweight and this is for heavyweights." With God's help, he understood, and said something so I didn't have to do that any more. But I still didn't get the casual replacement work as a grader or trimmer.

In the spring of 1958 I was elected to the local union balloting committee and put on the union payroll for two weeks during the union elections. According to the union contract, vacancies for key positions had to be posted on the notice board. The head foreman chose to put up three vacancies for lumber graders while I was away. Here again the secret help came, because on the balloting schedule I had to go to my own mill, along with another fellow, to ballot the graveyard shift. It was a cold night, and when the rush was over, I asked the other fellow to take care of the late-comers while I went to the punch-clock room to warm up. As I was standing over the heater, I looked up at the notice board and saw the vacancies. The next morning I brought an application to Mr Moncur, the personnel manager.

I went back to the mill on a Monday afternoon shift, and the head foreman put me on the dry chain. On Tuesday I reminded Mr Moncur, "I want this job. I have already proven to be a good grader. There is no reason I should be denied it." On Wednesday I told him that I would even go to the company headquarters in Vancouver and publicize the matter through the union, and he promised to really press the head foreman, but it didn't make any difference. So on Thursday morning, around eleven o'clock, I took that sheet of production stoppages from my bedroom and went to the mill to see Mr DeMan, the mill manager. It so happened that the Super Power arranged for me to walk through the yard to the manager's office as Mr Moncur was leaving, and we met half-way. He asked, "Tara, where are you going?" and I told him. "Here is the sheet. You can read it." When he saw what I had, he didn't want me to show it to Mr DeMan because it wouldn't be good for the head foreman. "Well," I said, "I'm not after his job. I just want the grader job." Mr Moncur asked for one more chance. "If he doesn't give you the job tonight, you can do whatever you want tomorrow."

That evening, near the mid-shift break, Charlie, the night foreman, said, "You go do the grading on the sticker." The mill had two stickers and needed seven men to operate them – a feeder, a planer-setter, and a grader for each machine, and one bundler. They were small machines that did specialty lumber, mouldings, and small orders that couldn't be done on the big machine. After I had worked for a couple of hours, the head foreman himself came over. His approach was friendly, but he suggested that I wouldn't want the job because the vacancy was not on the sticker but on the Stetson Ross machine, handling heavy lumber, and I would have to take the graveyard shift. "I know you don't like that shift because of the bedding conditions at home." (It was difficult to sleep during the day with other batching fellows coming and going.) "That doesn't matter," I said. "When I challenged the job, I had to accept the conditions."

He started me on Monday, working on the day shift with the two boys who had been given the job ahead of me. One boy had been bumped down to trimmer. The other was working beside me as a grader because the Stetson Ross machine employed two. On that machine, to equalize the work the two graders would trade positions every two hours, after coffee breaks and after lunch break. I began the day in the second position, further down the flow of lumber, picking up everything that the other grader left. The machine was throwing out a thousand lineal feet a minute, and the boy I was working with was deliberately wasting time, going slowly and putting pressure on me to finish what he did not do. Every five minutes I had to stop the machine to catch up. He was making me look inefficient so that senior management would think I couldn't handle the job. I put up with it for half an hour. Then, when he was clearly slacking, I said, "What are you doing?" He looked at me and said, "I don't understand your language."

Finally, relief time came, and we exchanged positions. I began to play the same cunning game, shirking at my position and forcing him to stop the machine. It didn't take him ten or fifteen minutes before he spoke. Coincidentally, he repeated the same sentence: "What are you doing?" So I said, "I don't understand your language either." I added the word "either." Then we compromised, and the work went smoothly after that. But the head foreman and the boy's father, who was a lumber inspector, were flying rumours that my grading was not up to standard. I knew it because quite a few fellows told me. After three weeks we went on the graveyard shift, the two boys and myself. On the last shift of the week, which was a Thursday, the head foreman came up to me and stopped the machine. "For tonight," he said, "you do the trimming and the trimmer man will take over your grading. On Monday you go on the day shift on the other machine."

That night the lumber was two-by-twelve Douglas fir, number three grade, which generally doesn't have to be trimmed very much except when there are big splits or breaks. But the head foreman told us to do as much trimming as possible to improve the grade, and that tripled my work because the two boys took their cue and sent me as many pieces as they could, keeping the pressure on all the time. The load was so great that I must have stopped the machine many times. A trimmer couldn't walk over to the tap whenever he was thirsty, but he had water nearby in big glass wine bottles. In six and a half hours I drank at least five gallons. Fortunately, it was the last shift of the week, and I was going back on the day shift on Monday, which gave me an extra twelve hours of sleep. This happened in March, and after I walked home on a cold night, I had so much perspiration I could squeeze it from my socks and clothes as if I had been travelling through water.

When I came to work on Monday, they put me on the planer machine that I had started with when I began grading a year before. My old friend Art Roe, the lumber inspector, was there. "Be careful," he said. "I'm told that your grading will be checked by the roving inspector from the Pacific Lumber Bureau." On Tuesday, when I was grading construction lumber, two-by-four hemlock studs, they pulled out load and took it to the yard so that a supervisor could regrade it with the help of two workers. That load had come off the planer machine at the rate of four hundred or five hundred lineal feet a minute, and I had done it in fifteen or twenty minutes, assessing the grade of each piece and marking it with chalk. The supervisor with his two assistants took an hour and a half to check it over. At coffee-break time Mr Roe walked up and patted me on the shoulder. "Boy, you have done well." If a lumber grader was 95 per cent accurate, with the balance only one grade out, he was very good. On that load I had been 97 per cent accurate.

After that I was more confident and relaxed, but the head foreman did not quit yet. I came to work one morning and he said, "Make sure the lumber is done properly." He had arranged to put small pieces of dry cedar through, and the machine was no good for it. He knew it. It was set up for heavy green lumber, and even then some of the shorter pieces would turn sideways on the roller and come through horizontally. The stuff was too light, too thin, too short, and too narrow, and it was constantly turning on the rollers and becoming entangled. After a while the head foreman told me I was stopping the machine too often. I wanted to know how I could go any faster, and he gave me a lecture of a minute or more on the kind of work he had done in the past and how good he had been. "Well, fine," I said, "but you give me a demonstration for a while and I will follow what you do." So he started grading. Within a minute I could see eight or ten pieces with the wrong chalk marks, and I pulled them to the side. He stopped the machine and asked me what I was doing. "Just sampling your

good grading,"I told him. When I showed him his mistakes, he
threw the chalk-holder on the floor, angrily, instead of handing it
to me, and he said, "Do as you like." "Fine," I said; "make sure
you don't bother me again."

The batching people in our house used to invite Mr Moncur for
dinner at Christmas time. He was very fair to us as personnel
manager, so we would offer him a gift like a good table lamp, or
something like that, to show how we felt and to respect the spirit
of Christmas. Generally we East Indians had to compliment our
bosses with gifts for fear of losing our jobs. In those days some
managers would take big gifts, although I never had any experience of that. During my feud with the head foreman I brought a
turkey to his house for Christmas as a goodwill gesture. He accepted it happily, but he didn't understand that it was given in
friendship, and that cost me a lot of hard time and hard feeling,
and it cost him as well.

In those days, because my family wasn't there, I read a lot. I was
getting quite a few Punjabi monthlies from India – *Aatam Science*,
from Calcutta, a very spiritual magazine, *Sant Sipahi* and *Gurmat*,
two religious magazines from Amritsar, and *Amar Kahanyan*, with
stories emphasizing Indian moral values, social discipline, and
creating a better sensitivity of living. In English I read the *Vancouver Sun* every day, *Life* magazine every week, and *Reader's Digest*
monthly, and I would read the odd magazine from the market,
like *Time*. I also read *The Sikh Review*, from Calcutta, every month
in English, and after I came to Port Alberni I started the weekly
airmail edition of *Hindustan Times*. The postal efficiency was so
good then that I would get it regularly by the next weekend.

In Nanaimo I joined the Canadian Legion. I told them, "I am
loyal to Canada, but India is my birthplace, and I must be loyal to
that." So they didn't ask me to swear allegiance to the queen. The
best thing they did was to collect used articles for the poor. Generally they just had get-togethers with a lot of drinking. I didn't
have the habit or the leisure, so I didn't join at Port Alberni. But I
attended another organization as a representative of the Sikh community. This organization was based on culture – Italian, French,
and so on. Quite a few Sikhs lived in the Port Alberni area, and the
chairman, who was a lady, wanted some representatives from the
Sikh community. My namesake, Tara Singh Bains, and I were well
known for our union activities, so she approached us. I went to

the meetings regularly, and at the annual meeting in 1958 she asked me to give the keynote address. She wanted me to speak on the Sikh religion, but I chose the topic "Survival Today" and spoke for an hour to about fifty people. That was a major debut for me, going outside union circles to an audience of various backgrounds.

Although I didn't have any family life of my own, I had close relationships with union friends in the white society. Mr Colwell and his family in Nanaimo were so affectionate in their relationship with me that I considered Mrs Colwell my younger sister. When I went to Nanaimo I stayed with them, and one time Mr Colwell called me by telephone because he had been offered a post by the lumber company and he wanted to discuss it. He thought he could not help the common man if he were in company management, but I told him he was wrong: "In company management you can do more." Finally, he took the job. When I left for India, his family gave me a forty piece Melmac dining set that I took with me and still have in our home in Kultham.

I had a very good impression of the white man's society at the time. Family life was disciplined; people were honest and had good work habits. If someone threw something in the street or spat, you could caution him nicely. Very few women smoked or drank, and most had long hair and wore no ornamentation. Only married women or engaged women wore rings, and quite a few married women wore scarves. After I went back to India, whenever I spoke on the stage, I praised the Canadian way of life. But I expected it would change because the world was changing. I told my relatives in Cloverdale, "Within thirty years, this dairy milk delivered at your door will not be secure." I wanted the unions to establish an education fund so that people would think about the future and uphold the family structure, which is the backbone of everything. When I was living in Nanaimo, I was elected as a delegate to the Island Labour Council, which had its headquarters in Parksville, between Nanaimo and Port Alberni. For the next four years I was re-elected nearly every year, and at the annual general meeting I used to put forward a resolution about an education fund; but my arguments were ignored, and it always failed.

My union activity and my welfare society activity put me in the spotlight among the people in Port Alberni, and they wanted me to lead them in other projects. One project was to build Sikh crematorium on a piece of land donated to the community by a good

Sikh who had died. We formed a committee and collected donations to build a chimney and a shed, and to put up a barbed-wire fence with a gate that could be locked at the entrance. The chimney was a brick and concrete type for cremating the dead, and the shed was for shelter if it rained.

We didn't have a gurdwara in Port Alberni, but we organized a religious festival for the first time in 1959 and rented a community hall for a complete weekend. We had a sports tournament as part of our festival, with children's athletics and youth athletics. About twenty or thirty Sikh families lived in Port Alberni, but people came to our festival from all over the province, and teams came from all over to participate in our tournament. We had our own soccer team of youth in their late teens and early twenties, which I had organized a few months beforehand. After this festival people started to think of building their own gurdwara, and by the time I left in 1960, a campaign was under way to collect money.

While I was in Port Alberni, three babas came to Canada to raise money for the Desh Bhagat Memorial Hall in Jullundur city. These Sikhs had been members of the historical Ghadr Party of North America, the revolutionary party that sent emigrant Sikhs back to India in 1914 to fight the British. One of them was Baba Sohan Singh Bakhna, who had been president of the Ghadr Party. Another was Baba Gurmukh Singh Lalton. By this time these three babas had inclined towards socialism in their thinking. Some people called them communists, but they weren't actually. I believe that Sikhism propagates spiritualism plus socialism. Baba Sohan Singh Bakhna was a very communicative person. He was happy and he made everyone else happy. But Baba Gurmukh Singh had a fiery nature. He hated to see demoralized Sikhs who had cut their hair, and when he did, he was very critical and sarcastic. For that reason he wasn't very popular with the Sikh leadership in British Columbia. These babas stayed a couple of weeks, and we collected twenty or thirty thousand dollars from Sikh workers and families in the Alberni area. Generally the babas didn't come out with us. Their names were enough, and we didn't have cars to drive around. It wasn't easy; we did a lot of trekking. Desh Bhagat Memorial Hall later became the centre of Communist activity in Punjab, so it didn't keep the status that the babas intended.

We didn't come from India to settle in a far-off land among people with religious, cultural, linguistic, and even colour differences without trouble and pain, but the economic lure was there. I wanted to bring my brothers in, starting with Piara Singh, who was next youngest to me. He was a machinist on the government railway, and each time I applied for him to come, he became involved in an accident. Once he cut his index finger and required several operations. When he recovered from that and we tried again, he got a brass splinter in his eye, and the treatment affected his hearing on that side. He was a good Sikh, a good worker and disciplinarian, and he figured that God didn't want him to go to Canada. So he said, "Better give a try for the younger brother."

Altogether, we were six brothers and three sisters. After Piara Singh decided not to come, we applied for the second youngest brother, Jagjit Singh, who was eighteen or nineteen at the time and had only a grade-four or -five education. My sister and brother-in-law visited India and arranged for all his immigration examinations because it is difficult for a young fellow with only a little education to come down to a big city like Delhi and manage those things. When he arrived in Canada, my sister phoned me and invited me to come down to Cloverdale for the weekend. My nephews, sister, brother-in-law, and I had a frank and open discussion about his hair, with no pinching remarks. They had a point and I had a point. They said that he didn't know anything about Sikhism, so it wouldn't be very helpful for him to keep his hair and feel inferior at work because he looked different. My point was that he lacked knowledge and experience and that his beard and turban were a barrier that protected him from juvenile influences. My eldest nephew, Mac Singh, had opposed my hair, but he was a man of integrity, and when he gave my view a vote of confidence, the others accepted it.

I took Jagjit Singh to Port Alberni and applied at the mill for work for him. For the first few months he got casual weekend work, but it turned into regular work later on. With the big gap between my knowledge and experience and his, he always had hard feelings towards me, but he could depend on me and I used the right approach with him, so that he hung on, with the two of us living together until I went back to India in 1960. We had a two-storey house, and my room was upstairs in the attic, which was more convenient for peace and meditation. One weekend, just before I was going to leave for India, he came up to me and, without saying anything, burst into tears. With clasped hands he apologized and begged forgiveness for his rude behaviour. He said,

"Now I realize what kind of personality you are," and he fell into my lap. I was sitting on the bed. "Well, fine," I said. "I have no hard feelings. I know that with your lack of education and social experience, the reaction was bound to be there. So, with this forgiveness, I give you this advice: don't take to social drinking, and as for sexual need, you can get married. Don't fool around at all."

7 My Birthplace Village

When the first space flights were launched in 1957 and 1958, I was living in Port Alberni. They made an impression on my mind, and I had a dream in which I happened to be with two whites who were about my age and we got into a spacecraft. They were the drivers, and I was the companion. I hadn't known them before, but we worked together cohesively and as friends. These two white fellows took the spacecraft on to the surface of Mars. As soon as we landed, I saw a field of sugar cane in which each stalk was as high as a tree. I was amazed. We decided to explore, each in a different direction, and we set a time, before sunset, when we should meet to return to earth.

In this dream I came to a village of mud houses and a large room that was in good shape except that one wall had fallen down, so I could see inside. A mixed class of students – men, women, and youth – were sitting on benches while the teacher wrote Punjabi letters with chalk on a wooden blackboard standing on a tripod. Looking at him from behind, I had the impression that the teacher was Guru Nanak, and when he turned around, he *was* Guru Nanak. I could not move or say anything, and I was so absorbed that I forgot the time. All of a sudden I felt I should go, so I hurried to the landing-spot. The village was to the south-south-west, and the sun was on the horizon shedding a golden light.

I was surprised, I think, to see that the spacecraft was already leaving. But I didn't feel very sad. I looked at the field of sugar cane coloured by sunlight, and I thought that I should find some place to stay. As I got beyond the canefield, which obstructed the view, I could see, four or five miles in the distance, a gilded city of tall domed buildings. At the moment I started towards it, the dream broke. I accepted the dream as a gift and a reflection of my own state of mind. The happiest part was that I saw Guru Nanak. And I felt that my white companions on the flight must have been Chitra and Gupta. In Hindu philosophy Chitra and Gupta sit on the left and right shoulders and record the thoughts and actions of human beings. I knew that I was on the track of spiritual earning, that the destination was there and that I should work towards it.

After my second youngest brother came to Canada, I applied for the next older one, Chatter Singh, who had spent ten years in the Indian Army and had a family with a couple of children. He arrived in the spring of 1960. Then, early in the summer of that year, my wife, my daughter, and my middle son became ill with typhoid fever. My wife wrote and sent telegrams pressing me to return to India, although I had not intended to go back so soon. "The money cannot help now," she wrote. "We need you to look after us." I took this as a command from God, so I quit my job and prepared to go. When I did this, I decided to make my future in India and not return to Canada. My difficulty wasn't with the white society but with the Canadian Punjabis who were ignorant about their own faith. My brother-in-law and sister had moved into Vancouver and were living on Kerr Street, so instead of going to the farm I stayed with them in the city for a few days before my flight. In the old Sikh gurdwara at 1866 Second Avenue West, I asked the priest to perform a prayer for my success in India and for my never having to return to Canada. Finally, departure time came. My sister cried because she knew my views about coming back. I was touched and tried to console her. "You can come to India and we will meet there."

I returned via the Pacific to complete my circuit of the world. From Vancouver I flew to San Francisco and then to Honolulu, where I took a twenty-four-hour tourist break. In Tokyo I took another break and did some shopping for my brother, who had requested some particular machine tools. My family was seriously ill, but I believed in the secret help of Almighty, and I figured I would never have a chance to see those places again. You can tend to people, but you can't save them if they are not fated to live.

Even at Delhi, at the request of Mr B.L. Nijhawan, the travel agent who arranged my ticket in 1953, I stayed an extra day because he had arranged a lunch at a premium vegetarian hotel in Connaught Place.

My brother Piara Singh met me at Delhi and then returned to Bina Junction, where he was stationed. I arrived at home on the train from Delhi on the morning of 18 June. My wife was recovering from her fever. When she was in her twenties and I was in the army, she had a serious attack of typhoid, so this one was light. My daughter was getting better too. But my son Tarsem, who was eight, was dangerously ill with his second successive attack. He had medication, but he needed someone to nurse him efficiently and to keep him pumped up with courage. As soon as I reached home, I set forth to do that. Privately I advised my wife never to say anything discouraging. I said, "If you can't control yourself, go somewhere else with your tears, please." After a month he came out of this attack, but he had two more later on.

Because my father and I differed in our approaches to life, I had decided to settle in my wife's village. But I went to visit him as soon as I could, which was a few days after I got home. At that time Sikhs were protesting against the central government, which was purposely creating a split between Hindus and Sikhs. The government wouldn't recognize Punjabi as the regional language of Punjab if it were written in Gurmurkhi, the script of the Gurus. In Canada, reading the weekly airmail edition of *Hindustan Times*, I had no sense that the problem was developing to the extent it was. Four days before I reached India, Master Tara Singh, the unchallenged leader of the Sikhs, led a protest march in Delhi. Hundred of thousands of people participated. It was the largest procession of Sikhs up to that time, and the Delhi administration ordered a lathi charge. (A lathi is a six-foot rod of solid bamboo.) The movement got into a pitch of protest throughout Punjab, and peaceful protesters were arrested every day. My father was a veteran of the Akali Lahar, the protest movement against the British. He got involved in these demonstrations and was arrested and put in jail. This created a problem in my birth village, Sirhala Khurd.

My two young sisters were living at the farmhouse at Sirhala Khurd. They sent a Bengali fellow, who was living in father's orchard, with a message for me to come quickly. So I had to go. I

stayed a couple of days and made arrangements for one senior elder to sleep at the house at night. Then I came back to care for my
sick son. During the next two months or so I had to travel back
and forth at least half a dozen times. A couple of times when I was
in Sirhala Khurd and the situation with my son became dangerous, my father-in-law came to get me. He rode his horse. He was
fond of horses, and I had sent him money from Canada to get a
good one. So I was tangled between two places. The direct distance between the two villages was fifteen miles, but I had to take
the indirect bus route, which was fifty miles, and the last five
miles from Mahalpur I did on a bike that I borrowed from a
friend.

I mentioned these things in letters to my younger brother, Piara
Singh, who was employed by the railway at Bina Junction in central India. He arranged for leave and came home to visit father in
jail in Hoshiarpur. Then he came to Kultham to convince me that I
should settle in Sirhala with my whole family. I was a little hectic
about that because I knew that father wouldn't mend his ways,
but Piara Singh assured me that father would abide by an agreement if we discussed it. At this time my son had another relapse of
typhoid fever. Piara Singh and I went to Hoshiarpur jail and interviewed father. We made a verbal agreement. I had four conditions.
1) Father must never use any foul language. 2) He must stop lending his money and scaring up court cases, but lead a relaxed life
and keep his money with him. 3) He must never interfere with my
management of land and family affairs, but I would consult him
when needed. If something was not being done properly, he
should caution me, and if it was not corrected, he had the full
right to take over. 4) I would take charge of the ancestral land at
Sirhala only, and not the mortgaged lands he had acquired in
other villages. (I believed that a Sikh should not exploit the weak,
and father's business of lending money to the poorer people of the
community and charging them interest was exploitation.) Father
had only one condition. He wanted good, rich food all the time.

For seven or eight months father remained in jail in Hoshiarpur
without being sentenced. During that time I would bring him
good dried food and fruit and money, although there was not
much he could spend it on. On this occasion, after Piara Singh
took me to see him, I discussed the matter with my wife and father-in-law. Father-in-law said he would stay behind. He did not

want to go to Sirhala with us. My wife also put up a strong resistance, and she was right in foreseeing the same old dictatorial habits with father. But I was able to convince her. "We have full economic independence now," I told her. "If we see any recurrence of the old behaviour, we can move back here." So we loaded up a bullock cart with necessities and took up residence at Sirhala. In all we stayed two years.

During those two years we took charge of the land and the houses. In our combined family we had the four children, my niece, my two younger sisters, my youngest brother, and father, after he came home from jail. The big, three-storey brick house in the village needed work, and I did a heavy renovation that cost around eight thousand rupees. In the summer I would stay at the farmhouse with the boys, and I did some cultivating as a hobby, as well as producing vegetables and fruit. Most of the land I would rent to other people. We had a servant helper-boy, a very good boy, and a gardener helper, the Bengali fellow. I bought two nice milk buffalo, and we had a lot of fruit from the orchard and vegetables from the garden, and I could buy many food items as well, so it was a good life for everyone. The agitation for a Punjabi Suba (a state based on Punjabi language boundaries) lasted close to a year and was on the minds of Sikhs all that time. But it was peaceful.

In Sirhala we had one gurdwara, and everyone went there. It was a gurdwara in the real sense, because sect and caste made no difference. Generally we had a big congregation on the first day of the month (in the Indian calendar) and on at least one other day, such as Gurpurab. On these occasions I would speak. In Canada I gave quite a few religious talks at Sikh gurdwaras or at welfare society general meetings, and by the time I returned to India I had no hesitation about going to the stage if I found some usefulness in doing it. I didn't want to be an orator just for the sake of being one. In Sirhala the village people were impressed with my views and my approach. They had great faith in me, but I didn't want to get involved in the administrative games of the village. Two elders came out to the farm one day to persuade me to take the lead on some village projects. I told them I would do my best to contribute personally or economically, but I refused to be the head person. They said, "If you don't agree, we will carry you by force to the village." And they actually stepped forward to carry the cot

I was sitting on. At their insistence I agreed to one project, which was school development.

In Punjab the village panchayat (council) was elected every five years, and the panchayat elections were coming up. The government had decided to give a bonus to any village that elected its panchayat unanimously. About one hundred women and two hundred men from the village gathered at the gurdwara and wanted me to be the sarpanch, the head of the panchayat. (The total village population was seven hundred or eight hundred.) I defended myself, through all their insistence. Finally one village elder stood up and said, "All right, Tara Singh, I am going to say something other than you being the sarpanch, and don't try to refute that. It is very simple. You nominate the future sarpanch of the village." That put me on the spot because it was clear that, among the various factions and sections of the village, I was the unifying factor. So I said, "Okay, uncle, I need your help on that."

I asked him to stand in front of Guru Granth Sahib and to perform an ardas, a standing prayer, and to ask for the secret help in bringing the right name to my mind. Everyone stood up, and he performed the ardas, and the priest took a hukam-nama (an order) from Guru Granth Sahib. With a humble feeling, and total surrender in my mind, I came to a person by the name of Sansar Singh. When I did so, the congregation cried out their approval: "Bole son Nihal, Sat Sri Akal." But the outgoing sarpanch and a couple of his friends were not happy, so unanimity was torpedoed and the seed sown for an election. In the election we ran two slates, the outgoing sarpanch's slate and our opposition slate. Sansar Singh defeated the outgoing sarpanch, but there was a tie for one of the positions on the panchayat. The tying vote came in by bike from a far-away orchard farm near closing time. Otherwise, the outgoing sarpanch's wife would have been elected. Both parties agreed to a draw, and God guided the hand of a child towards our candidate and the outgoing sarpanch's wife lost. Nearly the whole village was waiting for the results at the primary-school building. I came out immediately and stood on the brick steps and said, "The election is over. We are all one." And I asked everyone to go to the gurdwara to perform a prayer. From then on I was responsible for keeping the panchayat vehicle moving.

We had two projects – to raise the school from primary to middle level and to pave the dirt streets and construct a surface drainage system. The government gave a grant for street improvement, but the villages had to provide free labour and quite a bit of material. Fortunately, we had the evacuated houses of the Muslims who had lived in the village until the partition of Punjab in 1947. Some of them had built big brick houses with money they had earned in Malaya and Indonesia. Now these houses were held by the government. We dismantled them and used the bricks for paving, even though these houses were not legally ours to take down. We were able to do it because one of the men from our village, Harjinder Singh, was an air vice-marshal and the right-hand man of Krishna Menon, the defence minister. Harjinder Singh appreciated what was going on and helped to convince the authorities that it was a good thing.

Whenever we had difficulty in the street work, where corners were too tight or the street too narrow and we had to alter a wall or remove a projection from a building, Almighty graced me to be the negotiator, and the people co-operated 100 per cent. There was only one street in the village wide enough for a car, and that was our street. Even a bus could go through there. But all the other streets were much too narrow for motor vehicles, and we could widen them only a bit. In one case we had to push a complete brick wall back eighteen inches to make the street four and a half or five feet wide. In a couple of other cases we needed to move families out of their houses, and they agreed to go on to evacuee properties. After we dismantled the rest of the evacuee buildings and pulled away the material, the government auctioned off the land. Harjinder Singh wanted a walled garden and orchard to attach to his home, which was back-to-back with the gurdwara. In the auction nobody bid against him, and he got an acre or an acre and a half. He wasn't able to enjoy this garden for long because he died soon after he retired.

Our village had two ponds, and we decided that the east side should drain to the east pond and the other side to the north. During the rainy season these ponds were used for cattle. Harjinder Singh and his friends on the east side wanted to divert more of the drainage to the north so that they could keep their pond clean. I was not the only one to object, but the others did not raise their voices as much as I did. They were a little hesitant because he was an air vice-marshal. At that time thirty or forty of the village youth had been recruited into the air force through him, and that was a big part of the village economy. All their relatives were under his influence. Besides that, he brought many benefits to the village from the government kitty. When he wanted to divert one channel, I challenged him in an open forum, and it was done the way we had planned. But he was eventually able to drain that water to the north because the other villagers were not so independent.

He changed many decisions that we had already made. And when we wanted to name the school Havaldar Khem Singh School, he did not like it, although he could not object openly. Privately, he wanted his own name. That hurt me. Havaldar Khem Singh was a great personality, a real patriot, who uplifted the village in all fields and provided the village children with free education in his own buildings. The air vice-marshal himself had gone to Havaldar Khem Singh's primary school. And Havaldar Khem Singh had been a real pillar of the independence movement. Through him, our village was the centre of so much activity that it was fined five thousand rupees and blacklisted by the government under the British. (After independence the village got that money back for village development.) So when Harjinder Singh was not happy to call the school after this great human, that put a big rift between us. Gradually, I resigned from the school committee and became a little passive in village projects.

After that, during one of his visits to the village, when things were going a little haywire, Harjinder Singh called a meeting of the village gentry early in the morning before sunrise. A messenger came to me about two hours of darkness before sunrise. I told him, "I will perform my prayers and then I will come." After an hour the same messenger came again to say that all the village gentry were waiting in Harjinder Singh's house. So I went to his house for the first time. About fifty people were sitting there. I had just got inside the door when I heard him saying, "Some people are calling me a dictator. Well, people call Mr Nehru a dictator. But I don't like it." There was still space on the floor for me to sit; people pointed to it, and I sat down. Then he said, "Who thinks I am a dictator?" I waited for pretty near a minute and nobody dared to speak, so I stood up. "If nobody says it, then I say yes, you are acting like a dictator." And I buried him with the deviations he had made from decisions he had agreed to. He tried to beat around the bush, saying, "Well, sometimes you have to change this and that. You are taking it too serious." I said, "No."

Despite this rift I tried to support the good projects in the village when people approached me – like acquiring land for a stadium, and school promotion. After some negotiations the government of Punjab did agree to name the school Havaldar Khem Singh Government School. On one occasion the chief minister of Punjab, the defence minister of India, and the deputy commissioner of the district of Hoshiarpur visited in a big defence helicopter because our village had been declared a model village. But we could have done more, economically, educationally, and socially, if Air Vice-Marshal Harjinder Singh had not tried to push things his own way.

The village sarpanch, Sansar Singh, was forty-eight or fifty years of age and had one daughter but no male issue. After a year's hard work in the service of the village, he was blessed with a son. "You have been rewarded," I told him, "so the best way of giving thanks is to make a good amount of ladoos [sweets] and take them to the gurdwara and make announcements in the village." In Punjab, when a child is born or someone dies or an official comes with a message, the village chawkidar (watchman) goes to every street and corner, blowing a trumpet or beating a drum, and calls out in a loud voice. Generally he is a low-caste fellow, a singer or bard, a leatherworker or a sweeper, and his pay isn't much, so people give him some cash or remuneration in kind. "Let the chawkidar make the announcement," I told Sansar Singh, "and let the children come to the gurdwara and after prayers distribute those ladoos. Fill their bellies and make them happy, and surely those children will pray for you, and the Guru and Almighty will be pleased."

Sansar Singh said sure, it would be a nice thing to do. But within a few days he took the advice of some of his friends and colleagues and tried to unite the two factions in the village by holding a big drinking party in the evening. What he got was a big shot of mischief. When those people began drinking, instead of uniting they began fighting, swinging clubs, and some were seriously hurt. In the early morning both sides were going to take their injured on bullock carts to the police station at Mahalpur, five miles away. The sarpanch was at their feet, with begging hands pleading with them not to take their cases to the police. That was how he celebrated the birth of his son, with drink for the men instead of sweets for the children.

About that time the son of a panch (a member of the village panchayat) got into trouble. There was a village playground between Sirhala and the adjoining village of Rasoulpur. After the evening soccer game four or five of the youth would sit out near the playground talking until it was very dark. The ringleader was the son of the panch. I used to shuttle my bike home for supper and back to the farm for sleeping, and I could hear their voices as I went by. That was a big pinch in my mind because the ladies of the village generally went out for their bowel motions as soon as it was dark. A couple of times I walked up to those boys and admonished them. "Why are you sitting here while the village femininity is coming out into the fields for their bowel movements?" When I did that, they dispersed without argument, but afterwards they kept a vigil, and when I returned from the farm on my bike, they would keep quiet while I was passing by.

Finally, the ringleader was caught with a girl from the other village. Nearly two hundred people from both villages gathered in open session at short notice. This was on the first day of the month on the Indian calendar, so I was busy with the family prayer before Guru Granth Sahib on the third storey of our house. A messenger invited me to join the process of this case, and I came after completing our prayer. The boy's father, the panch, admitted his son had done wrong, but he wanted to minimize it, so the village elders asked for my opinion. I asked the father, "If it was your daughter instead of your son, how would you decide?" (In our culture, responsibility is generally with the boy.) For a while he said nothing, and then he agreed that his son should be punished. By this time the girl's father had gone to the police on the recommendation of his relatives. So we either had to get the legal complaint withdrawn and decide on punishment ourselves or let the case go to court.

In a village, every boy should regard every girl like a sister. Otherwise the punishment is to blacken his face with soot, garland him with shoes, and parade him on a donkey. The boy's father wanted the village forum to decide the punishment, but not that one. He said, "If you do that, the boy might jump in a well and kill himself. Please show some leniency." So we decided to let the court take care of it. The boy's father preferred that to public shaming. The boy got a year in jail, and after that he waited a couple more years before he dared show up in Sirhala.

In 1961 Almighty gifted us with a daughter, our last child, Parkash Kaur. So I had my five children and my brother and two sisters in my charge. Our boys, Surinder, Tarsem, and Manjit, were going to the village primary school along with my youngest brother, Santok. We tried our best with him, but he was very poor at school. Destiny surrounded him with all the resources for higher education, but he could not get passing marks beyond grade four or five, and he quit. My two sisters were sharp and wanted education. The elder one, Ajit Kaur, was studying at Khalsa College, Mahalpur, and the younger one, Avtar Kaur, was going to Girls' High School at Nangal Kalan, a mile and a half away, along with my elder daughter, Kuldip Kaur. The girls rode on their bikes, the automobiles of India in those days.

In the spring of 1962 I arranged for my sister Ajit Kaur's marriage to a boy from a village thirty-five miles away, north of Hoshiarpur city. He came from an educated family, (one brother became a director of education for Punjab), and they didn't demand any dowry. But we were able to afford it, so we gave one thousand rupees cash and furniture, kitchenware, clothing, and bedding – all good quality. My uncle in Malaya had died two years earlier, and I held the money he left in trust for the marriage, so father said that was his contribution. My brothers Jagjit Singh and Chatter Singh sent money from Canada. My brother Piara Singh, who was at Bina Junction, gave what he could, and I put in the rest. Because the groom was the youngest brother in his family, they all wanted to come. They said, "We don't worry about the dowry, but we don't want to leave anybody behind." So they brought eighty people by chartered bus, and we lodged them at the gurdwara. It was quite an occasion. People came from all over our village and from surrounding villages for the reception time, and they also came for the wedding time and the see-off time the next day. We brought in one of the topmost chefs to feed the wedding party and our friends and relatives. Instead of bringing a wedding band, the groom's side let us arrange it, and then they paid for it. With all those people there, we appreciated their discipline and their religious approach.

In the fall of 1962 I took my family to my wife's village of Kultham. My wife did not want to go. "After we have settled here and made so much effort, why go back?" But I had given father verbal notice before the marriage of Ajit Kaur. I told him that I would fulfil my duties in arranging the wedding, and then I would go to Kultham permanently. Father had begun to deviate from his promises. Within a year I had seen that it wouldn't be easy to keep him in line with what we had agreed. I did not want to confront him, but a point of challenge did come. He wanted to borrow money from me for a project in another village, and he wanted me to lend money to some of his friends. I refused because it wasn't a good project and he had wasted money putting up buildings in our mother's village, Barian Kalan, a static village where no more buildings were needed and where he had troubles with adjoining owners. Once I had to go there to convince the other side in one of his disputes. So I wouldn't lend him money. He got up and tried to show me a stick, so I took a few steps forward and gave him a lecture. "All these years no son of yours has dishonoured you. You are trying to terminate that." I am thankful to Almighty that he receded from his intention and stepped back. But I decided then that I would have to leave Sirhala Khurd.

8 My Wife's Birthplace Village

I came to know Subedar Sohan Singh from Bahar Mazara, a small adjoining village on the Phagwara road, because I sent my elder son and daughter to schools in Phagwara. This was after we moved back to Kultham. He had once been the personal driver for the commander-in-chief of India and for some time a teacher at King George Royal Military College at Jullundur, and he was doing volunteer teaching in Phagwara. Subedar Sohan Singh was a man of the same approach and discipline as myself. He had a friend, Dr Jagat Singh Marwaha, who was a retired executive engineer from the military engineering services and also a homeopathic doctor. (He was the president of the homeopathic association of Punjab.) Through Sohan Singh, Dr Jagat Singh became a friend of mine.

One day in 1964 when I visited Dr Jagat Singh, his brother Dr Bhagat Singh was also there. He was a homeopath as well. Jagat Singh said, "Today I want to feed you people with good sweets." I agreed, so he quickly went to the market and bought sweets, fruit, and milk. He had the milk boiled and everything prepared. Then he called an elderly gentleman from an adjoining room to join the table – his house was a big one with many rooms. This gentleman was a Hindu between seventy and eighty years of age. Dr Jagat Singh introduced him as a Hindu sadhu from Patiala whose children didn't understand him. "At present he is suffering from very chronic piles and we have welcomed him here. It is a great benefit to us." Dr Jagat Singh told this gentleman that I was from Canada, even though I was dressed in simple Punjabi clothes. (People in Punjab are generally impressed if they know you have lived in Canada.) "Well," I said, "it is nothing special being from Canada. It is not a degree or any honour, simply experience about the world." Then I told him that before I left Canada, I performed a prayer in the Vancouver Sikh temple that I would never have to return there.

This Hindu sadhu was wearing bifocals, and his eyes were fixed on my face. When I finished, he spoke with wonder. "Samundar par ek bar or jana parega" (It will be necessary for you to cross the sea once more). Without hesitation Dr Jagat Singh said, "The sadhu has seen the picture of your future and it will happen." These comments stunned me. "My goodness," I said. "Too bad." Then the sadhu spoke again. "Parmatma bhalai karega" (Almighty will do good). So that restored my shaken mind a bit. According to the teachings of the Guru, one should not work for the acquisition of occult powers. To the contrary, one should live in the world as a simple householder. But people with occult powers, like the sadhu, can see into your future. In the years that followed I kept working to avoid returning to Canada, but destiny brought me back.

One day Dr Jagat Singh and Subedar Sohan Singh arranged a trip to Ludhiana to visit an astrologer friend of theirs because Sohan Singh wanted to consult him about some coming event. Just for the fun of it, they took me as well. Jokingly, they said, "No harm in it to know your future." I didn't agree. Why know it? Let it be the will of God. If you know something bad is coming, you have to be very strong, and few people are. But I showed the astrologer my hand. He looked at it and read his books, which were written in English, and then he told me, "You will retire a completely defeated man." "In which way," I asked, "spiritually or in a worldly way?" "No, no," he said, "it is your worldly aspect. You will have no benefit from those you help." "Well, that is fine," I said. "That is good." And he said, "Actually, it is your spiritual aspect that is the cause of it."

Subedar Sohan Singh and Dr Jagat Singh gave me a connection with the Ramgarhia Educational Council at Phagwara. This council ran a big school complex at Phagwara as well as a few village high schools like the one at Kultham. Kultham is a bigger village than Sirhala – more than three times the population. A branch line of the

railway from Phagwara to the Shivalic Hills runs through the village, and the main road from Phagwara to Chandigarh is close by.
By 1963 Kultham had a co-educational high school, Desh Bhagat
Memorial High School, with three hundred students. We also had a
government primary school, and I sent the younger boys there, but
the educational standards of Desh Bhagat Memorial High School
were very poor. One year thirty or forty students wrote the matriculation exams for university entrance and they all failed. That is why
I sent my elder daughter and eldest son to Phagwara. We bought a
bus pass for the daughter and a rail pass for the son because the
Ramgarhia school in Phagwara was near the railway station. But it
took extra effort to get them back and forth each day.

The Ramgarhias are Sikhs of the carpenter caste, and they are
more sectarian than the Jats when they name their schools and
gurdwaras. If some Jat Sikhs organized a school, they wouldn't
call it Jat Sikh School. Generally the Ramgarhias run good schools.
But Kultham was a backward village, illiterate and superstitious.
The village caretaking committee didn't have a single high-school
graduate on it, and they were divided factionally. So they were not
able to look after the school adequately. And when all the matricu-
lating students failed their exams, that created a big backlash
everywhere.

The headmaster of the school had an ongoing feud with one of
his senior math teachers. One day, when this feud came to a head,
he called in the village committee and got them to sign a petition
to the Ramgarhia Educational Council for this teacher's dismissal.
Coincidentally, the committee was just leaving the school as I was
coming home from Phagwara on my bike. The school was on the
outskirts of the village near the railway station, about half a kilometre from the northern perimeter. The headmaster got a student
to stop me, and he showed me the petition. This headmaster was a
friend of my younger sister's husband, who had given him a reference in case he needed my support. When he showed me the petition, he wanted me to sign it as a member of the village gentry;
and because it was a Friday or a Saturday he wanted to hand the
petition in right away. I knew the teacher, and he was a man of
loose moral and religious character, so I agreed with the headmaster's petition. But I gave him an excuse. "I am not a member of the
education committee," I said, "but I will bring in another petition
to be attached to this one."

The headmaster had a bachelor of teaching degree, but his petition in English carried quite a few errors in spelling and so on, and I didn't want to be associated with it. To me, his English wasn't adequate. Also, he had written, "that teacher trims his beard." A Sikh should not cut any hair, but I could see that the headmaster had trimmed his own beard. The math teacher did it obviously and the headmaster did it craftily, but how could one criticize the other? So I didn't want to be part of that petition. At home I drafted one and a half legal-sized pages of my own and signed it "Tara Singh Bains, Canadian." This was the first and only time in my life that I put "Canadian," although people do use the terms "Canadian" or "American" profusely when they go back to Punjab. I did it to show the council that I had some knowledge of other parts of the world.

This happened a couple of months before the students wrote their matriculation exams and got a zero result. After that disaster the village committee asked me to come to their meeting. They wanted me to get involved. I refused because I had been in Kultham for a year and a half and had taken the trouble to get my children educated in Phagwara after finding out what the school at Kultham was like. Why should I be part of that deteriorating situation? "So please excuse me." The discussion went back and forth. Then a member of the committee said, "Sardar Ji, the president and the secretary of the Ramgarhia council told us that they won't listen to anything we say unless we bring in Tara Singh Bains." So I said, "That is fine. I will go and see them. But how do they know about me?" "Well," he said, "they inquired about you after they got your petition."

We went to Phagwara and met with the president of the council, Sardar Mela Singh, a sincere hard worker with a deep-gifted psychology. He was not an educated man, but he was able to run all those institutions. The secretary, Mr Sagoo, had an MA and was also an industrious, good man. They wanted me to head the village committee. Otherwise they wouldn't keep the high school in Kultham. "This is a big responsibility," I said. "The school is totally run down. We have to stop withdrawals and bring up discipline and educational standards. It won't take months but years to bring it back to normal." Also, I knew that the high school had been brought under the Ramgarhia council through Swami Purna Nand, a Jat Hindu who wore the garb of a sadhu and had an ashram in Kultham. The swami was an illiterate man, but a total politician with a great influence with the council. So I told them my terms. First, I wanted to sit on the selection board for teachers and headmasters with a veto power. Second, I wanted full support from the council. And third, I wanted the exclusion of Swami Purna Nand from the school affairs.

They accepted my conditions and appreciated them. Within a year we had a few second-division results in the matriculation exams. After two years we had very good results. We went to each neighbouring village like missionaries, to convince the parents to send their children. In one instance I arranged a few meetings with the people of Mandhali, an adjoining village, when they planned to build their own high school. "We don't need two adjoining co-educational high schools," we told them. "Instead we have a golden chance to have one for boys and one for girls." They agreed, but someone from our committee must have played a secret role to make that project fail. It was too bad, because co-education at the high-school level has undermined the standard of education and moral discipline in Punjab.

In Sirhala a friend and I started a small-scale poultry business with fifty pullets, and when I came to Kultham, we split it and I took my share. At Kultham, we had some income from the land that we leased on a fifty-fifty basis – 50 per cent to the cultivator and 50 per cent to ourselves. For more income I wanted to build a poultry shed on the farm and to keep five hundred or more laying hens, but our land was divided into two plots, and neither one was large enough. At one time every owner in the village had at least five or ten plots according to ancestral inheritance. In the 1930s the land had been redistributed, but it wasn't done very well. Only 10 per cent of the owners got all their land consolidated into one plot, while 90 per cent were left with two plots.

Today, all the acreage of Punjab is aligned with the north pole. My own village of Sirhala is an exception because, when the land was redistributed in 1935, the job was done so well that nobody wanted to change it. But when I was living in Kultham and planning to start a poultry business, the land there was reconsolidated and realigned according to the new system. The villagers put me on the committee. One man had worked on the previous redistribution and knew how to do the demarcation, but he was too hesitant, so I said, "All right, I will take over." The village supplied the labour, and I was director, with instructions from the government consolidation officer. Before we redistributed among the landowners, we allotted land for the common utility of the village – for roads, cremation grounds, schools, gurdwaras, the village bank, a playground, refuse dumps, ponds, and an area designated for the use of low-caste people. We had to straighten the roads and mark out a perimeter road around the village, connecting with the roads from adjoining villages.

The whole process was very slow. People took a lot of convincing. The village achieved some of its goals but not all of them. The village elders lacked foresight or education, and they let factional and selfish interests come first, so we didn't get proper drainage or allocation of refuse-disposal sites, and Kultham is still suffering. On one side of the village the water has nowhere to drain and just goes into low-lying spots. That is where the Ramdasias or leatherworkers live. Kultham has a concentration of shoemaking, and two-fifths of the people are Ramdasias. The rest of the village, including half of the Ramdasia households, drains into one pond. We needed a bigger drainage pond to look after the whole village, but the land we would have used near the village is premium land. It is rich with human excrement. So the village elders wouldn't allocate any of it.

The drainage system had another problem too. People used to have to go to the village wells for drinking water, and they didn't use too much, so the surface drains would dry out in the summer and flies wouldn't breed. Then people got artesian wells for their own households, and they began using water freely for bathing to cool off in the heat. The drains became waterlogged and never dried out, and the fly population went up. I noticed a big difference between the 1950s and the 1960s, and it has become worse since then. The surface drains should be cleaned every day or every second day, or the village should have a tube well or a storage tank at the highest point and use the water to flood the drains to wash them clean. I used to clean the drains personally as a service and an example. But I was a son-in-law to the village, and people would say, "Please don't shame us. You are an honoured one. We will do it ourselves." And they did. But the time would come when it wasn't done soon enough, and the fly population would go up. Rice production, with flooded paddy fields, which started in the 1960s, added to the problem. We started to get mosquitoes as well as flies. Finally, some of us brought in a Bhangi family, a sweeper family, and paid them five rupees a month per residence to do the surface drains every fourth day for the whole village, which had about five hundred households. The poorer families didn't pay; they might give him a chapati (a kind of Indian bread) if they could; so he would make five hundred or six hundred rupees a month.

During the rainy season the main road connecting the railway station to the motor road would get waterlogged. In 1963 it was very bad. The residents of other villages would have to go through mud and water on their way to the railway station, and if they met a member of the village panchayat or some elder of the village, they would say, "Shame. Is there nobody who would think of doing anything in this village?" With the grace of Almighty, I had the idea of organizing the village youth on the weekends when they were not in school. Every weekend we would work around two hours in the morning, and I would take tea and sweets and biscuits for them to eat. We started after the water receded at the end of the rainy season. During the autumn and winter we dug a channel about a yard deep along the main road, and we used that soil to build a footpath five feet wide right up to the railway station.

The land consolidation in Kultham went on for three years, so I had to wait to expand my poultry business. In the third year of my connection with the school I brought my son back from Phagwara Ramgarhia High School and enrolled him in grade nine at Kultham. By then my elder daughter had passed grade eight. I figured that crafts education would be better for her than more education in literal subjects, so we didn't send her to grade nine. With the help of the education officer for the local development-block area we were able to bring in a few industrial classes. (Each development block had twenty-five or thirty villages in it.) A couple of times I was able to bring in a sewing teacher for the girls. The village would provide accommodation and some funds, and the rest came from the government side. After my daughter finished grade eight we got a teacher of sewing, knitting, and embroidery for a year, and my daughter learned that and got a certificate.

I took an eight-week poultry course in Jullundur at a government educational institution that had a big farm just past the Royal Military College. The classes were four or five hours long, and I would go by rail every day. But with everything that had happened since I came back from Canada, my cash resources were depleted to a point where I couldn't see any easy recuperation through poultry. To establish sheds and other requirements on the farm would take 10,000 or 15,000 or 20,000 rupees. When I came back to India from Canada, I had 40,000 rupees. After that I had income from the farm but no profit. At Sirhala I spent 7,000 rupees on house renovations and 3,000 on the marriage of my sister and on expenses. At Kultham I bought an acre of land for 3,500 and put an extension on the house. And I donated a lot of money in service at Sirhala and Kultham. My elder son and daughter were eighteen and nineteen. I am a feminist by nature, so I discussed it with my wife, and we decided to arrange their marriages with the money we had left.

The boy we found for Kuldip Kaur, my daughter, was from the village of Hakoomatpur, only a couple of miles from my birthplace village of Sirhala. His name was Balbir Singh Dhanda, and he was a very handsome young man employed in the air force through the air vice-marshal of my village. When we met to make the arrangements with his grandfather and father on one side and myself, my brother-in-law Sawaran Singh (my wife's close cousin), and my father-in-law on the other, I found out that the boy had trimmed his beard. He was about nineteen. We had a frank and fair discussion. I explained my desire for a marriage with a Sikh observance of life. I had in view the order of Guru Gobind Singh, the Tenth Guru, that a Sikh should marry his children into Sikh families. When I came to the trimming of the beard and the keeping of the hair, his father and grandfather repeatedly took responsibility, but I refused their promises. "No," I said, "I can't put you in that situation. He has to live his own life. He might keep his beard for some time, but later he might not want to. You can't induce him to keep it intact right now, so how could you induce him to keep it then?"

He was an only son, and I could see how obedient and helpful he was to his family. If he could keep Sikh discipline, then I could visualize a good match for my daughter. So I gave them some time. "If he decides he can do it," I said, "you can send me a message. If I don't receive a message from you in four weeks, only then will I look for another match." But I told them that if he decided he was going to keep his Sikh form, then we could not tolerate any violation. "It will hurt the relationship." And I told them that he should not expect to immigrate to Canada through the marriage.

After three weeks they sent word that they were 100 per cent willing. So we went back and each side gave their word, and we fixed a time for the betrothing ceremony. This was in 1965. On the day of the ceremony I gave a lecture and said, "You are pledging before Guru Granth Sahib that no violation should be done." He was a very good boy, but he had a disappointment soon after that. When he was near the upper Burma border, on the north-east frontier of India, he injured his hip. He was playing soccer and somebody hit him with a boot. After that he got news that he had been accepted for training as a flight lieutenant. But, with his injury, the military medical authorities classified him as category C, which meant he couldn't go. During this time we had a regular exchange of letters. In one letter he wrote, "There is no God." So I just had to coach him through. He wrote to say that I should find some other match for my daughter because his future was very uncertain. I told him in reply that a Sikh will never turn away from a resolve taken before the Guru, and I gave him some quotations from Sikh history and tried to lift his spirits.

The marriage took place at Kultham in the spring of 1966. When I spoke from the gurdwara stage, I used to advise people against spending money on costly jewelry because they would overdo it whenever there was a wedding. My sister sent five hundred rupees from Canada, and in her letter she told us to spend it all on gold jewelry. So that pulled my leg. From then on, when I was on the stage, I never said, "Don't use gold." Instead I would always say, "Be a little cautious when you go to gold." My wife also gave some of her jewelry – not too much, just three or four things. I didn't object. I couldn't say anything against it when it was so important to her.

The wedding party came by bus and stayed overnight. Some of the groom's uneducated relatives were drinking and playing lokgit (popular Indian music) over the loudspeaker system. For them a wedding was a chance for entertainment, and they didn't worry about interfering with others. The groom's father was a very soft person, so I went myself and gave them a little harsh caution. Then they stopped. Even if the loudspeakers are used for religious recitation, I'm not in favour of it if it is late at night or early in the morning. People have to work. Why disturb them when they are sleeping? Only a few will listen. Why disturb the rest?

When my son was married, I did not arrange an overnight stay because the bride's village was only thirty miles away, and we could manage to go and come back on the same day. We hired a bus and I cautioned all the members of the wedding party. "There will be no drinking at all," I told them. "This can be done when we come back." I said that because I couldn't put a curfew on my father-in-law. Instead, we gave him some money, and when he came back he made a party for himself. So we had a good time.

After that I wrote to my sister to pay for my passage to Canada. I needed her assistance, and she was happy to give it. Before I left, I had to hand over my education duties. The village called an open session, and fifty or sixty people gathered on the broad platform in the shade of the village banyan tree. The education committee and the panchayat were all there, and they thanked me for my services and gave me a clay statue of Dr Rabindranath Tagore as a little gift. They asked me to stay in England for a while, on my way to Canada, to collect donations to blacktop the link road and build new rooms for the high school. For that purpose they gave me a letter signed by the village gentry.

On 30 June 1966 I started my journey from Delhi to Vancouver, with a stopover in England to carry out my fund-raising mission. At London my relatives from Kultham met me at the airport. In 1953 the Kultham settlers in England were all batching people. By 1966 they were mostly families. The first of them had come to do foundry work in Birmingham, and they were still mostly settled there. But quite a few were living around the outskirts of London, at Southall and Slough. At Birmingham we held meetings to explain the village projects, and the people there promised over seven hundred pounds in donations. I did not handle any of the money myself but set up a local collection committee. Coming back from Birmingham, I spent a night at Leamington Spa with a fellow from Kultham who was an autoworker, and he gave me fifteen pounds for those projects. After that I came to London to arrange some meetings there. But I had to cut my time short and leave for Vancouver right away because my brother and sister in Canada called for me.

Before I went, I handed over those fifteen pounds to the collecting committee. We had a final meeting in a pub. Most of those fellows were illiterates, but good fellows – not mischievous. Later, one of them wrote to tell me he had heard a story that I had taken some money for myself. I sent a very detailed letter in reply, and after that nobody said that I took a penny. I didn't go back to Kultham until 1976, and after a gap of so many years I saw no purpose in investigating what had happened to the money – how much had been received and how much had been spent. But people told me that the amounts were never disclosed to the public.

My sister and my second youngest brother, Jagjit Singh, had written from Canada to urge me to come quickly because he was sick with kidney trouble, and the doctors said he could not survive without a transplant, which had to be done in Montreal. First Jagjit Singh sent an urgent request for me to come. "Perhaps if I can see you," he wrote, "it might give me something." He wanted me for my spiritual, moral, and psychological impact. I wrote to my sister to explain that I needed a couple more months to complete my mission. Then a telegram came that said, "Come immediately. I want to see you before my end." So I had to cut short my mission, because one must comply with such a request. It is a good thing to feed the hungry bodies, but it is far more important to feed the minds.

PART TWO

A Canadian

9 Modern Sikhs

My flight reached Vancouver on 19 July 1966. As soon as I landed, my brother-in-law and elder sister took me to their home in Cloverdale. My younger sister Avtar Kaur was with them. (I had sent her to Canada for marriage in 1963, and she was living in Port Alberni.) That afternoon, when we reached the house in Cloverdale, everyone was so happy. Nobody had expected I would come back. At suppertime my brother-in-law said, "I am so happy that I want to toast a drink of wine." I said, "Well, I don't drink, actually." A practising Sikh should not take alcohol or any intoxicant. My brother-in-law knew that. So then the discussion started. "Well," he said, "you know that I don't mean you are a drinking person, but for the sake of pleasing a person's wishes it doesn't violate your principle."

I asked him, "Does it mean it will bring real depth to your happiness if I do take?" He said, "Yes." He had a special sweet wine, a cherry wine or something like that. "All right," I said, "dear brother-in-law, I will take a few drops for your happiness." When he poured a little in my glass, my sister spoke. "Ho! Younger brother! You don't drink. How come there is some liquor in there?" I had hardly half an ounce. "I am not drinking alcohol at all," I told her. "It is only the wishes of a person. And there won't be a second time." Then they told me that they had talked about this before I came. My brother-in-law said that I would accept a drink if he requested me, and my sister said no I would not. "He is a man of very solemn resolve." So they made a bet. And when I took the drink, my elder sister and my younger sister lost a hundred dollars. After that I never in my life took any more.

My sister and brother-in-law had moved back to the farm because they were tired of city life. They owned two pieces of land: forty acres with the house and buildings, and behind that another twenty acres backing on to Coast Meridian Road. At the entrance gate they had a barrier with a lock, and they had a lock on the gas tank, which was near the barn and garage, eighty yards from the road. When I saw that, I asked them why. They said that thieves had been stealing their gas on a regular basis. All of a sudden I thought of what I had said when I first came to Canada – that the time would come when milk would not be safe at the front door. Two or three days later, at lunchtime, brother-in-law came down to the house to say that someone had stolen a load of corn from the corn patch beside Coast Meridian Road. So I laughed at my nephews and reminded them of my predictions. A couple of weeks later thieves broke into a shed and stole an irrigation pumping set and some tools from my niece, who had 130 acres on River Road in Delta. I wasn't happy to be right in my thinking about the future. Actually, I was alarmed that things were deteriorating faster than I had expected. When I looked at Punjab, with so many people, where the quality of police was low, I saw far less stealing than in Canada, where justice served very democratically but people were losing their social, moral, and spiritual values.

I saw my younger brother Jagjit Singh in Vancouver General Hospital, and I gave him a big lift. He was very happy to see me. Within a few days the doctors sent him to Montreal for his transplant operation. Here again, the Secret Hand worked for his benefit. He had to wait a few weeks for a kidney, and he got one through a motor vehicle accident that killed some white person whose two healthy kidneys were donated. The specialists chose two candidates from the waiting-list. One was my younger brother Jagjit, and the other was a white lady from Quebec. The transplants were carried on pretty near simultaneously. As soon as Jagjit got out of the operation room, he had a feeling of relief in his system, and from there on he never faltered or experienced any setback. He was under intensive care and on medication but on a constant progressive route. The lady from Quebec was of the same race as the donor, yet her body rejected the kidney, and it had to be pulled out. Both were diagnosed as fit to receive those kidneys, but only one had success, and his was so good he survived over five years after that operation.

When Jagjit got sick, his wife moved from Port Alberni, where they had been living, to Vancouver. Her name was Kalwant Kaur, and she was from the village of Sansarpur near Jullundur. I had arranged to send her out to Port Alberni for her marriage with Jagjit. In 1966 they had two little daughters. When I came back to Canada, my aim was to get a job at Port Alberni where I had worked before. But my brother-in-law and sister repeatedly asked me to stay in Vancouver to look after Jagjit's family. My brother-in-law knew Mr Munro, the manager of a cedar sawmill in Vancouver, Nalos Lumber Company, at False Creek, right by the Granville Street bridge. My brother-in-law had worked for him quite a bit and was a longtime friend. So he talked to him, and he showed him a letter that I got from the MacMillan and Bloedel mill in Port Alberni when I left my job there.

A big company like MacMillan and Bloedel carries a lot of respect with its letters. But when I quit that job at Port Alberni, back in 1960, I didn't know that I should ask for one. On my last day I went to Mr Moncur's office for my time-check. He gave me a chair opposite his table, and we had a good chat for a few minutes. He appreciated my behaviour and work and had good wishes for my family. When he held out the time-check, he didn't put it into my advancing hand. He was gazing into my eyes, and I could see that he expected me to say something. He said, "Do you want a company letter?" I said, "If you think I should have one, yes. Otherwise, I won't request one." He said, "You deserve one," and he did it right away, had it typed on a company letterhead and signed it.

That letter helped me to get an interview at Nalos Lumber and a job as export grader. I had to handle big pieces, but the flow wasn't that heavy, and the lumber was all red cedar, which is much lighter than any other species in British Columbia. The management at Nalos Lumber were very happy with my performance, and I enjoyed working there. This time I learned driving, immediately, and I bought a car. That gave me independence and freedom and made it feasible for me to go to the gurdwara at 1866 West Second Avenue to attend congregation there.

In those days very few practising Sikhs lived in British Columbia. I tried to count many times when I was in Nanaimo and Port

Alberni before 1960. Among the elderly Sikhs, two or three dozen kept the complete Sikh form, but among the men in their twenties, thirties, or forties, I knew of no more than eight. And those elderly Sikhs, who had been in Canada from the pioneer days, did not have much knowledge of Sikh scripture and Sikh history. They were just carrying on religious performances on a routine basis. So British Columbia looked to me like a desert place with only scattered oases. If I may measure my own standard at that time, I was just a beginner. But I was known to the people from my previous stay in Canada. And because they respected my spiritual and moral approach, they had started calling me Giani Ji – even in Nanaimo after my first lecture there. Such was their knowledge of Sikhism that they could call me a giani, a scholar, when I was at grade one compared with what is required.

In the early days, during the Ghadr Lahar (revolutionary movement), the resolute Sikhs from Canada and the United States went home to liberate India, and they left behind a barren stage of spirituality and integrity. The ones who stayed started to cut their hair and shave, and gradually their numbers superseded the bearded Sikhs. Those clean-shaven Sikhs wanted to attend congregation in the gurdwara without wearing turbans. In those days, in Western society, gentlemen wore hats, and they would take them off when they greeted someone or attended congregation in a church. Those clean-shaven Sikhs wanted to do the same thing when they went to the gurdwara. They made an arrangement of nice wooden pegs for hanging hats inside the veranda at the entrance. This was at most of the gurdwaras. Abbotsford did not have a veranda, so the hats were hung in the basement. Hillcrest did not have one either, so the hats were taken inside. But Vancouver had a great many pegs. A well-dressed, white-bearded Sikh would stand as chobdar (guard) at the entrance, and if some stranger or new person came, he would ask him to take off his hat. The management committee thought that wearing a hat in the gurdwara showed disrespect to the Guru. That was their level of understanding of Sikhism.

When I was living in Port Alberni in 1956, Sant Teja Singh visited Canada after more than forty years. He had led the Sikhs in Canada and in California in their early struggles. He was shocked when he saw the state to which Sikh practice in Canada had fallen. He spoke at the Sikh gurdwara at 1210 Topaz Avenue in Victoria, and I was there. At one point, when the clean-shaven

Sikhs did not want to cover their heads, he became so irritated that he called them "Gande ande," which means "bad eggs" in English but has a stronger meaning in Punjabi. People protested to each other. "Does a sant say that?" they asked. They didn't think that a person of that calibre with such a rich life behind him would ever say anything like that.

The white community at large called us Hindus. I tried to explain whenever possible, "We are not Hindus. We are Sikhs." But most of the Sikhs in Canada, whether clean-shaven or turbaned, did not mind. Even when they were talking among themselves, they would refer to themselves as Hindus. Dr Arjun Kirpal Singh from the United Kingdom visited Canada a year or so after I came back. He was a young man in his late thirties or early forties with a PhD, and he stayed only a short time, but the notion that we could be called Hindus was so evident that he became aware of it. When he spoke at the gurdwara, that was his main theme. He said, "There is a hidden conspiracy to bury Sikhs in a sea of Hinduism,"and he expressed his feeling in a very impressive speech. After that we began to talk about this issue, not generally on the stage, but privately.

In our community most of the people were batching people right up to the time I came. When some families did settle, starting in the 1920s, the men forced their wives to adopt the Western way of life by wearing skirts. Giving up Punjabi dress and wearing skirts seemed odd to those ladies and caused them grave anguish, but they had no other recourse. When they attended the gurdwara, they could not sit on the floor in the right position without exposing their thighs. The management bought heavy curtain cloth in long pieces up to twenty yards each, and the ladies would sit in rows and pull the cloth over their knees to keep warm in winter and to cover their legs.

I was attending the Vancouver gurdwara regularly, and people used to ask me to give religious lectures. Because we didn't have many pathis – people who could read the scriptures for akhand path (continuous reading) or sahaj path (slow reading) ceremonies – I would do that voluntarily as well. In 1967 I was drawn on to the gurdwara mangement committee along with some of the younger educated men who had come to Canada under the quota system. Sometime during the following year a few ladies attended the gurdwara wearing Punjabi dress. A couple of the clean-shaven young men on the management committee came to me after the congregation while I was dining in the common kitchen. They said, "What do you think of these women who have come into the temple in Punjabi dress?" I didn't say anything. After a couple more questions and a silence of a minute or more, I said, "Instead of giving my opinion on this, I am concerned with my own appearance as bearded and turbaned Sikh."

"No, no, no," one fellow said, "the turban and beard among men is well accepted." I asked him what was wrong with women in Punjabi dress, and he answered that these women were the first to come that way and they would not be accepted by the general Canadian society. "What is the oddity?" I said. "It is just within the gurdwara, and then they drive home." He couldn't find an answer, and walked away with a grin. Later on the conversation came back to my friends and relatives in some twisted version that I had to clear up with explanations and reasoning.

For a while, in 1969, the gurdwara did not have a proper granthi (priest), only an elderly caretaker granthi who couldn't do performances on stage. I used to supplement him. At annual ceremonies, when Sikhs celebrated Guru Nanak's birthday at Abbotsford or the martyrdom of Guru Arjun at New Westminister or Independence Day at Hillcrest, granthis of all the gurdwaras would go. I represented the Vancouver gurdwara at Victoria at Christmas time, when Sikhs in Canada had a function as a goodwill gesture towards Christians. When I was about to leave, the treasurer and one other member of the Victoria executive asked me to take fifteen dollars for travelling expenses. I told them it was very wrong. They insisted. In the smaller village gurdwaras, where granthis are not paid salaries and just depend on volunteer contributions, it is the custom. But in cities they should not accept because they are well paid. So that was the discussion for five or ten minutes. Finally they became very humble and said, "Please complete our records. We don't want to create an exception. We have been giving to others." I said, "All right, you can write down there and put that money into the Guru's treasury." They said, "No, you just take it in your hands." Then I became a little cautious, but I was still too innocent. "Okay, give me the money," I said, "and I will put it in the Guru's treasury myself." Again they insisted that I should sign the registry.

I had a feeling that they might misuse this in the future. Early in 1970, at a funeral at the new Ross Street gurdwara in Vancouver, while a group of people were standing in discussion outside, that treasurer from Victoria said to me, "I know you take money for doing akhand path performances." I said, "Where?" I understood immediately that he was going to bring up that instance, and he did. I said, "If you have any integrity as a human being, let us go in front of Guru Granth Sahib. Let ardas (prayer) be performed. I will say what I did, before Guru Granth Sahib, and you say what you said, and we will see who gets punished from heaven." That shook his heart. The people around knew who was right, and that thing never surfaced again.

In 1968 a Punjabi Hindu fellow named Visva Malhotra came up with the idea of a community newspaper. He had worked in a press and knew something about journalism, and he was a very nice religious gentleman. The other traditional Sikhs weren't interested, but I thought it would be a good opportunity for the community. So the two of us started a tabloid-sized newspaper in English and Punjabi that we called *Punjab Weekly* and, later, *Punjab Times*. I wasn't familiar with the press, but he took the press and field responsibilities and wanted me to be editor. We printed cuttings from Punjabi papers, which I was getting daily by air from India. And we wrote articles and editorials, but not in every issue, because that was hard to do with work and family responsibilities.

Somehow, with the help of Almighty, we ran thirty-five issues, starting with twelve pages and reaching up to twenty. We did have some advertising, but not that much, and we did have some subscriptions, but mostly we gave free distribution. I was putting in the money as well as the work, and he was putting in no money but a lot of work. Our house was our office, and I gave him free accommodation. On seeing the success of our paper, the leadership of the bare-headed, modern Sikhs thought it should be a joint community effort. First they convinced Mr Malhotra, and then they convinced me. We established a board of directors, and Mr Malhotra became a paid employee. They wanted the paper to be, in their words, a secular paper, not a Sikh paper. For the sake of the community I swallowed my objections. Mr Malhotra was a good man, but he was a wall of sand that needed strong protection. The other people began to interfere, and when I found out, I told Mr Malhotra that I was going to shut the paper down. So we killed a good enterprise and a good effort that was most needed.

I was living in my own house by then. When I first started working at Nalos Lumber, I lived on Kerr Street in my brother-in-law's house with my nephew and his wife. Then I moved to a basement suite on Main Street, where I lived with my younger brother Chatter Singh's father-in-law, who got a job through me at the same sawmill. After a while I was able to buy an old house at 3135 East Forty-fifth Avenue in the Killarney district in South Vancouver for $14,000, with a down payment of $2,000. The house had a low basement and an attic over the main floor, and it had been newly painted for sale. I stayed there as a single person for six months until my elder son, Surinder Singh, who was nineteen, with his wife, Gurdarshan Kaur, and little son, Iqbal, joined me.

To bring the whole family over was not too easy. It took several years of earnings for a careful person to pay the passages, to get a good house, and to keep the family going. My father-in-law was by himself. His wife had died before I married his daughter. They had two daughters, but the eldest died in Kenya, so my wife was looking after him in Kultham as well as our own children. I brought my eldest son over with his wife and child so that his income would supplement mine and his wife could relieve me of the cooking and housework.

When I first applied to the immigration department, the officials questioned me. They said, "Why don't you get your immediate family over here? Your son is married, so he isn't part of it." I tried to convince them that our family system was different, but they said, "Well, it is not within immigration department rules that we can admit him to Canada." My sister suggested we get a lawyer, but I said, "Why spend money on that? I would rather do it myself." So I wrote a petition of nearly two pages, legal size, in which I explained my situation and my plan to rejoin the whole family step by step as we got the money. In the concluding paragraph I said that I would stake my citizenship on my story. "If an investigation proves it wrong, let me be deported. If it shows that I am truthful, give my son's case a compassionate consideration, because the immigration department here has shown a lot of discrimination over and above department rules." Honesty and truth are always valued. The department approved my application, and my son came to Canada at the end of 1968.

A few months before my son arrived, Mr Munro, the manager at Nalos Lumber Company, died, and the new manager brought in a foreman who was a real chippy personality. This foreman wanted to increase production without any regard for quality, and for the export market it couldn't be done. He pushed too much, and he was prejudiced and tried to create false imagery. At various times he put checks on my grading, and every time I was right and he was wrong. So he bore a big grudge against my quality of work, and he wanted to get rid of me. But the assistant manager and the other foreman were sympathetic and wanted to keep me on. Once a customer in Australia rejected a shipment on reinspection. Mr Ritchie, the manger, called in the export graders from both shifts. We told him that this foreman was pushing, pushing, pushing, which was not the way to keep up quality grading.

Through the goodwill of the other officers in the mill I got casual employment for Surinder. I tried to conceal him from the chippy foreman, but somehow, after a month or so, he found out who he was, and he sent him home for no reason. I went to the Vancouver local office of the IWA on Seventeenth Avenue. Jack Evans was the secretary. When I explained the situation to him and told him about my union activities during my first stay in Canada, he said, "Where the hell have you been hiding for so long?" Actually, I didn't want to get into union activities any more because in many cases the union was just another bureaucracy in a power struggle, and the unions were going most of the time for more money and not doing enough to get safe working conditions, particularly in smaller operations. Jack Evans gave me a job steward's button. I asked him to tell the real job steward, so he wouldn't be put out, and I stuck that button in my turban over my forehead. When the chippy foreman saw it, he called me into his office. He was steaming, and he tried to threaten me. I told him to leave me alone. "You can't find any fault with my performance, and you should not force me into retaliation." But that chronic mind did not understand.

I could see that the company would not survive if the management did not maintain the quality of their grading, so I started to look for another job. The first place was Bridge Lumber, a Crown Zellerbach mill on Mitchell Island on the north arm of the Fraser River in south Vancouver. When I showed them my letter from MacMillan Bloedel, they said, "Come right away." I took two days"leave from Nalos Lumber to try the new job, and it was all right. The next week I tendered my resignation. Aside from that foreman, the management were sorry to see me go, but I told them the truth about my reasons.

At Bridge Lumber I worked in the green chain grading. Later, they needed a grader in the planer mill, and because I had sound experience, they gave me that job. This company put out a newsletter every now and then, and they put my name in, in a very nice manner, because I had the A certificate for grading. Somehow this newsletter got into the hands of Transco Lumber Company, which was only three doors away. The foreman sent a message that he wanted to see me. When I came, he said, "You can start immediately." I told him I would give the other company a chance to find a replacement, which took a couple of weeks. Then I left Bridge Lumber after working there only two or three months.

Transco was a remanufacturing plant for upgrading lumber. They bought low-grade dimension lumber from other mills and cut it into two-by-four studs. The odd time they did three-inch cedar decking. Because it was a smaller operation, with only fifteen or twenty men on a shift, I was more important, and I thought of getting employment for my son. But within three or four months Streiling Lumber in Burnaby offered me a permanent day shift, handling one-by-eight-inch cedar siding, which was lighter than the two-by-fours at Transco. An East Indian fellow there named Gurnam Singh knew me from Nalos Lumber. He was working as a grader, but he had been offered a promotion to yard supervisor if he could bring in a good planer-grader in his place.

I told the foreman at Transco that I had an easier job. He said, "Well, it is not easy to get a replacement." I told him, "They might not want me for too long." So we worked out a schedule with the day-shift grader at Transco. He agreed to continue for the first half of the afternoon shift, from 4:00 until 8:00, and I would come on after the break at 8:30. We did that for about six weeks, and it was a good supplement to my income. When I used to come off the day-shift at Streiling Lumber, my daughter-in-law would have my food ready, and after prayer I would go to bed for two or two and a half hours of sleep. Then I would work from 8:30 in the evening until 1:00 in the morning. (I could get home in ten minutes and be in bed by 1:30.) After four or five hours I would get up for my day shift.

Because Streiling Lumber were running only one shift, I couldn't get a regular job for my son, but they employed him from time to time as a casual worker, and later on he became regular. We stayed there until the next summer, when the mill shut down because the market was poor. When that happened, my brother-in-law arranged a job for us at Cloverdale at a Chinese farm next to his own. The farm job paid only a fraction of what we got at the lumber mill. Both of us could have drawn unemployment benefits, but we didn't. When you are prepared in your own mind to carry your own load, you don't go fishing to find easy ways. We drove from Vancouver to Cloverdale every day, and I kept trying to find something better. Early in 1970 I phoned Mr Schiller, the Transco foreman, and he said, "Sure, I'll try to get you on. The sooner the better." We didn't have to wait long before he called me to start, and soon after that he employed my son on the lumber pull-off.

While I was working on a steady day shift at Streiling Lumber, I would go a few miles extra on my way home to visit the construction site of the new gurdwara and watch the building and the materials being used. The gurdwara society had acquired land from the city, at a reasonable price, on the 8000 block on Ross Street at Marine Drive. The old brass in the gurdwara, being mostly illiterates, wanted the educated youth to take over the project, and these younger men were modern, clean-shaven Sikhs who had immigrated from India in the 1950s. Among the youth who were active in the affairs of the gurdwara, only three were turbaned. The people on the building committee wanted to use the gurdwara as a community centre. According to Sikh tradition, a gurdwara is for religious performances – marriages and paths (readings from holy scripture) – and for education, and a gurdwara can sponsor sports, but nothing like entertainments or social parties. The original plan included a sacred room for Guru Granth Sahib on one side of the main congregation hall and a room for akhand paths on the other. When the roof went up, I could easily judge that there wasn't sufficient space for those rooms on the main floor or for all the rooms we wanted on the basement floor. We called a meeting of the executive and asked a member of the building committee what had happened to the sacred room for Guru Granth Sahib. "When you build a palace for a king," I said, "how can you eliminate his private room?" He couldn't hide from us, so he said, "Guru Granth Sahib is not a big person, and we can put it in some corner." The session got hot. Someone said, "You are just a few adherents. We will use the scissors to trim your beards into alignment with the rest." It became quite evident that those rooms had been taken out wilfully. So we began to publicize those discrepancies by word of mouth.

The building was supposed to be ready for the quincentenary of the birthday of Guru Nanak in November 1969. On that occasion, with a new gurdwara, Sikhs would come from all over British Columbia and donate wholeheartedly. We watched the progress of the building closely, with an eye on the celebration. When they were ready to put up the laminated beams, they started to bulldoze dirt around the outside. We questioned it. "What the hell is going on?" They said that the beams were so heavy that the cranes needed a base, but after the beams were installed and the roof was on, they didn't remove the dirt. Instead they brought in more to build a dike that hid the basement level of the gurdwara from the street so it could be used for parties or even as a dance hall.

We were close to the quincentenary celebration date, and the walls of the congregation hall were all open, just framed and not finished. We asked the building committee what was happening, and they said, "Sure, you will get it in time. It is prefabricated and it won't take too long to fill in." Just a few days before the celebration they put in big eight-by-eight-foot glass sheets around three-fourths of the main floor and basement, like a big business showroom. "Why is the temple being built like an exhibition building? It should be a sanctuary for prayer." The building committee said that they would have curtains inside. "Why the expense of curtains?" we said, "and the window panes will be broken by vandals. We will have constant trouble and the unnecessary cost of repairs and high rates for building insurance."

They had designed a cafeteria-style common kitchen, which was not according to tradition. How can you perform seva (service) in the Guru's kitchen if it is all self-serve? When we looked in the courtyard for a base for a flag-post to fly the nishan sahib (the Sikh flag), we couldn't find one, and they said that they would have two small posts at the entrance. "Why two?" we thought. "There are never two." These people were born into Sikh families, but they were not practising Sikhs. At heart they were materialists who accepted the imagery of modern science and progress and saw no future for religious moral values. But they didn't have a hold on the public psyche yet. The Sikhs in Canada were mostly first-generation immigrants, rooted in the religious culture of Punjab, and although they were clean-shaven, they respected Guru Granth Sahib and gave generously to the gurdwara. The influence that the modern Sikhs had came from ties of friendship and family, but their strength was not that solid. They couldn't build a community centre because people wouldn't give it precedence. We needed a new gurdwara because the old one on West Second was too small. We needed a community centre too. I said, "Let us build a community centre after the gurdwara, but let the gurdwara be a gurdwara." But they were thinking that whatever they decided, they could bring about.

For the quincentenary ceremony we cooked food at the old Sikh gurdwara and transported it to the new one. Five or six thousand people came from all over, and we had the largest Sikh gathering in North America ever. The grounds were in bad shape, with big holes everywhere, and mud, and the building was unsafe, with no railings around the galleries. The congregation hall accommodated three thousand with an overflow of two or three thousand, Nobody was injured. That was a miracle. Two children fell into a big puddle, fifteen feet deep, and were not even scratched.

I was treasurer of the building committee at that time. The old treasurer had resigned when people objected that the committee were too slow with their reports of receipts and donations. The committee employed some girls to do the work. At one meeting we found out that they were being paid. "Well," the people on the committee said, "no one else will do it." So a group of religious Sikhs came to me. I didn't want to do it, but they said it was a service. Then they went to the building committee and said, "We have a treasurer." That was the first responsible office that I held in the gurdwara society. The building committee was supposed to give me all the account books, but they didn't. They were very polite, humble, and nice, but they were playing the juggler with me. Perhaps they thought I would give up in a few days and run away. Nobody knew that I was a qualified army ordnance accountant. I opened a new ledger and started from there. Nearly every three months I would put out a cyclostyle copies of a report, all individual effort.

In 1970 one of the members of the building committee became president of the gurdwara society. We had a joint meeting of the executive and the building committee in January. Before the meeting I went to the Guru's room and performed my prayer and took guidance from the Guru, and the guidance was clear. You can't carry on with the materialists. So I pulled a piece of paper from the notebook kept beside Guru Granth Sahib for page counting during sahaj path ceremonies, and I drafted a letter of resignation. During the meeting someone asked about an old donation. I stood up and said, "This happened prior to my taking over." The old treasurer had to explain, and during his explanation the newly elected president intervened. He said, "This is not a nice set-up. The books should be in one place." Then he said, "The old treasurer worked so long, the books should be with him." "If that is the situation," I said, "then I resign."

The new gurdwara was ready for possession by Baisakhi day, 15 April 1970, so we brought Guru Granth Sahib from the old gurdwara on West Second to the new one on Ross Street, which was a distance of eight or nine miles. We could have carried Guru Granth Sahib in a slow procession, singing hymns, to the beat of drums and rattles. The city of Vancouver would have been happy to let us do that. In the early days, on Guru Gobind Singh's birthday, the pioneer Sikhs used to come in walking procession from Fraser Mills, eighteen miles away. But the leadership wanted to muffle the event rather than exhibit it. They had a procession of cars and bundled the Guru Granth Sahib on to a bus. The president of the gurdwara society and the president of the building committee displayed their names on their vehicles, but nowhere, on any vehicle, were any religious mottoes shown. When we celebrated Guru Nanak's birthday and the building was in poor shape, nobody got hurt. Now all the work had been done and the building was in good shape. But we no sooner entered the gurdwara and installed Guru Granth Sahib on the throne than we had an accident. Some kids were playing in the gallery, running around. An eleven- or twelve-year-old boy ran into the sound-proof glass we had up there, and we had to rush him to the hospital. A lot of blood spilt on the floor. Religious people were saying that the start was not propitious.

That summer my sister arranged a private meeting with me along with my younger brother Chatter Singh and my maternal uncle's daughter's husband, Bikar Singh. They wanted me to pull out of gurdwara functions. That was the issue. They saw a danger of serious conflict that might involve me in physical situations. They were sincere in what they were saying. "After all," they told me, "if you become involved, we will have to stand behind you." When my chance came, I said, "Okay, I am very thankful for your advice. I never requested and will not request anyone to help me if I am involved in some adverse situation by doing selfless service. If anything does happen, it will not be caused by my mistake or intention."

10 Community Strife

Getting landed immigrant status became much easier in the late 1960s and early 1970s than ever before. Visitors could come to Canada and apply for permanent residence after they arrived, and it wasn't long before almost every Sikh family had one or more relatives from India staying with them. These people had a big impact on our family and community life, and the problem was at a pitch in the fall of 1970. When the Canadian East Indian Welfare Association held its annual meeting that fall, one of our educated younger men spoke up. That was Ujjal Dossanjh. He was studying law then, but he was motivated by sympathy with working people and very socialistic. He wanted to know what was being done to address the situation. His questions were very forceful and factual, and the executive could not answer. He really bombarded them. He asked why we weren't helping the visitors and why we were allowing them to be exploited by our own people. His attack was very righteous because some professional people in our community were charging high fees for immigration cases or selling services that these visitors could not afford or would not have chosen if they were not in a dependent position. And employers in the community were paying minimum wages.

The modern group controlling the gurdwara building committee and the Khalsa Diwan Society, which managed the gurdwara, were maybe two dozen of the already settled Sikhs, with another two dozen behind them. Their extended family links gave them influence over the flooding population of visitors. Then, when the public learned of all the deviations and discrepancies in the building of the gurdwara, opinion among many of the visitors switched. There was a split in the community, and many people rallied behind those of us on the religious side. The support that the leadership expected after completing the gurdwara was shattered. Though the vast majority of the visitors were clean-shaven, they gave religious morale a big boost. Even in Punjab then, about half of the Sikhs trimmed their beards. When they came to Canada, they may have trimmed or been clean-shaven, but their feelings were mostly oriented towards religion, and gradually quite a few regrew their hair and became turbaned Sikhs.

Vandals were breaking the big glass panes of the gurdwara, so the executive put up a fence around the perimeter, and they got the place landscaped. But when the first rains came, the main roof started to leak profusely, and the exterior tiles started to fall off. The executive were slow to do anything about it, and they defended the contractor. They would argue as if they had built it themselves. They would lean on lame excuses, saying that this had happened because of this, and later on they would have a new explanation. There was deep disappointment in the community, and people got behind us. We were surprised when the time came for the election of a new executive, because the modern Sikh group started to nominate our people. They nominated me, first for president, then for vice-president, and then for general secretary, but I declined each time. Other people from our side were chosen unanimously. Batan Singh Bilga, the president, was clean-shaven but religious-minded. So was the vice-president. The general secretary, Moola Singh Patara, was a practising Sikh. All were good people. When I saw these religious personalities already elected, I accepted nomination as recording secretary. So the complete slate was from our side.

We learned soon after the election why the other side had given up control. The treasury was empty. There was less than fifty dollars in the bank account, and we owed over three thousand to the architect, close to fifty thousand to the contractor, and about nine thousand to the landscaper; and we had a big mortgage with the Imperial Bank of Commerce. They all sent us collection notices right away, and we became busy convincing them that the old executive, who were really responsible, had left us with no funds.

Paying the bank was our first priority, then the landscaper. We told the landscaper that we would comply as funds came in. But we challenged the contractor and the architect because there were defects in the building.

The modern Sikhs figured that our group was not competent to handle this kind of adverse situation. They thought that it would not take too long before we would fiddle out and they would be able to come to the stage in the gurdwara and tell the people that we were just empty howlers who complain and can't do anything. After that they would explain again that when such a big project is undertaken, there will be problems. It is just the norm. That is why those people put us into office – just to nullify our effectiveness once and for all. But our challenge to the architect and the contractor was something they hadn't expected.

It took three or four weeks before we could get any records pertaining to the construction of the gurdwara from the old executive. Finally, to avoid further damage to their side, they gave us some books in which the contract, maps, and designs were most important. Every piece of correspondence that I received I took up to the stage and translated into Punjabi. People from their side would get up and object. By the time of our big congregation for the annual anniversary of our martyr Mewa Singh, people from the opposition group were standing up in the gurdwara shouting slogans against us. They knew by then that we were not incompetent and that they would have to fight it out or there would be more disclosures. The more they protested, the better our position grew among the public.

We employed the services of an engineering firm to prepare a report on the building because the walls were damp during rainy season, the roof was leaking, and the tiles were falling off. On the basis of that report we hired a lawyer and started some legal correspondence. We met the contractor with lawyers from both sides. We found out that there was no warranty on his work, but he had to agree to keep replacing the tiles when they fell off – for five years – and he had to repair the roof. And we met the architect, Arthur Erickson, in our office, along with the assistant architect and one or two representatives of the building committee, as well as a few people from our side. I explained to him about the major defects and discrepancies, and I appreciated his personality at this meeting because he was always nice and honest. The assistant architect had worked on the project when the building committee eliminated the sacred room for the Guru and a buffer room that had been in the plans so we could hold a simultaneous service if needed. I pointed my finger at him, and I declared, "You are the one that violated the faith." And I told Arthur Erickson, "We don't have a complaint other than one. It was your duty to keep an eye on the project and you trusted your subordinate too much and now our community suffers." He said, "Yes, Mr Bains, you are right."

Donations came in from the Sikh public, and by mid-term we were in a very sound position. We did a few alterations to the gurdwara. The first was to create the Guru's holy room. We did that by closing down the back hallway to create two rooms: one for the Guru Granth Sahib's night retire and one for the holy accessories. The old executive had built a six-foot almira that stood in the open hallway on the south side, and they used to put the Guru Granth Sahib and holy accessories there. We were able to establish a library out of a room that perhaps they wanted to be used by the ladies. We put in cupboards, and it became a library room and a boardroom, and we put in a flag-post for the nishan sahib (the Sikh flag). Jagjit Singh Dhillon donated the cost of the library-room modifications, and Kernal Singh Johal donated the cost of the flag-post. They favoured the modern Sikh side but joined hands with us for our honest and righteous work.

While we were in office, we tried to eliminate membership dues. The old executive had registered a constitution with the provincial registrar's office in Victoria late in 1970. Due to my knowledge of English and my religious and other volunteer services, I had been a member of the constitution committee, not to begin with but at a later stage. The original English draft said that the executive would be elected by donors who gave so much money. Then it was amended to read, "for so long as the debt is not paid." When this draft was sent to the people, they said that it should be translated into Punjabi and circulated, and then a general meeting should be held to finalize the constitution. But I never saw any Punjabi draft, and the constitution was never approved by the public. After we took office, we found that it had been registered. The people who did it just wanted to get their own way, whereas people like me, who opposed them, wanted gurdwara management to be an open affair. That caused a lot of feuding in the community. Why should the constitution be imposed without the knowledge or approval of the public? We didn't want any membership restrictions at all, but later in the year, to avoid more feuds, we compromised and agreed that anyone who donated a minimum of twenty-five dollars would be a voting member.

When we moved into the new gurdwara, the building committee and the executive at that time convinced the public that the old gurdwara property was of no use and should be sold so that the money could be applied to the mortgage held by the Canadian Imperial Bank. They put up two big billboards saying it was for sale. We found out from several people that the money was really going to be used for a community centre on the corner of Marine Drive to the east of the temple. They had bought a couple of houses in that location, and in 1970 we saw that those houses were being used for parties. We saw liquor bottles and kitchenware with meat refuse. If a community centre were built on that site adjacent to the gurdwara, then what went on in the community centre could come over to the gurdwara. Once any precedent is set, it is hard to eliminate.

While we were on the executive in 1971, we worked hard to sell the old gurdwara. We were lucky that a fellow from the old leadership helped us. This was Surinder Singh Sangha, who had become a real estate salesman and who was a very nice fellow, very compromising and lenient. It was a big blow to them when we sold the property and applied all the proceeds to the bank loan. The building should have been preserved as historical commemoration of Sikh history in North America. But we had to sell it while we could so that the next executive could not sell it and use the money to build a community centre near the new gurdwara.

In the spring of that year a Hindu swami gave a lecture at the new gurdwara and mentioned Yogi Bhajan or Harbhajan Yogi. We didn't know anything about him and thought he must be a Hindu. With the grace of Almighty, Harbajan Yogi came to Vancouver that same spring, and he was dressed in traditional Sikh form – kurta pyjama, turban, and loose beard. He gave a very impressive lecture, and we learned who he was and what missionary work he was doing. According to his explanation, he was a senior customs officer in the Indian government, and he studied yoga and became a qualified practical yogi. He came to Toronto to take a job teaching yoga. The immigration officer who interviewed him told him to shave, but he was strong enough in his belief to give precedence to his religion over a high-paid job. So he went to Los Angeles to stay with his one-time good friend Dr Marwaha. Through his yoga he created quite a following among the white youth there, and he set up the 3HO, which means Happy, Healthy, and Holy Organization.

After we got to know him, we had constant liaison with Yogi Harbhajan, and whenever he came back to Vancouver, we asked him to speak at the gurdwara. A few months later, in the summer of 1971, Baba Amar Singh came with his troop of spiritual musicians. We didn't know he was coming either until some Sikhs phoned from Malaysia, where he had been preaching. He arrived a couple of days later with his companions, three boys and one old man. Two of the boys were about thirteen years of age, and the other was eighteen or nineteen. Amar Singh was around thirty-five and a bachelor. He had been trained at an institution in Punjab called Nanaksar, which had been founded by Baba Nand Singh, a real saint and a simple-living person. Seven or eight missionaries had been trained at Nanaksar, and Amar Singh was the youngest. As far as I know, his group was the first preaching group to Vancouver from India.

Baba Amar Singh performed services mornings and evenings every day for ten weeks or more, and during the evening session the numbers started to reach close to one thousand, and generally, within a couple of weeks, people started to cover their heads! There was no strong preaching from our side or from Baba Amar Singh about it, but informative preaching, which made people understand that it showed disrespect to the Guru to go bare-headed. We made a few thousand scarves from the society's funds and kept them cleaned and placed them at the front entrance for people to use to cover their heads before they went in. That became a bone of contention with the modern Sikhs on the other side. A few times those scarves were stolen away, and we had to make new ones. We had to keep our eye on them and never put too many out during the day.

Amar Singh was very punctual, very accurate in performance, and very effective. Every time I entered one of those sessions of kirtan, I was absorbed in it totally. He had a great impact on the whole public. A few hundred would come in the morning and a big crowd in the evening. At the end of the evening session Baba

Amar Singh and his group would have the food that had been prepared for them. Gradually people became so enthused that they started to prepare food for everyone. This wasn't right. Normally, in our homes we eat at 6:00 p.m. or 7:00. People would come home from work at 5:30 and eat and then attend the evening session, and they didn't need to have another dinner at 8:30 or 9:00, when the session was over. The Guru's kitchen is for the needy or for travellers. It is not for the residents of the local area. If we partake of the Guru's langar (food from the Guru's kitchen), then we must be able to contribute in kind with physical service, whether on the stage or in the manual work, which is called seva. Otherwise people become selfish, and freeloaders come for dinner only.

I was working at Transco Lumber then, and generally I worked on the afternoon shift steadily. My counterpart, the grader on the other shift, agreed to stay permanently on days. I was doing a lot of work for the gurdwara, and by working the afternoon shift from four until midnight, I could have time for morning prayer and for other business. My three sons were all with me. Surinder, the eldest, had come out with his wife at the end of 1968, and he was working at Transco. Tarsem and Manjit had written their matriculation exams in 1970. Prior to that, my wife had written to me to get them into Canada after the exam because, she said, she could not handle their higher education at college. So they came early in 1971. Manjit was under eighteen and Tarsem was a little older. Neither was married, and there was no problem with immigration. I figured that, for the time being, I could get Tarsem a job at Transco. And I put Manjit into Killarney High School. But I kept sending Tarsem to English classes, depending on what shift he was on.

By the summer of 1971 we were ready for the rest of the family. My wife and I discussed it in our letters. We got some relatives in Kultham to take over the house and land to maintain it so that my wife could leave. And I arranged for my wife and father-in-law and our daughter Prakash to come to Canada as visitors, to sidestep the requirement of travelling back and forth from Punjab to New Delhi for immigration and medical examination. There was only one immigration office in all of India, and that was in Delhi. They arrived in Canada in August. At Vancouver airport the immigration authorities said, "Why did you get them in on visitor terms?" I said, "My father-in-law is too old. He may not like the winter here. It may be that we may have to make some other arrangements." So the immigration authorities agreed and gave them permission for a six-month stay. And we didn't have any problem extending it. Father-in-law liked Canada, and my wife was happy to be with the family. She took English classes for around ten weeks and learned some, but there was a lot of work at home, so she stopped. Prakash had passed grade four in Kultham, and she went into primary school in Vancouver.

My younger brother Piara Singh and his family also immigrated that summer, and they arrived ahead of my wife. Twice before Piara Singh had shown a desire to immigrate, but each time he had an accident and couldn't come. Piara Singh was a foreman commanding over forty mechanics and artisans in a locomotive-repair shed in Jhansi in central India, where there was a big railway-coach factory. He was the one brother in the family in whom I had the deepest confidence, and vice versa. Yet after his arrival in Canada it took only a week before relations were strained. I never dreamt that, after so many years, it would happen. That was a big lesson to me. I learned that a relationship is not in your own jurisdiction.

Piara Singh had a very good life in Jhansi as a blue-collar supervising officer who was provided with all the facilities available. And he had lived all his adult married life away from home as an independent unit. He just came to visit the family in Sarhala Khurd on annual leaves or casual leaves. When you are close to a person but never live together, you never come to assess the inner being. Piara Singh expected to find a good employment situation for himself in Canada because Canada is an advanced country, and he thought that there would be a good demand for his kind of qualifications. But he came when there was high unemployment. The cycle of boom days was over. I had an old two-bedroom house with a newly rebuilt attic and a low basement. Altogether we were six, and Piara Singh with his wife and two children made four more. So we were ten in the house, of whom seven were adults. And Piara Singh's son was a pretty big boy too. I moved myself into the attic and my eldest son and his wife and child into the back bedroom. My other two sons were in the basement, and Piara Singh's boy went down there too. I gave Piara Singh and his wife and their other child the front room. After living on their own for many years, they found it a strain to live with so many people, with so little room.

Piara Singh arrived on a Sunday. Monday was a busy day for me at the gurdwara. We had arranged for a bulldozer to open a driveway to the main kitchen of the gurdwara. To put that driveway in, we had to remove a big bank of earth twenty feet high. When I went to the gurdwara that morning, I saw a crowd of opposition people, and they had stopped the bulldozer. Batan Singh, the president, was there, but we were just two against the rest. So then, back and forth, we discussed it, and the tussle took two or three hours before we agreed on a solution. So I had no spare time for Piara Singh on Monday, and that was unexpected. On Tuesday evening I sat with him, and we talked very comprehensively and amicably, and we decided that Vancouver was the best place for him to live, find a job, and educate his children – better than Cloverdale, where my sister lived. If he stayed in Vancouver, he would be nearer the gurdwara, and he would have a good religious environment. The only difficulty was the tight accommodation.

On Wednesday I was busy again at the gurdwara because we had our meeting with Arthur Erickson, about the discrepancies in the construction of the gurdwara building. My sister and brother-in-law took Piara Singh and his family out to Cloverdale. They had phoned and invited him to stay the night, and I said, "Why not?"

When I came home from work on Thursday, I was thinking that everything was fine. Then I learned that, after visiting the farmhouse in Cloverdale, Piara Singh and his family had decided to move there. That was a big sudden blow, and I had no cure in my hands. I had to ask him for what reason this sudden and drastic change. He blamed me. He said that instead of looking for work for him and for his wife, I was spending more time elsewhere – that is, at the gurdwara; and he said that I did not tell him about the work situation before he came. I would blame him 75 per cent on that point because I wrote to him to say that there was unemployment but some arrangement could be made. He thought of Canada as a very rich country and did not visualize any difficulty as a settler. I was on my way to take a bath when he said, "I owe you for the money you sent from your tithe." That remark was a piercing one, and it had added sharpness because he said, "from your tithe." I had to clarify what had happened, but he was prepared for a long session. For eight hours we talked. I was ready for the bath, wearing just my shorts without even a vest, but I sat in the living-room with my brother and his wife until the next morning.

In India, before Piara Singh received his immigration papers, the doctors found a spot in his wife's lungs, and she had to undergo treatment. During that time the extra expenses – specialists, X-rays, travel to Delhi for treatment – were a heavy burden for him, and I sent him extra money. At one point I was very tight, so I thought I would mention the situation to sister. I told her, "I have only a couple of hundred dollars in my tithe account, and by the time I get my next pay it will be too late." Generally, I never sent tithe money to my family. But sister didn't volunteer to help. She said, "Why not take money out of the tithe account?" So I did, and replenished it later. She must have told Piara Singh when he went out to Cloverdale. It was a reproach to me that I would only pay out of my tithe money for a brother or sister.

There was some misunderstanding between sister and myself. It had to do with our brother Chatter Singh. She had a complaint against him, and I felt he was innocent. That caused a strain in our relationship, and it was a second family trauma for me. The third trauma was at the Ross Street gurdwara, handling all the situation there. And I was pushed into the secretaryship of the East Indian Welfare Association, handling the visitor problems. With all that, there was too much burden on me. All these problems caused some health upsets. Always in my mind was the feeling I would break down some day. Within two or three months the hair of my beard started going white. I looked like a very young man up till then. That summer my face shrank, my beard started to go white and my weight reduced.

A couple of months later, after Piara Singh moved out to Cloverdale, I was involved in an incident at the old Sikh gurdwara on 1866 West Second Avenue. Visitors were living there in the residential quarters, and I was in charge as caretaker of the facility. Neighbours complained to the city about the mischief-making of some of the visitors, and the city complained to the gurdwara society. Naturally, I was the one to redress it. I lectured the visitors, and then I went to city hall and spoke to the authorities. They were sympathetic, but they said that we had a sanitation problem as well as a mischief-making problem, and they wanted both corrected. I spent some money on sanitation equipment, and I appointed a committee of the visitors to maintain good conditions. Unluckily, on a check later on, I found that some of the bad characters living there had arranged a drinking party in the kitchen and were cooking chicken, which is forbidden in the gurdwara, where all meals must be vegetarian. As an elder, I talked to one of them like an angry father and showed him a broom and told him, "Your type needs some harsh handling."

He was four yards away, standing on the floor of the kitchen, and I was slightly lower on the porch when he threw his shoe at my turban. It is a great insult to a Sikh. It was a glancing blow, but I later found that it broke my comb. Everyone was very upset. The rest of the visitors were all apologizing. But the man who threw the shoe had run away. It didn't take more than five days for him to change his mind. They must have run around night and day to the gentry of the community to put pressure on him. At the weekend he apologized very humbly, running to touch my feet. I said, "No, no. That is not enough. It can't be left like that." When it first happened, I said that this was not an insult to Tara Singh Bains but to the secretary of the gurdwara society. He knew it, and he promised to be a good man in the future.

This story reached Piara Singh in Cloverdale. One day Piara Singh phoned me, and at a fixed time I went there. After a brief discussion he said that a great dishonour had been done to me, yet I had said nothing to the family about it. I explained what had happened and that the whole community had felt the insult and that it had been reconciled. "Why should you feel the dishonour of the family?" I asked. At this point Jagjit Singh – my youngest brother who had the kidney transplant – came in, and he had a very light type of greeting. I could see that he had something on his mind. It didn't take too many minutes more in the discussion before Piara Singh said, "I have heard that there are generally ten gundas (hired goons) behind a secretary and fifty behind a president." That was a shocking remark. I told him, "That means, pretty near directly, you are calling me a gunda." He said, "No, no." Then all of a sudden Jagjit Singh said, "Oh gunda, you are a gunda." In the past, when he had disputes with his wife, I would not take his side, and naturally he had not liked it. That is what poisoned his tongue. Piara Singh admonished him. But the damage had been done. It seemed to me that Piara Singh had called him to our meeting purposely, although he later tried to convince me that Jagjit Singh had just come in by chance.

This was a real breaking-point in my mind. I told Piara Singh, "You can justify yourself, but you cannot satisfy me. This was planned by you." They had put some sweets on the table. I told him, "I won't take anything." Jagjit Singh left, and I told Piara Singh, "This is my last visit to your house. On the basis of misinformation and misjudgment you have hurt my feelings so much it will never encourage me to be the same in future." After that we had only formal meetings. Quite a bit later the eldest nephew, Surjit (Mac) Singh Gill, tried to patch things up. He persuaded Piara Singh to have a sahaj path bhog (a prayer ceremony) at his house and to invite all brothers and sisters and families to remove any differences. Piara Singh had to comply. But it still stayed formal. It wasn't close again.

Piara Singh went on working on the farm at Cloverdale with Mac Singh, and his son went to a school where there were no Sikhs at all, not even clean-shaven ones. When I told Piara Singh, "This is the last of my visits," I also said, "One day you will leave this place in tears." Just all of a sudden that thought had come from the gravity of my heart. I could visualize what would happen if his son grew up there. And it did happen that, within a couple of years, his son became a little mutinous. There weren't many places where a Sikh family could find a good Sikh environment, and Canadians didn't know that much about Sikhs.

In 1971, when the municipality of Surrey started to expand, a lot of East Indians moved there. Previously very few had lived in Surrey. The Sikhs bought an old church building near Scott Road, and they modified it as a gurdwara. They called it Delta-Surrey Sikh Temple. That became the centre of a new residential development. It didn't take too long before some hooligans, some white kids encouraged by some older people, began to make trouble for the East Indians in Surrey, who happened, particularly, to be Sikhs. Hooligans set the Sikh temple on fire once or twice and vandalized so many houses, some very seriously. At school East Indian children were also subject to jeering and discrimination. Later on the Ku Klux Klan were involved in some of the hooliganism. It became a very big problem for the authorities to handle.

There are God-gifted people who are inspired with exceptional thought and methods to remedy such situations. One of them was Mr Sid Bentley, a teacher at William Beagle Junior Secondary

School in Surrey. He believed that, if the school gave students knowledge about the faiths and cultures of minorities, then we would have a better atmosphere of understanding. He went to the principal, who was a good and thoughtful man, and to the staff, and he got the go-ahead, even though this wasn't his subject. To begin with, he invited Sikhs, Hindus, Muslims, and Buddhists to speak at the school. I happened to be the one to speak for the Sikhs because I was recording secretary and public-relations man for the Khalsa Diwan Society, and Sid Bentley's request came to me.

I gave quite a few lectures and made quite a few visits to his school after that. He intensified his project so much that the ignorance, which is the cause of prejudice, started to whither away. Later in the school year I gave a lecture to a senior class and came out to my car just as lunchtime recess started. Instead of driving off right away, I sat in my car. In front of a house on the other side of the road, opposite the schoolyard, a young Sikh lady wearing her Punjabi dress was raking the soil for a new lawn. I watched all of the students, and I didn't see a single one look at her in a queer way or point at her. They were walking out in groups and droves, grade nine, ten, and eleven students – all puberty age – and not one paid any attention to her. Some of the youth were pretty mature, seventeen or eighteen years, but they didn't even cast a stealing glance. I was so happy and thanked God for such a good result. It showed me that once the average person learns the facts and the reality about minority people, then negative feeling evaporates.

Another place where I spoke was at the Marpole Kiwanis Club in south Vancouver. The gathering was in the evening, and they had a very nice dinner. I spoke about Sikh and Indian religion and culture for about an hour, and then we had a question-and-answer session. Afterwards they sent me a certificate of appreciation in the mail. That evening was the first time I had horseradish. It looked so nice and I took a good mouthful. O boy! I had to use my handkerchief quite a few times to wipe my eyes. My son was with me, and I told him, "Don't eat that!" But it didn't matter. If people of various religions can sit together and discuss their common beliefs, then a common platform of understanding is formed in a very comprehensive and friendly environment.

About that time an amritdhari (baptized) Sikh had to appear in court, and the officials told him that he couldn't take his kirpan in with him. That created an impasse, and someone from the court called me in from the Khalsa Diwan Society. When I got there, I learned that the justice people, who didn't have any knowledge of Sikhism, had decided to get copies of the Sikh sacred scriptures, Siri Guru Granth Sahib, for the administration of oaths to Sikhs. Some misinformed Sikh had told them where to buy them, and they had spent money to get some from Amritsar. When I went to the courtroom, I discovered that they had the presence of the Guru in there. I explained that Siri Guru Granth Sahib has the status of a living Guru in spirit and can't be brought into the courts. The officials agreed instantly that they had made a mistake, but they insisted that there should be something for Sikhs. It wasn't necessary, but I didn't know it. I hadn't been in the courts before and didn't know that an oath could be affirmed without any scriptural presence. We discussed it in the Khalsa Diwan Society and decided to give some small booklets of everyday ablutions in place of Guru Granth Sahib. I made the officials understand the discipline of cleanliness. They should wash their hands and there should be no smoking when the booklets were used. So we gave them the booklets and took away the copies of Siri Guru Granth Sahib and installed them in the gurdwara.

We had problems with amritdhari Sikhs wearing hard-hats at work. One fellow was a truck driver, and all of a sudden they wanted him to wear a safety hat. There was the case of a student at the British Columbia Institute of Technology, and a couple of others concerned with the compensation board. I made presentations to the authorities, but with very limited success. The human-rights board accepted our view, but not the compensation board. The senior official there wanted us to find some alternative to a complete turban. He wanted something devised so that a hard-hat could be worn over a small turban – to which I never agreed.

At the end of the year our group decided not to contest the election for the next year. We were an informal group of the religious-minded, some clean-shaven and some not. Most of us were working people. Our opposition, the modern Sikhs, aligned themselves with Naxalites, who were communists. They used the Naxalites to create an environment with too much stress. Naxalbari is a town in West Bengal. That is where the Naxalite movement started, and it spread to Punjab. The Naxalites slipped into Canada through the visitor system. Their philosophy was very straight – total vio-

lence to achieve their goal. At one point they were distributing literature on the gurdwara premises, and we wanted them to be on
public property. One fellow agreed to stand on the road outside
the gate. You could discuss with him, decide something, and
stand on that. The others you could never trust. We had too much
trouble. If it had been civilized, we could have continued. But we
had vandalism at night and hooliganism during congregation. We
had shouting, fisticuffs, and beatings during congregation when
many people were there, and we had to call in the police frequently. We knew that these things were well organized. That is
why, although we were in a very consolidated position to win the
election, we decided as a group not to contest it.

11 Community Service

My elder son, Surinder, rented a place on the other side of the Kingsway, not too far from us, and moved there with his family after my wife finally came to Canada in August 1971. We still had eight in the house, father-in-law, my wife, our youngest daughter, Parkash, two sons, Tarsem and Manjit, and we had Mohan Singh Kang and Baldev Singh Chahal. Mohan Singh Kang was a neighbour from Kultham and a relative of my wife. I didn't know he was coming to Canada until, all of a sudden, he showed up at my door. Baldev Singh Chahal was my younger brother Piara Singh's son-in-law. He came a little later on his own, without his wife. He was a qualified draftsman, but Mohan Singh had only grade six or seven education. They came to Canada with visitor's permits and stayed with us until they were given landed immigrant status. My wife was the only one cooking, washing, and housekeeping. I did the grocery shopping – that was my duty – and the boys would help one way or another, but my wife had a lot of work. She didn't have to look after milk buffalo like she did in Kultham, but the family was much larger.

I was working at Transco Lumber on the afternoon shift and also working odd hours at a little planer mill named Stadco Lumber. Tarsem and Surinder also worked at Transco until they got jobs at a big bottling plant for Seven-Up and Pepsi on Boundary Road, where they learned forklift driving. Manjit worked there too on weekends. We were able to get these jobs for them through the production manager. His name was Manmohan Singh, and he had lived with me for five or six months when he first arrived in Vancouver. Manmohan Singh had experience with the Coca Cola bottling plant in New Delhi. He immigrated to Ontario and worked for Pepsi Cola there, but his wife was feeling lonely because she didn't meet many Sikhs. So he moved to Vancouver and at first he stayed at the old Sikh gurdwara on Second Avenue with his wife and daughter. That was early in 1969, and I was in charge of the residential quarters at the gurdwara and doing religious performances as well. He was quite impressed. He was a turbaned Sikh, and in those days there weren't many Sikh youth with complete hair.

Manmohan Singh was looking for a place. He said that he needed a practicing Sikh as a landlord, and he wanted to stay with me. At that time I had Surinder and his wife with me. So I put a toilet and a washbasin downstairs and moved them down there to make room for Manmohan Singh and his family. At times like that I generally kept a record of household expenses and at the end of the month divided them up among all those living in the house. Manmohan was a knowledgeable personality, and he respected me as an elder. During his stay we were always discussing religious and social matters. Later on Manmohan Singh consulted me on a special subject. He wanted to run his own business instead of working for someone else. I suggested he start a restaurant, a nice clean one that was up to date. He said that, as he wasn't a citizen, he couldn't get a liquor licence, and a restaurant without a bar would not be a success with white people. So I guaranteed a loan for him and acquired the liquor licence in my name. He opened a restaurant on Main Street serving East Indian food. When he became a citizen, we transferred the licence to his name.

I worked at Transco until the early winter of 1972, and then I changed jobs. Transco were buying a very poor grade of lumber and upgrading by splitting the pieces. That meant that the lumber graders had to do more handling. When I told Mr Schiller, the manager, that I wanted to go, he said that was okay, although he didn't like to lose me. The new job was at a mill on the north arm of the Fraser River, at the foot of St George Street. I knew a Sikh who had been an electrician at Nalos Lumber and who had some shares in this new mill. He also worked there as an electrician, and he did first aid. He wanted me to work there because he knew about my grading ability and my work habits. He offered more money than I was getting at Transco, so I agreed to go.

I started in on the afternoon shift. They were buying big, third-grade logs. A good grader could get a lot of clear lumber out of those logs, but it required experience. In my first eight-hour shift I was able to pull out as much clear lumber as they used to get in a whole week. When the manager came the next morning, he got to know. He said, "Is it all clear?" I said, "It must be 95 per cent on grade," which is the best requirement. So he was very pleased, and I had an easy time there. I coached the other grader, and they got a big return.

In February 1973 I had a car accident. My middle son Tarsem used to go to the Kitsilano area for English classes, and he would drive my six-cylinder Valiant, but he would bring it back in time for me to take it when I left for the afternoon shift. On that day he was held up in the traffic, so I drove in the second car, an English Vauxhall, which was smaller than the Valiant. At the sawmill the chipper machine broke down after three hours of operation. They tried to repair it but found that they needed a part that they couldn't get until the next morning. Around 8:30 p.m. they sent us home. One fellow went the same way I did, so I took him in my car. There is a main intersection at Fraser and Marine, only three blocks from the mill. I was ten or fifteen feet from the intersection and going twenty-five miles an hour when the light turned amber. So I accelerated to go through before the red. I had hardly entered the intersection when I saw a big Pontiac zooming down the long slope on Fraser. If you don't brake a few times coming down Fraser, your speed easily rises up to seventy or seventy-five. With some secret help, I steered to the right and applied my brakes successfully. The other car caught my bumper and dragged me a few feet in its path and then carried on another twenty-five yards before it ran up on to a curb in front of a gas station and stopped. I had a whiplash from the jolt, and I was dizzy for five or six minutes. If I had been driving the Valiant, I would have projected further into the intersection, and he would have hit me more squarely. By catching my son up in that traffic, Almighty saved me from a worse collision.

The light changed a couple of times while I sat there, too knocked out to move. I was still sitting there in a dizzy spell when a pick-up truck approached the intersection from the south. The driver who had hit me was a twenty-year-old boy who had had his licence for only six months. Instead of coming to find out how

I was, he went over to the driver of the pick-up. They had a long discussion. I saw the light change at least four times, and I could see them pointing at the intersection and nodding. Then the pick-up pulled over to the side. The man in the pick-up became the other driver's witness, although he had not been there when the accident happened.

Two East Indian workers from the sawmill were walking along Marine Drive, and they had just crossed with the lights when the accident happened. They came over to my car right away and stayed with me. After I recovered a bit, I went to the gas station on the southeast corner and phoned the police. While I was phoning, a patrol car stopped and a young policeman spoke to the boy and his fixed-up witness. When I came out of the gas station this policeman handed me a ticket. He wanted me to sign it, and I refused very emphatically. I said to him, "How in the hell can you register a violation against me without getting any statement from me? You just have a one-sided story." He said, "There is a witness." Then I told him about that witness, when he had arrived and what he had seen. To prove my point, I told him to drive up to the intersection in the direction the Pontiac was going. So he got me into his car and drove around and approached it from that side, looking at the whole situation and the position of my car. He hadn't talked to the fellow who was riding in my car or to the two fellows who had seen the accident from the other side of the street and who were still standing by my car. He couldn't talk to any of them because they didn't speak English. But he became convinced that I was telling the truth. Even so, he said he couldn't quash the ticket. He said he would be on my side in the courtroom, but I would have to prove my story because the other driver had a witness.

On the day that the case came up in traffic court, I defended it myself. The fellow who was in my car was a witness and also the two fellows who had been walking home from the sawmill. I had another witness too, a Punjabi lady who had been there with her children. I hadn't noticed her, and the policeman didn't see her either, but she sent her husband afterwards to tell me that she had seen the accident and could be a witness if I liked. She was a good witness because she knew English. My other witnesses weren't much help. The interpreter was a Canadian-born Sikh girl with a real Canadian accent in Punjabi, and her pronunciation was so confusing to one of my witnesses – who had never been in court before – that he wouldn't answer. The magistrate let me interrupt a couple of times, but in my position I couldn't do too much. Now that there are more highly educated people among the East Indians, these things don't happen so often. In those days it was very poor. So it was hard to make a strong case against the other driver, and he was never charged. The magistrate dismissed the charge against me, but in his concluding remarks he said, "Mr Bains, had your passenger in the car not mumbled, the procedure would have been very different."

About the time of my car accident the mill got a custom cutting contract from a Japanese firm. These Japanese fellows would buy big number-one-grade spruce logs and cut them into heavy-dimension lumber for remanufacturing in Japan. They wanted to create jobs at home. On their order we were cutting eight-and-a-half- by sixteen-inch timbers twenty-four feet long. Of course, the whole log could not be cut into pieces that size, so we were also doing four and a half by four and a half studs, which they needed for posts, and then cutting the balance into smaller sizes. With all of those large timbers, our production increased twofold – 150,000 board feet – with the same crew.

It was too much for a grader to handle manually. In other mills heavy timbers could be turned by automatic kickers, but in this mill, where the largest sizes they had been cutting up till then were two by twelves, they didn't have that system. I spoke to the management about putting in an automatic kicker. They said, "Yes, the green chain is an old one, and we will replace it with a new roller and kicker." But they didn't do it. The pull-off crew always had a hard time with those big pieces. Every now and then they would stop the green chain, and that would force me to stop my table. The mill production would continue, and my table would get crowded. Odd times I would have to shut down the mill, and they would put on extra crew to clear up the green chain. In that kind of hustle tussle, I began to feel pain in my back. Some muscles had been pulled. Twice I reported this to the Sikh who had hired me, but he never recorded it. He would very politely say to me, "Giani Ji, you are so experienced, you don't have to turn all of the pieces." But I said, "I am an honest worker. I can't let go by any production that is suspicious." Of course, some times, when I was very sure – knowing the whole log – I didn't turn over all the pieces. And there was no pressure from the management. They respected me. But they wanted to keep the mill going, and with all this, my back got shot.

That year in August I bought a new house on Amethyst Avenue near Matthew McNair Secondary School and No. 4 Road in Richmond. It was bigger than the house in Vancouver, and it was on a sixty-six- by one-hundred-twenty-foot lot. I sold the old house for $30,000 and bought this one for $42,500. On 31 August, I worked my last shift. My back had been getting very bad, and in mid-August I told the management they could bring in a grader to replace me on a prolonged basis because my back was so bad and I wanted to claim compensation. I told them clearly about my position, which most people don't do because management doesn't like compensation cases. In a few days I received my time-check in the mail, which meant I had been dispensed with. I had been promised a talleyman's vacancy, but it was given to someone else. So I phoned the manager, and he said he didn't know anything about it. Later on he said, "Come to my office." When I went to see him, he was very nice. The company kept me on their list, and I agreed to go on a sickness benefit.

When I visited my doctor about my compensation case, he said, "No, no, you are fine. You can do the job." He was a good doctor, but he wouldn't send me to a specialist. I saw him a second time, and he told me then that my case would not succeed because the company didn't have any record of my reporting an injury. He signed the papers for me, but that is what he said. I applied anyhow, and they sent some assessors to my residence. In late December I got a reply. The compensation board stated that my back injury was not attributable to my work but that, if I did not agree, I could appeal.

A year later, in August or September of 1974, I was driving to the gurdwara from Richmond in someone else's car. My door was half-way locked and rattling. When I approached No. 5 Road intersection on Westminster Highway, I stopped at the light and, without putting the car into neutral – it was an automatic – I tried to reset the door by opening it and then pulling it. The first time I didn't succeed. The second time I pushed it farther out and pulled it harder with a jerk. The door did lock, but something happened in my shoulder. I felt serious pain, something broken, not in the bone but in the flesh. Although I saw the doctor and the orthopedic specialist and had X-rays and manipulative treatment, things did not rectify. Gradually, by November, my shoulder was semi-jammed. It could be that I made it worse by working with full zeal in the gurdwara services, like washing toilets. I had many duties. But it became so bad that, by December 1974, I couldn't even turn to tie my turban, and for washing my hair I had to have help from my wife. At night I couldn't touch my bed with my shoulders and had to keep propped up with pillows. This condition continued over a period of a few months. Then, getting tired of it, I thought of going back to India permanently, because the damp and cold were aggravating my back, shoulder, and neck.

In the fall of 1973, not long after I quit my job at the sawmill, I got a phone call from Paul Janulus, who was in charge of the official interpreters' association and knew pretty close to thirty languages. He had met me a couple of times at Sikh temple ceremonies, particularly at a wedding in New Westminster where I was performing the recitation and giving a lecture on the marriage aspect of life, partly in English and partly in Punjabi. That might have impressed him, or he might have called because he was stuck for an interpreter. He didn't know I wasn't working. When I told him, during our conversation, he said, "Well, if we could join hands in this court interpreter's job, I would be happy." So I agreed, and that work carried on until 1983. In the first few years I did quite a bit.

A lot of cases were in family court. We had some in which young children had deserted their parents under the pretence that the parents were too harsh. I remember one in which the social worker – a person with just virgin education, not education combined with experience – had encouraged the children to make complaints instead of trying to get a reconciliation. There were two girls and two boys, and all of them had been taken away from their parents, although the youngest one didn't like it and wanted to go home. The father was working out of town, up north in a sawmill, and the mother was a farm worker. They had bought a house and had to make the payments. Because they were working hard and didn't know English, they couldn't check the children's performance at school. The oldest boy was sixteen, and he was the main problem. I could see that he was the type that would drop out of school if he could. When the judge learned about the situation, he thought that reconciliation should be given a better chance. He asked me to help because I had been in family court quite a few times by then and he knew me. I talked to the younger three children without their older brother, and it didn't take too long to convince them to go home. Then I told the social worker to give me a few minutes with the parents, and I said to them, "Don't worry about the elder boy." When I spoke to him, I explained that these social-welfare services are not a green pasture for nothing, and I really gave him a comprehensive picture of what would happen to him away from his parents. I said, "Now you decide." It didn't take more than fifteen minutes before he became positive. Then I brought in the social worker, and we went back to the judge and the case was decided.

Some times, when people saw that I was the interpreter, they would come up to me in the corridor or in a waiting room to explain their case to me. I would tell them two things. I would advise them about the right approach and the wrong approach, but I would also say to them that once I was under oath, I would add or subtract nothing from the statement they gave. It would be their performance that would affect the result. I faced some people who couldn't put into words what they felt. Then I would ask for permission to stop and explain and not just carry on blindly. Once, in a turban versus hard-hat case before the human rights commission, I knew that the witness was expressing a key point that did not make complete sense in translation. In Punjabi he said, "Mera jhatt langdha reha," which in English means "I could live or I could manage or I could make both ends meet." I translated it as "I could make both ends meet." One of the lawyers on the witness's side was very sensitive, and he interrupted. "I have the feeling the interpreter is having difficulty." I said, "Yes. I have given a literal translation, but it doesn't carry the full meaning. This fellow had been fired for not wearing a hard-hat. He means that it was very hard to live with the money he got. It is a very comprehensive, short idiom that carries a long sense." When the case was over, some of the Sikh gentry asked me why I didn't complete his statement for him without hesitation. I said, "Well, I was under oath to be truthful. How could I add – which is falsehood?"

I started doing this interpreting work before I received a reply from the compensation board. I am sure I could have appealed their decision and obtained compensation, but something else happened in between. Our group of religious Sikhs had not been on the gurdwara executive in 1972 or 1973. The modern Sikhs were in control. But we were building up, and finally we were a force that could contest an election. This thought was given to me from within: if you appeal the compensation decision, you might succeed in winning dollars, but the duty of service at the Guru's house will suffer. And I was given another thought: in the spiritual arena, according to Sikh teachings, any money that you get that you don't earn by your own effort will have a negative impact on your inner being. So I did not appeal, and in the year that followed I spent most of my time in handling the affairs of the Sikh gurdwara.

In the summer of 1973, while I was still working at the sawmill, our group organized a demonstration during a visit by Indira Gandhi, the prime minister of India. By then the Sikhs were very aware of the injustices of the central government to Punjab in general and to the Sikhs in particular. This awareness was not limited to the boundaries of India but went very deep among the Sikhs world-wide. Mr Ikbal Singh Sarah, a lawyer and a dedicated liberal, consulted our group, and we decided on a peaceful demonstration with some placards showing our dissatisfaction with her government. Mr Sarah found out her schedule, and on the evening of 21 June he phoned to say that she was coming to Vancouver by air from Ottawa and arriving a little after sunrise the next morning. It took me a lot of effort over the phone to get some people out on a working day at such an early hour. Somehow I was able to mobilize at least twenty people.

At that time there was only one road to the airport, and on that road there was a small swing bridge. We decided that the bridge was the strategic place to stand. Her motorcade couldn't go any other way. We had about half a dozen Sikh ladies, about half a dozen turbaned Sikhs, and the rest were clean-shaven. We stood peacefully about five or six yards apart on both sides of the road. As soon as her motorcade approached, we picked up those big placards, which were nicely worded in English, with nothing offensive. They were simple and to the point – "Stop Injustice to the Sikhs. Sikhs are Dedicated Patriots" – something like that. We did not shout anything.

Around noon she spoke at the Ross Street gurdwara. The modern group on the gurdwara executive had a special cordon in the gurdwara to protect her. They were afraid of the Naxalites. But I didn't agree. In the Guru's house, everyone comes as an equal and sits as an equal. The Naxalites had a big contingent, and they were standing with big placards and shouting very aggressively from the time she approached until she left the premises. The police were in the gurdwara in civil clothing and outside in uniform. Our group did not demonstrate at all in the gurdwara because the gurdwara is a place of worship, and anyone coming there should be allowed to come in peace. At Ross Street, Indira Gandhi spoke in nice terms of Sikh sacrifices and of how Sikhs were hard-working people and so on. She was a smart politician. But in Ottawa, when she had spoken to the joint houses of Parliament a few days earlier, she had omitted any mention of the Sikhs, although she had included the Hindus, Muslims, Buddhists, Christians, and Parsis when she talked about the cultures and faiths of India. That gave us a real pinch, because she had accompanied her father when he visited Canada in 1950, and the Sikhs in Canada greeted them with a real deep heart and big pomp and show.

Her next public address was at Queen Elizabeth Theatre. Fifteen of us went there with our placards. A lot more would have come, but we didn't want to bring too many. The officer in charge of security knew me well and walked up to us as we stood quietly with our placards. He really appreciated the way we were demonstrating, unlike the Naxalites beside us, who were shouting and crude, and he said I should go inside to hear the speech. I didn't have a ticket. He said that tickets didn't matter. "You can even take a couple more people with you because I know you are not a security risk." I thanked him for his courteous and appreciative gesture, but I didn't go in. Afterwards I learned that when she spoke, she was very vocal in her appreciation of the Sikhs. Later she was upset with the BBC for showing the demonstration, with quite a few turbaned Sikhs in it, on its international broadcast.

In preparation for the gurdwara elections the religious Sikhs held a lot of meetings in private residences. We circulated a newsletter, and we called on key people at home. If you can turn a few key people, they can turn the others. We had two clear-cut issues. One was respect for religious values, and the other was the building. Two or three weeks before the election day we came to the question of our nominee for the presidency of the Khalsa Diwan Society. This was a well-attended meeting in a private residence. One of our companions named a man who had feelings, but no strength to meet what was required – a kind of floating instant leader or sloganeer rather than a lasting resolute candidate. This was a man I had known longer than anyone else. We had lived together in Port Alberni. I was totally upset, and I stood up and strongly opposed him and walked out. Mr Mota Singh Jheeta walked out with me. My contention was that we should have a candidate with religious integrity, public support, and a previous record, and this man didn't meet any of these criteria. It wasn't a question of a turbaned or clean-shaven candidate. I would have accepted either. Most of the members of our group were clean-shaven, pretty near four to one. Turbans were not the issue. We opposed the modern Sikhs on the basis of religious ethics and values, which the hard core of their members lacked.

After that I didn't attend meetings, although people consulted me on the phone, particularly on the presidency, because some of the members of our group knew I was right. I had calls from both sides, from leading hands in the modern group and from our group. To the faithful I suggested the name of Gurdial Singh Neel. Even when I was talking on the phone to a leading fellow from the other group, I suggested Gurdial Singh Neel. Everyone agreed but wanted me to approach him. I said, "No. If you want, I will come with you, but I won't take the initiative." I didn't want Mr Neel to have the impression that it was his neighbour and friend pushing him into this controversial situation. I wanted him to see that it was the people at large.

On election day the modern Sikhs and the religious Sikhs each nominated several people for the presidency. The meeting was heavily attended; the main hall was packed; and while it was a good meeting without high tempers, it was a tense situation, and both sides could feel that success would not be easy. Behind the walls of the assembly hall, half a dozen leading people, two or three from each side, held consultations. While this was going on, Mota Singh Jheeta, who was sitting close to me, asked me to nominate Mr Neel. We were near the stage, by the west wall, and Mr Neel was about four yards away, closer to the stage. I walked up to him. It wasn't my own self; it was the hidden force that induced me to do it. I sat by his side and requested him to accept the nomination. He flatly refused, and he was justified. He said, "How in the hell, in this kind of situation, could it be possible to do it?" I said, "You are right. But at the same time, it is the call of the time.

A person of your liberality and ability can help to improve things." This discussion lasted three or four minutes. I impressed upon him two points. I said, "It is not me, it is spiritual force that has brought me to you. If it were me, then I would have done it prior to this quite a few times." I explained what had happened on the phone. And I said, "I don't want to put you into a voting contest. You should accept nomination only if it is unanimous." He didn't say anything. He didn't even nod. But he did not object. So I stood right up there and asked for a couple of minutes from the stage to go on the mike. When I put Mr Neel's name forward, the response from all quarters was overwhelming, as if the community had solved a big problem. The people who had already been nominated were most exuberant, and immediately, one by one, they withdrew their names. Then someone proposed that Mr Neel should conduct the rest of the meeting.

The next office was vice-president. I nominated one fellow, and he declined. I was trying to convince him when Mr Neel read the list of nominees, and I was surprised when he read my name, because I hadn't heard it proposed. Some of the leading candidates withdrew in favour of me, and it became a unanimous approval from both sides. I also declined, and tried to clarify that I should stay out of it for the sake of neutrality. People from the other side said, "We know you are not a partisan person. It doesn't matter that you belong to one group." Even so, I stood strong in refusing. At this point Mr Neel made a declaration over the mike. He said, "If Tara Singh Bains doesn't accept, then I will withdraw. He induced me to do it, so how can I take it on without his support?"

So I accepted. After that, most of the other positions were decided without too much difficulty. For secretary we chose Gurcharan Singh Dhaliwal, for recording secretary Mota Singh Jheeta, and for treasurer Joginder Singh Sidhu. When we came to the position of assistant secretary, we had a contest, and we took a lot of time to counsel the candidates, but they were strong in their right to keep their names in. When we took a vote by raising hands, a fellow from the modern Sikh group won. That caused quite a lot of frustration in my group, particularly with the losing candidate, who kept that grievance for a long time. The rest of the executive got unanimous approval, so, with the grace of Almighty and the Guru, we avoided a serious confrontation in the community.

12 White Sikhs

A lot of things were gone from the gurdwara when we took over the management in 1974. We didn't make too much fuss, but tried to convince the old executive to give us what they had. We never saw the records of the building committee. Some relics were missing – particularly some historical pictures from the old gurdwara and some ceremonial sword belts. Luckily the old minute book was available, although it disappeared after our term was over. We got a good start, and our planning was two-pronged. We wanted to do something about the flaws in the building, and we wanted to improve religious observance. To investigate discrepancies and faults in the building, we again employed the services of a very good engineering firm, and I arranged to get copies of the 1971 engineering report for the new engineer. In dealing with the building question, we tried to keep fair representation, and we formed an advisory committee with people from all groups – the modern Sikhs, some neutrals, and some from our side, the religious side. We also formed a small subcommittee and put a couple of people from the old building committee on it. We thought that the engineering report, when it was completed, was strong enough to support action against the contractor and the architect, but it was around the middle of the year when we got it.

On the religious side, we decided that it should be mandatory for speakers or performers from the stage of the gurdwara to cover their heads. The annual commemorative day for our martyr

Mewa Singh came in February. On that day one of the modern Sikhs, Dr Gurdev Singh Gill, wanted to speak from the stage bareheaded. He had been president in 1970, and when people asked him to put on a head covering, he took a firm stand. This created some hard feelings, although not to any aggressive level. The president, Mr Neel, was ready to resign along with the whole executive. He was saying, "If a person of Dr Gill's calibre does not want to respect the Guru, then how can we work as a neutral committee?"

I was at the door when this situation came up. Dr Gill hadn't spoken because we hadn't let him. And while there hadn't been any tussle, some people had got up on their feet. Dr Kesar Singh Khalsa, who was not a member of the executive or associated with either group, walked up to me. He said, "Giani Ji, put the matter to a vote right away – instead of resigning. That is the best solution." So I went up to Mr Neel and the secretary, and they immediately called a vote. Mr Neel put it very simply: "Those who are in favour of bareheaded deliverance from the stage and those who are opposed." At that time only 4 or 5 per cent of the people in the congregation were turbaned Sikhs, and the congregation included people from all sides, supporters of the modern Sikhs and our supporters. Some of the clean-shaven Sikhs had covered their heads when they entered the gurdwara. Others had not. But when they all voted, there was no need to count the hands, because an overwhelming majority were for covering the head at the stage. That settled the matter, and Dr Gill did not speak. The vote showed great support and respect for the Guru, although I did see one fellow from the other group, a turbaned old man, who raised two hands in favour of his bareheaded friends.

At every congregation, large and small, I would always stand at the entrance as the doorkeeper of the Guru's house. It is a must. There should be someone in a congregation to take care if anything goes wrong. We have children in our congregation, and it takes an effort to control them politely and to convince the mothers to watch them. And when I was there, any person who had drunk any liquor would not come in. Gradually, in January and February, the congregation started to become very calm and peaceful. When people entered, we asked them to cover their heads, but if they didn't want to, we let them go in. We didn't stop anyone. That was our policy. But from the stage, every now and then, we would say something in a nicely worded way.

In 1974 the white Sikh youth were the real force behind Sikh re-generation in BC. These were the followers of Yogi Harbhajan Singh. When he had settled in Los Angeles, through his yoga approach he was successful in creating quite a following. The white youth, with the influence of the hippie movement, were trying to seek peace of mind wherever they could get it. Some of them started to attend weekend congregations at his residence, and within a short period of time these became well-attended regular events. There used to be langar in the common kitchen taken by those who came. It so happened that these young whites, with their honest and sincere approach, liked the simple and truthful teachings of Sikhism, and they became involved quite deeply. Members of Yogi Harbhajan's 3HO – Happy, Holy, and Healthy Organization – attended preliminary yoga classes, that included yogic exercises along with chanting nam simaran and reciting gurbani, according to Sikh tradition.

When Yogi Harbhajan first came to Vancouver in the spring of 1971, we didn't realize that he had a following of American Sikhs. But he was able to establish quite a few branches of 3HO through-out North America, and his followers set up an ashram in Vancouver. After it was established, I tried to give whatever possible in financial and moral support. I attended the white Sikh ashram frequently, and even in 1974–76, when I was no longer on the gurdwara committee and we did not have the gurdwara stage, I would go there two or three times a month. Sometimes two hundred people would attend. It was a mixed group. About 25 per cent were white – the white Sikhs and their kindred spirits – and the rest were Punjabis, members of the traditional group and people who didn't want to be involved in political activity but who would go to a religious function.

Of course, Yogi Harbhajan was a target from two sides. *Time* magazine ran a very demeaning article about him, and so-called Sikh leaders tried to undermine him. Among the modern Sikhs, some were very much opposed to the approach of the white youth in the 3HO because they had adopted Sikhism in its real traditional way. In our language we call whites goras, and we refer to white Sikhs as gora Sikhs. I mentioned the gora Sikhs in a discussion with Dr Gill, following a meeting in which his side had objected to putting the phrase "tenets of Sikhism" in the constitution. We came out of the meeting in a friendly mood, although apart in opinion, and we stood talking in front of the gurdwara. The subject was the outer form of a Sikh. I said, Even the goras are accepting the form." Mr Gill said, "They are hippies. In a few years they will go to where they originated. It is a wave that will die out." My answer came all of a sudden, naturally. I was in front of the doorway, looking back into the gurdwara at the Guru Granth Sahib, and I said, "Dr Ji, note it down in your mind that it won't take more than fifteen years before there will be turbans back again." And the turbans have come back among the Punjabi Sikhs. About the gora Sikhs he was wrong too. They haven't progressed in numbers after a good start in Vancouver, but their ashram has stayed at a static level.

In 1974 Yogi Harbhajan asked us to sponsor a North American tour by Sikh leaders from Punjab to commemorate the centenary of the organization of the Singh Sabha movement and the Sikh renaissance that began then. He said that he wanted to see the Punjabi Sikhs do it. Otherwise, the gora Sikhs were eager to take it on themselves, although they wouldn't get a very good impression of us if that happened. He was sincere because he wanted to see the whole community together, whites and Punjabis intermingled. After some discussion, we were able to convince the other three gurdwaras on the mainland, New Wesminster, Akali Singh, and Abbotsford, to join in. So we agreed to do it.

The tour group included Hukam Singh, Surjit Singh Barnala, Gurcharan Singh Tohra, and Giani Mahinder Singh from India, along with Yogi Harbhajan Singh and a troop of about twenty American Sikhs who performed kirtan. Hukam Singh was ex-president of the Akali Party and Surjit Singh Barnala was general secretary. Gurcharan Singh Tohra and Giani Mahinder Singh were president and secretary of the management committee for all Sikh shrines in Punjab (the sgpc). They stayed about fourteen days in bc and preached in at least one gurdwara each day, starting on Vancouver Island, then going up to Kamloops and Merritt and coming back to New Westminster and Vancouver. Mr and Mrs Jheeta, Mr and Mrs Neel, and I went with them.

On this tour Yogi Harbhajan had the strength to give the message that people should not go bareheaded before Guru Granth Sahib. At the Khalsa Diwan gurdwara in Victoria, despite repeated appeals – which succeeded at least in getting the secretary to cover his head – many people did not do it. The response wasn't good, and as a result the white American Sikhs refused to take food in the langar hall. At the other gurdwara in Victoria, the Akali Singh gurdwara, three American Sikh couples were married in one ceremony. By custom, at a Sikh wedding people give money to the bride and groom. Our people were so happy to see young whites getting married according to Sikh rites that they were giving openly, and the laps of those three couples were pretty near full of currency notes. With my own eyes, immediately after the ceremony, I saw the newlyweds count the money and place one-tenth before the Guru, and I haven't seen any preacher or musician from Punjab do that.

Around midnight Yogi Harbhajan told us that these American Sikhs would not go on to any of the other gurdwaras unless we had complete assurance that heads would be covered during congregation. We tried to convince them that the practice was taking root but it needed more preaching. They said no. "This custom of going bareheaded into the gurdwara doesn't exist anywhere else. It is a deliberate violation of the tradition. It shows total disrespect for the guru, and it should be abandoned all at once." After a long discussion we persuaded them to continue on the tour. But Yogi Harbhajan told us that they would walk out if even one person was bareheaded. We had to convey this message to all the gurdwaras. We phoned, but we had difficulty in changing that kind of tradition with one phone call or even with two or three.

There were seven Sikh gurdwaras on Vancouver Island at that time, and we went to all of them. At the Khalsa Diwan gurdwara in Port Alberni nearly everyone covered their heads. Two teenagers refused – a brother and a sister – and their father, who was a fully formed Sikh, could not induce them. One mature fellow about my age, a nice fellow, too, also refused. Finally the three of them agreed to leave, and we were able to start. At the Alberni Valley Sikh gurdwara things went smoothly. At Nanaimo we had a two-hour delay because some people came in bareheaded and the president said he couldn't force them to put on head covering. In the end, the majority made them accept it. Some of the real stubborn fellows might have been pushed outside. At Paldi we had no trouble, but at Cowichan Lake we had a tough time again.

After Cowichan Lake we returned to the mainland, and we had a good congregation at the Akali Singh gurdwara in Vancouver and at the Khalsa Diwan gurdwara in Abbotsford. Then we drove to Kamloops, where the Sikh community used to hold congregation in a rented hall. At Kamloops we learned that the group supporting the barehead approach had sent three people to create a fuss. These people followed us to Merritt. One of them was a sawmill owner, and most of the Sikhs in Merritt worked for him. So he had a grip on the public psyche. People felt that if they openly opposed him, they could lose their jobs. This man and his two companions became adamant that neither would they cover their heads nor would they leave at the request of the congregation. Mr Tohra and Giani Mahinder Singh appealed for respect for the Guru, but to no avail. Then I stood up on the stage for the first time on our tour, and I spoke directly to the sawmill owner, whose name was Tara Singh like mine. I said, "Is it not a pity that, at the sawmill, which is in your jurisdiction, you make each and everyone wear a hard-hat, which is a heavy thing, and here, in this place of worship, you are so adamant you won't put a small piece of cloth on your head?" Then I spoke to the whole audience. "Do you think he is the breadgiver to you? Why are you so afraid of him?" And I explained the discipline of the Sikh gurdwaras throughout the world.

That started a lot of discussion, and people tried to convince the mill owner, but he did not budge. Yogi Harbhajan and the American Sikhs decided to leave without congregating. It was lunchtime, and we were thirsty too. The local people protested to Yogi Ji and the American Sikhs, and to the rest of us as well, that it was not their fault that this frustrating situation had developed. But Yogi Harbhajan was strong in his position. He said, "If you are such a weak sangat – such a weak congregation – that you give precedence to job security over reverence to your Guru, then we won't partake of any food or water." We bought some pop or cold drinks and carried on in our motorcade back to New Westminster. That was a drive of about 350 kilometres, and we arrived at the New Westminster gurdwara about suppertime. Langar was ready, and the first thing we did was eat food.

That evening at New Westminster a turbaned Sikh told us that the supporters of the barehead tradition were willing to meet us for face-to-face discussion that night. He had rented a hotel room, or a hall, for the purpose. It wasn't a good idea, and we said we wouldn't attend. Somehow he was able to convince Yogi Ji and the four from India that they should go, but the atmo-

sphere was quarrelsome and they pulled away from a hot discussion as quickly as they could. The opposition told the media
that these touring preachers were causing a big rift among Canadian Sikhs, and it seemed to us that they were trying to create
situations to show that it was true. The next morning we went to
the Ross Street gurdwara in Vancouver. The American Sikhs
started kirtan around 8:00 or 8:30 in the morning. People came in
good numbers, and the hall was pretty close to full. Everything
was peaceful until three ladies – wives of modern Sikh leaders –
and about seven or eight young fellows tried to get in the hall
with bare heads.

A few American Sikhs were standing at the entrance, ladies on
one side and men on the other. They were handing out cloths to
each and every one as they came in and asking them to cover their
heads. The people in this barehead group of ten or eleven were
rude and aggressive, and when the American Sikhs stood in front
of them and asked them to put something on, they thought they
could push through, and they slapped and hit them and pulled
their turbans. I was right at the door, and I saw two young fellows
in action against one white Sikh. One grabbed him by his hair and
pulled him this way and that while the other fisted him in the
back. I couldn't contain myself. "What kind of shameless thing are
you doing? You don't realize." I admonished them like a father.
The two of them grabbed me and threw me out the gallery door,
flat on the floor. From the floor I could see two of my sons standing just outside along with a nephew, a son-in-law of my brother,
and some other turbaned Sikhs. They were about to attack these
rowdies. I pulled my loud voice and warned them, "Don't move
till we say. They have a crooked plan to stigmatize us as the ones
who are causing disunity among the Sikhs." It is a good thing that
those rowdies hadn't used their fists on me. Otherwise I don't
think I could have restrained the wrath of the turbaned Sikh
youth. I later learned that a young lady from the congregation had
given a good slap to one of the bareheaded ladies while she was
pulling a white Sikh lady by the hair. But generally they were not
successful in provoking a fight, and they started to slip away.
Someone called the police, and when they came, they escorted the
rest of them out. The police were willing to lay charges, but we
said that we didn't want to proceed. Yogi Harbhajan took part in
the discussion with the police in a room downstairs. We told them

that it was all a plot by the opposition, and we didn't want to fall into their trap.

The touring group spent three days in Vancouver. On Saturday they were supposed to perform during the spiritual congregation in the evening. Around 1:00 or 2:00 in the afternoon we learned that the white Sikhs were resolved that nobody should come into the congregation bareheaded. They were prepared to repel people by force, and rather than take a beating a second time, they had obtained shovel handles and wooden sticks. We were alarmed because we had only a few hours to sort it out. We called an emergency meeting at the Akali Singh gurdwara with representatives from the white Sikhs, the Akali Singh Society, the New Westminster Society, and the Khalsa Diwan Society. This meeting began at 4:00 in the afternoon. Yogi Harbhajan wasn't there. The white Sikhs were very serious. We tried to tell them once more that we were dealing with a chronic mistake committed through ignorance and that, while it was a sacrilegious custom, we had to do a lot of educating before we put any ban on it. I remember very clearly that one white Sikh addressed the whole meeting and said, very forcefully, "I don't think that you deserve to be called good Sikhs, because you are timidly tolerating the insult of the Guru." After a long meeting, with the grace of the Guru and Almighty, we convinced them that they shouldn't get involved in anything. Luckily no one tried to interfere with the evening congregation. Some things happened later on that year that almost convinced me we had made a mistake. If we had taken a stand then, it would have settled the question once and for all.

Bibi Nirlep Kaur was in Vancouver at the time of this tour, but she could not find an occasion to make her presence felt. She belonged to a royal family, a maharaja's family. Her father had been the chief minister of PEPSU (Patiala and the Punjab States Union), and people said that she was close to Indira Gandhi. About a week after the tour left, she came to the Ross Street gurdwara for a marriage in the family of some of her friends. She wanted to speak from the stage, and the secretary gave her an appropriate amount of time. Within a couple of days we began to hear that she was complaining about the lack of recognition given her by the Khalsa Diwan Society executive. I received several phone calls, and Mr Neel got some. The next Saturday we arranged a meeting attended by the executive and by Bibi Nirlep Kaur with about a dozen other Sikhs, including some good-natured people from the modern Sikh side. At that meeting she criticized Yogi Harbhajan and tried to prove that he was not a good Sikh. After some discussion, we agreed to give her unlimited time from the gurdwara stage on Sunday. We publicized this from the stage, and her friends announced it on the Punjabi radio program that evening and the next morning.

The secretary asked me to take over the stage for this event. He was a little scared. When I introduced her, I explained frankly what had happened. I said that she figured we were not quite justified in the amount of recognition we had given her, so we had met to decide the right step, and that is why she had been offered open time. I also said that she had not been given the stage to speak on any subject other than Sikh religion. The hall was not packed, but it was sufficiently full, with over a thousand people, when she came to the stage. She began by reciting a couplet of gurbani, which she had to read from a note. After she had spoken for six or seven minutes, people started to walk away. After another two or three minutes, she became so frustrated she said, "It is hard for me to speak from a stage under the restriction that I should speak nothing other than religious preaching." A couple of minutes later she apologized and sat down. She might have wanted to demean the missionary efforts of Yogi Harbhajan, but she didn't have the religious background to do it.

The barehead supporters kept creating trouble for us. The head coverings that we kept in the galleries were stolen many times, but we kept on replacing them. One evening the gentry of the community were holding a meeting in the langar hall. Some drunk and rowdy people from the other side came in and began asking questions and interfering to disrupt our business and get a reaction. Then they became physically aggressive. Mr Neel said something about their behaviour, and one of them shoved him and pulled his turban down. Another time, during Saturday evening kirtan congregation, about midway through the kirtan a lot of cars drove up, and one hundred or so people wanted to go into the congregation bareheaded while under the influence of liquor. We didn't resist. We said, "All right, if you want to do that, sit there." Some of them came in for five minutes and then left and drove away. We had a lot of intrusions of that kind into our peaceful performances.

We had already found it necessary to employ guards and to shut the gates from 10:00 p.m. until daybreak. That was because one night, early in the year, while an akhand path (a continuous reading from Guru Granth Sahib) was going on in the nearly empty gurdwara, half a dozen white hooligans walked in smoking cigarettes and picked up all the altar money and then set fire to the altar decorations. During another akhand path, in the early morning, some hooligans jumped over the fence and set fire to the curtains in the gallery where the ladies put their shoes. A third time, also during an akhand path, some hooligans dropped a real bleeding, semi-dead person right in front of the main entrance. The fellow on guard duty saw them, but they ran off. Again we had to get up from our beds in the middle of the night. The guy survived, but he never laid any charges against anyone. Someone wanted us to get the blame for beating him to death. Of course that didn't happen because the police by then were well aware of our good efforts.

One of the guards told us that white hooligans weren't alone in causing trouble at night. They had seen East Indian boys jumping over the fence. Someone stole big quantities of rations from the kitchen quite a few times by breaking the glass windows of the storage room. How they did it we didn't know. Perhaps they slipped in during the evening and broke the windows from the inside. Quite a few times, when we were afraid of some kind of disturbance, we had a lot of young people sleep in the gurdwara to protect it. We did this particularly on the weekends.

The Naxalite youth were behind some of the hooliganism, and they were involved in a very serious incident at the celebration of Guru Nanak's birthday in early November. At an executive meeting a week before I had proposed a resolution to stop them from distributing literature on the gurdwara premises. We had always asked them to stay outside the gate, but they would walk in anyway. Then people would ask us, "Why are they allowed?" Someone told the Naxalites about the resolution, and they came on Guru Nanak's day to do something about it. The Naxalites claimed that what they were doing was lok sewa (people service), but ever since 1970 they had been like wolves among the sheep, and they were always changing colours.

People from all sides came to the Guru Nanak birthday celebrations, and we had a big attendance. A responsible person from the opposition told me that something was going to happen. He said, "We don't want to see any disrespect to you, so you should not be at the stage." That is how we knew we would have trouble. It began in the congregation when some youth gave a beating to Malkit Singh Parhar, who used to do the Punjabi radio program. Then one of the Naxalites stood up and demanded an explanation from me. "Why is Tara Singh Bains against the lok sewa people, and why won't he let them distribute their literature?" He wanted me to come to the stage. I could visualize what was going to happen, and I didn't come forward. I didn't want any dishonour done to Mr Neel or Mr Jheeta. Those people were bent on doing something, perhaps not that much to manhandle me but to dishonour those two personalities as well. In this explosive situation, one person from our side, Mr Paviter Singh Sumbal, walked up to stop it. As planned, some of those youth grabbed him and started a fisticuffs with him. Mr Avtar Singh Khalsa, a turbaned Sikh and a post office worker, couldn't stand by, and he got entangled in the fighting. That happened within four or five minutes. Then it settled down, and another calm prevailed before two Naxalites climbed up on the stage table and started shouting on the mike, "We want Tara Singh Bains to explain his approach against us."

We had sent all our strong people, like my brother, sons, sons-in-law, and nephews down to the kitchen so that nobody would try to do foul things in there. We had seen that some of our opponents would do anything to put us to shame. If the langar goes short on that annual occasion, the executive is blamed. Our people could hear what was going on because the acoustic system reaches downstairs. When they heard those Naxalites challenging me, they entrusted the kitchen to some other people, and eight or ten of them came upstairs and entered from behind the stage. My brother Chatter Singh was with them and my brother-in-law, Ajit Singh Nainar. At the same time a group of good people aligned with the opposition, Surjit Singh Gill and his brothers and relatives, came in from the main entrance. They were also upset with the behavior of the Naxalites, and they had been right on guard, waiting in case they made any physical movement on me or my companions. When they joined hands from their side, it was no less than a miracle. The Naxalites had a group of pretty near twenty-five or thirty, but they were surrounded from the front and from the rear and the third side was towards the ladies, so they couldn't run away there. Surjit Singh Gill's people and our people pushed them into the north-west corner and gave so many of them good beatings that they never interfered with any gurdwara congregations anywhere after that.

We called the police, and the congregation dispersed. People went home peacefully, thinking that at least something had been done. I stayed there in a state of thoughtfulness, communicating with the Guru. Into my mind came the idea that, if my arm and shoulder had been good, I would have drawn one of those cere-monial swords kept under the Guru's throne, bowed to the Guru, and said to those Naxalites, "Okay, boys, come out to the parking lot, because this is the Guru's house, and I will tell you what you want to know out there." I was pondering whether to continue to serve in the Guru's house with my arm as it was, and I spoke to another fellow, Muktiar Singh Gill, who was still there. I said, "Well, Mr Gill, it seems like I shouldn't get into executive commit-tees any more with my physical disabilities." I think he was there to make me solemnize that thought. Otherwise it was just an arbi-trary feeling.

He said, "Giani Ji, I'm sure you are thinking that. But it won't be long before you are there again." That is when the signal came to me from within. "He is right. People don't stand on their prom-ises." Without any further discussion I stood before the altar and performed a very short, heartfelt ardas. "Guru Sahib, he is right. From this term forward, please don't involve me in any executive committees here. Get service from me in other ways. Finally, give me the solemnity to keep this pledge." After that, whenever peo-ple asked me to run for the presidency of the Khalsa Diwan Soci-ety, I always mentioned that ardas. One time a fellow told me that he would bring a command from five Sikhs who wanted to nomi-nate me. "You can't deny it," he said. They are like panj piari." What he meant was that five Sikhs together represented the au-thority of the Guru, like the five beloved ones in Sikh history. To which I said, "No! Panj piari will never order a Sikh to break his pledge taken before the Guru."

After the Guru Nanak Day celebration in November we didn't have too much time left on the executive. We decided to hold an election in which none of us would run. It was too frustrating to continue, although we had made a supreme effort. In all the time I had been in Canada I hadn't seen any Sikh baptisms – any amrit ceremonies – except with Amar Singh in 1971. In 1974 we had an amrit ceremony during Yogi Harbhajan's visit and another one through Amar Singh. We also made improvements to the building. To maintain it we repaired the tiles and the roof. We also spent quite a bit of money on the acoustic system. Downstairs we put in a new kitchen adjoining the original one, and in the upper gallery we constructed a sound-proof glass wall to create an enclosed area with room to seat 200 or 250 people. After that we could hold two functions at the same time – a wedding or memorial service in the main hall and an akhand path in the upper gallery. And when we had two or three weddings on the same day, we didn't have the problem we had before with only one kitchen, when it always took time for one group to clean up before another could take over.

During the year we wrote to school boards and invited them to bring tour groups – teachers, students, parents – to the Sikh gurdwara to become acquainted with our religion. I have a list for 1974 that shows twenty-eight tour groups that year. A lot of school groups came and a lot of others, from the Interfaith Citizenship Council of Burnaby, the New Age Community Centre, the West Burnaby United Church, the Coalition for World Disarmament, Langara College, Canada International House, and so on. Gurdial Singh Neel didn't have that much time, and we didn't have too many people who could conduct tours in English, so I took most of them. We would show groups around and explain everything and give them a lecture with time for questions and answers, and then take them to the langar hall for hospitality and refreshments. The approach in lectures like that has to be totally positive. If you give one word that bites another, it is counter-productive. We intensified our efforts by publishing articles on Sikhism and putting them into a kit with the Khalsa Diwan Society emblem on it for tour groups and mailings and for distribution at big gatherings. We had eighteen articles printed up, most of them in English and all by well-known authors, explaining Sikhism at various levels of thought.

When we announced the election for the 1975 executive, some of the religious Sikhs sought a court ruling that only practising Sikhs should be allowed to run the gurdwara, so we had to put it off. The religious-minded gentry wanted us to carry on, but we told them we couldn't in the kind of situation we faced. Finally we held the election, with a police inspector present and two assistants in plain clothes. Attendance was very heavy, perhaps heavier than when we were elected the year before, because the gallery was totally packed in addition to the main hall. This time the Naxalites supported the religious side. At the head of the modern Sikh slate was Surjit Singh Gill, who had led the attack on the Naxalites on Guru Nanak's birthday. The contest was very close. Giani Balbir Singh, the head priest, was counting the hands, and it took him a few minutes with each vote. But Surjit Singh Gill's people won nearly every position. Once the pattern was set, it continued. It was a group pattern, with the neutral majority opposing all the candidates that the Naxalites supported. The ones who lost blamed Giani Balbir Singh. It is usual to blame. But he had done the counting in full view.

When we handed over to the new executive, Surjit Singh Gill agreed with us about continuing the case against the contractor. Another good thing that he did was to introduce Punjabi classes in the evening during the week. That was a project we had wanted to start, but we hadn't had enough time. And with his co-operation, I was able to keep on conducting lectures and religious tours at the gurdwara.

13 Living with Physical Injuries

In Sikhism politics without religion is a very shaky process. Sikhs are suffering today because they have subordinated religion to politics. With the continuing frustration of modern Sikhs versus traditional Sikhs, our group wanted to stay organized. We decided to form a new society outside the gurdwara and we named it the Shiromani-Akali Dal Society of Canada, after the organization that had fought for gurdwara liberation in Punjab. As soon as we decided on that name, I phoned the registrar of companies and told him to hold it for us. I was thinking that if it was caught by other people, we wouldn't be able to get it. The constitution of our society said that the directors had to be amritdhari Sikhs – Sikhs who kept the complete form and discipline. Such people were rare in those days, and restricting the directorship to them didn't seem satisfactory to some of the traditional Sikhs. So we held a couple of meetings and decided to form a second society with moderate discipline requirements to take in a broader group, and we registered it under the name Sikh Sewak Society. About seventy or eighty people actively participated in its meetings. Through these two societies we kept some organizational life going among the religious Sikhs.

In those days, when we did not have the gurdwara stage, we used to go to the Gora Sikh ashram (the ashram of the white Sikhs) on weekends. The Guru teaches that all humanity is equal. So it came to me, "Why not join hands with the gora Sikhs? Why not integrate with them? They are Sikhs, perhaps better Sikhs than we are." Through our effort Bakhshish Singh was invited to that ashram when he was in Vancouver. Ever since that Tohra-Hukam Singh tour in 1974, groups of spiritual musicians – kirtani jathas – have been coming to North America. Giani Bakhshish Singh from the Golden Temple in Amritsar was among the first. He came in 1975 with his troop called Hazoori Ragi, and he was performing kirtan at the gurdwaras. Yogi Harbhajan invited him to the ashram congregation, and he went there for the first time. Some of the traditional Sikhs have kept up these contacts, and the white Sikhs happily go whenever they are welcome. But the modern Sikhs did not want to have anything to do with them because they contradicted their modern view of Sikh life.

I was still targeted by the Naxalites, even when my term of service was over in the gurdwara and I was bedridden, with my back and shoulders pretty near jammed. They kept writing about me in one of the newly run papers, *Lok Awaz*. Someone brought me one of their issues, and when I read it, I was very upset by the false publicity. All of a sudden the atma from the seat of the heart questioned my individuality. "Hey. So far you have been thinking very wrongly that you give selfless service. Had you reached that stage, then these remarks wouldn't hurt you. It is your hidden desire for appreciation that is being hurt." In service one does not have to care for any honour or dishonour. If it is performed in the name of Almighty for his creation, he will take care of that.

I was lucky enough to be part of a society called Pacific Interfaith Association of British Columbia. The founder of this association was a retired citizenship court judge in Vancouver, Dr Black. He was a real Christian with no prejudice against any religion. Along with Len Burnham, Dr Charles Pares, and Val Anderson, all clergy, he started the idea around 1973 or 1974. I don't remember how I got involved. Dr Black must have called the Khalsa Diwan Society, and a few months later, in 1974, I was taken into the executive. In that organization all had faith in each other, faith in all faiths. We held the major annual event towards the end of February during Brotherhood Week. We would rent a church hall or auditorium, and members from all faiths would bring food, and speakers from each faith would deliver a short talk. Generally the attendance was over 250. One year it was over 300, and I brought 500 samosas. That is about 125 pounds of cooked food, and it took seven or eight ladies to prepare that the day before.

The Interfaith Association played a major role in the Habitat Conference held at Jericho Beach in Vancouver under the sponsorship of the United Nations in 1976. The association ran an information booth about the various faiths in BC and from the Sikh faith. With His grace, I was able to mobilize about thirty people to take turns working in that booth. Among the thirty, I invited two or three white Sikhs from the 3HO. The rest were Punjabis. At one event in the old air force base hanger set up as a hall, we had three thousand or four thousand people packed inside and more outside listening to the audio system. Each speaker had five minutes to present his faith, and I spoke for the Sikh faith. It was all positive throughout. People of all faiths were positive.

Father died a natural death in India in 1975, when he was over eighty-five. We were then three brothers and three sisters in Canada and two brothers in India. Jagjit Singh, the fifth youngest brother from me, had survived his kidney-transplant operation for more than five years. Then he became a little sickly and was admitted to hospital. The doctors found a fungal infection in his spinal column, and he didn't recover from it. His will power had been so strong before, but when he was near his end, he was in such a downcast mood, despite our encouraging, and the nurses and doctors, that the doctor said, "No, I don't think he will survive." Up to the time of his death he was the longest-surviving kidney-transplant recipient. So he made history. That left my elder sister, Karam Kaur, my two younger sisters, Ajit Kaur and Avtar Kaur, and my two next younger brothers, Piara Singh and Chatter Singh, in Canada. Piara Singh was working as a machinist in Vancouver, and Chatter Singh was in the construction business. In India, my third youngest brother, Mohinder Singh, was in the Punjab police, and my youngest brother, Santok Singh, was in the army. In Vancouver, all the brothers and sisters arranged a commemorative ceremony at the Ross Street gurdwara, with an akhand path and an open langar. In Sarhala Khurd, Mohinder Singh and Santok Sing arranged a ceremony, and I think we sent some monetary help because father was a well-known personality and there would have been a lot of people attending.

In 1975 my second eldest son, Tarsem Singh, married Rajwinder Kaur, daughter of Giani Jagir Singh of South Vancouver. I had talked to Jagir Singh a few years before when we had some meetings in his house. (He was also working in the gurdwara on the traditional Sikh side.) I could see that this girl of his could make a match for this boy of mine. Then, at the time of the elections for 1975, we had major differences in approach to the gurdwara situation. When we were discussing things like constructing rooms in the gurdwara or putting up flag-poles, if it was a good idea, he was more for taking action. I told him that people had to be convinced first. He said, "Well, these are good things. Why delay it? Do it and then we can get approval?" I said, "No. First put out circulars, and on the stage also give notice a few times." There is a big difference between government and a religious service body. When we say we are doing something for the Sikh faith, it should be the faith of everyone – total faithfulness. And in the gurdwara service, the political approach should not take precedence over religious observance.

When we had these disagreements, I just gave up the idea of a marriage between my son and his daughter. Then, all of a sudden, I got a phone call from him regarding the proposal. I said, "Well – – if we two want it this way. But I don't want our difference of opinion to have an adverse impact on the young couple." He said he wouldn't interfere and that we could make a resolve on that, which we did on the phone. And since then we have acted on that resolve, even in private discussions.

I consulted the boy, and he said he figured that a girl from Punjab would make a more faithful wife than a Canadian-educated girl like this one. I explained that I knew the family very well. That was the first point. I said, "Secondly, in this situation you get more benefits – education and professional earning." At that time she was working at BC Telephone. "Thirdly, you won't have any pressure from her family to sponsor relatives as immigrants to Canada. Fourthly, a girl from India with no relatives here would be a total burden on us economically, and it would take quite a while to train her to adjust to the Canadian stream of life. This girl is completely adjusted both ways." He had seen the girl. My reasoning appealed to him, and he agreed. He said, "Well, I have seen the girl. When you know them so well, there is no need for me to interview her. I can't find out any better than you did already."

Tarsem had completed his vocational training by then. He had worked for a few years to supplement family income while the younger son, Manjit, went to school. When Manjit finished high school, I put Tarsem back in the education side. By then Tarsem was over age, so I had to pay for his classes. He said, "It will be very tight financially." I said, "Don't worry. I want you to do it. Go full time, take exercise, play, study." When he finished high school, I gave him one year vocational training in electronics.

By then I had decided that I should go back to the warm and dry climate of Punjab. The damage to the cervical section had become a complete injury to the nervous system, and my shoulder since then is always so sore. During 1974 I attended first-aid classes, just to get a soft job. But they didn't give me the ticket, whereas my younger son Manjit, who was in class with me, got it. When I phoned, they said that it was because of my shaking hand. That was a result of my injuries. The damp and cold made my back and shoulder worse. Tarsem said, "You should change climates." He was married. My youngest daughter, Parkash Kaur, was in grade seven. Manjit had completed one year vocational training as a machinist and was pretty near two-thirds through his apprenticeship. So I made up my mind to return to Punjab, at least on a semi-permanent basis.

One day, when we were making these plans, Manjit came up to me and said he wanted to enter university. I quickly answered, "You have increased my life volume. That is what I have been looking forward to." When Surinder, the eldest boy, came here, I asked him quite a few times to take further education. "It doesn't matter that you are married," I told him. But he said, "Father, I am not quite interested in higher education." And he is doing well without it.

When Manjit spoke to me about university, I said, "Well, I have some reservations. If you can meet my terms, you can have full support. Keep your Sikh form and character. You will face a very tough situation of sexual involvement, which is very open in Western society, particularly in modern days. As you are a mature young man, this will affect you. So the safest way to satisfy that is to get married. Whenever you feel the sexual urge going beyond your control, let me know. Arrangements will be made, with your approval only, and your education will be continued even after the marriage." Then I said, "Can you keep to this?" He said, "Yes". I was very happy, and he started at Langara College to clear some subjects so that he could qualify for university. At high school, discussing his subjects with some of his counsellors, I had prepared him only for vocational training.

He began going to college quite a few months prior to our departure. This attendance at college changed his inner feelings. When I had been going to first-aid classes and he had been going with me, I told him, "Your mind is a little opaque to me. There is something breeding there." He would say, "No. No. Never." In the family, my system was that anyone going anywhere would tell the senior person in the home where and for what. This system has two purposes. One is communication and the other is to save embarrassment – having to say you don't know where someone is, which shows indiscipline in the family.

At one time he played like a magician. He told his mother he wanted to attend the birthday of a schoolmate in the evening. His mother told him he should get permission from his father. She was going out on a visit and just getting into the car with the rest of the family. He took advantage of that and walked up the stairs as if he was going to ask me, but he didn't. When my wife came back, I said, "Where is Manjit?" She told me what had happened. So I said, "Okay".

My room was very close to the stairs. He came around midnight, very sneakily. I was even sneakier. I knew immediately when he entered, and I went downstairs. In that house there was a small entry room, and he was still there, taking off his shoes. I asked him, "Where have you been?" He told me he had been at a birthday party for such and such a fellow. I said, "Did you take permission?" He said yes, he had asked mother. Then I called mother, and she explained the right story. "You are guilty," I told him. "You wanted to do the cheating, which is bad."

During the discussion I could smell some alcohol in his breath. I said, "You have violated the discipline. You have taken some alcohol." "Oh, no, father," he said. "Not at all." "I can smell it," I said. It was a nice play, a juggler playing with a master juggler. I told him to take a deep breath and release it. He did the opposite. Instead of releasing, he would take in. When he did it the wrong way three times, I slapped him with complete force, and my fingerprints stayed on his face for four or five days. He was shocked. He said, "I am twenty now. You shouldn't have done that." I said, "Hell with you. You can be thirty or forty. I am still father, and it will still come if you do wrong."

The family woke up. Tarsem was studying in his room on the ground floor. So the discussion started. Tarsem wanted to admonish Manjit. I said, "No. Don't say anything. You can do it if I am not here or mother is not here, but otherwise, you don't have the right. You can listen if you like. Otherwise go study. Don't waste your time." My younger brother's family was staying with us, and also my eldest daughter with her husband and two children. Everybody was up, and during the discussion this fellow Manjit finally said he wanted to leave the house. I said, "Well, I don't want to stop you. But so far you are a good man. I wouldn't say "You go!" Your choice."

He said, "I want to go."

"All right, anything from us?"

"Two hundred dollars, some clothes."

Right away I pulled out his paycheque. I had been carrying it in my pocket for over two weeks without cashing it because I knew he wasn't feeling right within. The cheque was for over three hundred dollars. He was working as well as attending partial classes at Langara College.

"Here is this amount, and I will give you more cash to make it at least six hundred, and that new car which I bought for you for three thousand dollars, I'll give you that also – and utensils, rations, bedding, and your amenities requirements."

He never expected that I would give him the car or that much money, so he was thinking he was very well set. I gazed at him and I said, "Now this is my last advice to you as a father. You are a very green sapling in this modern society, and with the rights and the care you have enjoyed in this family, you don't know what you will face outside. It won't take more than six months, at the most, when you will come back to this house as a totally humiliated person. We will admit you in because it is the duty of a good Sikh and a good human being. But remember, this is a very big family. There are about twenty households in the Vancouver area and at least two dozen youth of your age who have good company with each other. The type of respect that you command in the family now will all be gone when you come back. And why will you come back? Because the hawks will eat your flesh very quickly, and there will be no other place for you to go. So naturally you will come home. There is your choice. Either you stay here and become a good man and observe the discipline, or you can go now and come back later with very little respect in the family."

With Almighty's grace, sanity prevailed in his head, and he didn't move at all. But when we left in 1976, he shaved off his beard immediately. Tarsem, the middle son, was very upset. He called his uncles. They held a meeting, but it was a very tough situation for them to handle. Tarsem sent me a telegram and a letter asking whether he should keep Manjit in the house. I replied by telegram, "Keep him with you. Letter follows." In the letter I explained that, with expulsion, Manjit would become a total ruin, whereas in the family environment at least there was hope of bringing him back to form as well as into a good discipline of life. It so happened that, instead of getting into University of British Columbia, he went to Michigan, where he could complete an engineering degree in four years instead of five. At Michigan he felt homesick, and he wrote to me in India that he wanted some religious and spiritual books. I immediately went to Amritsar and sent him ten kilograms of books by registered air mail, which is quite a sum of money. But this young fellow, by getting into open Western society, seemed to lose his grain of Eastern integrity. He became like the Western youth.

Manjit was not the only one to shave. My son-in-law Balbir Singh Dhanda did it too. He used to trim his beard before he married my eldest daughter, Kuldip Kaur. When we arranged the match, he promised he would keep the Sikh discipline. Then, after a while, he started trimming his beard again. That violation of his word set my mind against bringing him over to Canada. But my innocent daughter wanted to be near her mother and brothers. And my wife kept pounding on me about the matter. Ladies have more compassionate minds. So I said, "Convey this message to him that he should not trim in Canada at all." He promised, and they came with their children early in 1974. After a while the same old story reoccurred, and that strained my feelings. After my wife and I left for India in 1976, first Manjit shaved and then this son-in-law.

While we were getting ready to return to India, I went to the junior high school and got a school leaving certificate for our youngest daughter, Parkash. Then I made travel arrangements for four of us, myself, my wife, Parkash, and my father-in-law. Coincidentally or, actually, by divine design, Yogi Harbhajan happened to be visiting Vancouver just before we left. Mr Gurdial Singh Neel, who was a teacher at Matthew McNair Secondary School and a neighbour of ours, had a get-together, and Mrs Neel prepared a very good dinner. Over fifty people – ladies and gentlemen – attended. There was a general discussion about the situation of

Sikhism and Sikhs, and it lasted about four hours. Yogi Harbhajan had come with about half a dozen of his gora Sikhs (white Sikhs). Generally, Yogi would go to India every year with his North American Sikhs, so at the end of the evening I just thought to ask him when his next visit to Punjab would be. He was about to leave, and we were standing just inside the door. Perhaps he misunderstood me, because he said, "I will be coming to Vancouver in December." I said, "I won't be here." He said, "Why? You are much needed here." I told him it was beyond my reach, and I explained about my disability. His reply was that something should have been done about it, and I said that I had done something, but it hadn't helped. With a slight touch of taunt I said, "I mentioned that at least twice to you also." He immediately could read what I meant.

"Ah-ha, so that is a very good taunt," he said. "All right, let us see what it is."

He sat me in the camel position – the yoga posture with the feet under the buttocks – and he asked me to join my hands with palms together and raise them in front of my face. He said, "Recite the Mul Mantra and keep repeating it, five times while slowly going down as far as you can to touch your knees, and five times while coming up." Mr Mota Singh Jheeta later on told me that, while I was doing this, Yogi Harbhajan was reciting something under his breath. Within one cycle he could feel what my trouble was. He said, "Bhatha hi bahal ditta." That is an idiomatic expression in Punjab. A bhatha is a brick kiln. When you start the fire for heating the bricks and it doesn't ignite properly, then the whole bhatha is ruined. Yogi meant, "You have ruined the whole situation. Out of this there is no recovery."

Then Yogi laid me flat on the floor with my arms by my sides. He measured from the tits to the belly-button and found out how much curvature there was in the body structure and which way it went. Although I always feel strain and pain in my right leg and foot down to the heel, he started with my left big toe. He gave a big jerk. That was his method of adjustment. He is a big man – 240 pounds. I was only 100 pounds. Next he pressed my left leg below the knee. Then he jerked the knee. Later on he put his foot on my pelvis and pulled my leg with a jerk. And he repeated the same process with the right leg. It wasn't intolerable pain. I could take it.

After that he sat me up again in the camel position and jerked the left arm. That was a killing pain. He was applying his whole strength. He was sweating, and I was sweating. I could not hold my tongue and I said, "This pain is more than death perhaps." He said, "Oh, very good." Then he said, "Then you won't feel that pain again when you die." He did the other arm. With each arm it was a jerk and a twist and that pain again. Then he took my neck in his lap and fixed the left side and then the right. There were crunching sounds, but the pain wasn't so bad. Mr Mota Singh's elder brother Jeewen Singh, who is a very tender-hearted person, couldn't stand what was happening. He thought, "Yogi will kill our Giani," and he went to the basement. Finally Yogi stood me upright and said, "Your body is totally straight, but you will have to do exercise and prayer."

When I reached home it was about 1:00 a.m. The session had taken pretty near three-quarters of an hour. I had a good sleep that night and didn't wake up until 8:00 a.m. Jeewan Singh Jheeta phoned my wife and said, "How was Giani Ji when he came home?" Then he asked, "How is he feeling now?" She said, "He is sleeping soundly." When I got up, I felt light; my arms were feeling better; my back and legs were feeling much better. Immediately my thoughts were of the orthopedic surgeons whose methods took over a year and actually caused the situation to deteriorate. Later on I learned that some good chiropractors do apply the same methods as Yogi Ji.

Within a couple of days I felt pretty light – more than 50 per cent better. That changed my mind about going back to Punjab on a permanent basis. Instead I decided to stay there for a trial period only. So I went back to the junior high school on Williams Road to enrol Parkash in grade eight for the next year. We decided to leave father-in-law in the care of my sons, but we took Parkash. I figured that this could be an educational touring trip for her. We left on 9 July via Air Canada to New York and thence via Air India to London. I never saw a more difficult airport in my lifetime than J.F. Kennedy airport in New York. For Parkash we took a break for a week in London and toured around. We visited many places – Buckingham Palace, the Houses of Parliament, Tower Bridge, the Tower of London. At Trafalgar Square, where there are lots of tame pigeons, some photographers took pictures of us, and they were honest and sent those pictures to us in India. Parkash was so happy, and I was so happy that she was on the trip and enjoying it.

When we alighted at Delhi airport we had a list of everything we were bringing with us – camera, movie camera, radio, two cassette recorders, and so on. The two striped customs officers who examined our luggage said, "Sardar ji, you have so many things. That will involve you in lots of customs duty." A person who is cheating is under stress and burden, and a person who is not cheating is relaxed. I said, "All right, it is evident I have lots of things and whatever is due I will pay." So he went back to consult, and a three-striped Madrasi customs officer returned. He said the same thing. I answered, "I am very happy to pay, because this is my real motherland and she breasted me to earning capacity. I am coming back. I have the money, and I will be happy to contribute something to her." The officer was so complimentary. People talk of corruption at Delhi airport and it is there, but you can't be forced into it. I never had any trouble. When I told this officer that my stay would be temporary, he gave me six months' permission with no charge. Later I got an extension. Eventually I did have to pay something, but when I went to see the customs officer in charge, he said, "Sardar Ji, we are here to serve you, not to punish you." And he told the junior officer, "Charge him only the minimum."

When the customs officer was going through our five pieces of luggage, he said to my wife, "Bibi Ji, do you have some jewelry? Are you wearing anything around your neck?" I said, "Yes, she is," and I asked her to open the buttons on her sweater. He said, "No. No – please, I didn't mean that." After we cleared customs I went to exchange some money at the State Bank of India counter at the airport. In the exchange box was a young Punjabi fellow. I had a Parker pen with me worth four or five dollars. While he was counting my rupees, this young fellow said, "Sardar Ji, you people bring very nice pens from North America. Please could I have one?" I said, "Not as a bribe. You are doing your duty." And he was so humble he said, "Not the least. You are just like my father." "That is fine," I said. "Have this one."

14 On a Pilgrimage

During the summer before she began high school we travelled all over Punjab with our youngest daughter, Parkash. We hired taxis, and we took a car from some relatives and paid them their expenses. When we visited Darbar Sahib (the Golden Temple) in Amritsar, Mahinder Singh, the secretary of the SGPC (the management committee for Sikh shrines in Punjab), remembered me very well from the time of his North American tour in 1974. He was very cordial and respectful, and we were given A-class accommodation with all modern facilities – even air conditioning – in a new addition to the Guru Ram Das Sarai (hostel) in the Golden Temple complex. The SGPC has a bus system that goes on a fixed route to quite a few historical gurdwaras within a thirty- or forty-mile radius of Amritsar. We saw so many places on these tours or travelling on our own, and all that time – nearly two months – I did not experience back trouble. There was some strain, but no real pain. At the end of that summer we sent Parkash back to Vancouver to start her classes at Hugh McRoberts Junior Secondary School. She didn't have any trouble going alone on the long flight because I knew Mr Nijhawan, the owner of Nijhawan Travel Agency in Jullundur and New Delhi, and his people were able to make sure she was all right.

Later on my middle son, Tarsem Singh, visited us for a couple of months with his wife and little daughter Harleen. Father-in-law was also with him. At the historic Shahidan gurdwara in my wife's village of Kultham there were no proper arrangements for bathing, and people were talking about putting in a tube well. It just came to me that we should induce father-in-law to give five thousand rupees, which was the estimated cost, and then put his name on a marble stone for his services. So we did donate, and the gurdwara committee installed a tube well and a power room for the pump.

While Tarsem was visiting, people began to insist that I should accept nomination as president of the Shahidan gurdwara. I generally don't want to take elected positions because elections cause groupism among the villagers. You can't keep your neutrality and impartiality through that channel of service. Tarsem's departure from India was booked for the same day as the selection of the gurdwara management committee, so I sent a message that I had to accompany him to Delhi to see him off. In the evening before his departure, he came back and told me that it was delayed. Then it came to my mind that God wanted me to do this gurdwara service. When I went to congregation the next day, I was appointed unanimously. I said I had a couple of reservations. "I will observe total discipline as ordained by the Gurus regarding performances under gurdwara Shahidan. This gurdwara will have no objection to anyone coming to congregation regardless of caste or creed – untouchables or whatever. No bias will be tolerated. I want to create unity. Once I see my neutrality is being jeopardized – if an account of some disunity does surface – I will resign right away." Everyone was happy and gave me the authority to select my own committee, which I did without delay.

For two and a half years I worked there. With the help of the committee I was able to get the whole village to volunteer labour to build up the perimeter road in front of the gurdwara. During the rainy season this road was a real marsh, with muck two feet deep in some places, and people in Kultham had to travel over it to get to other villages. At the end of the rainy season we filled it in three days with debris from some deserted village houses and a thick layer of foundry slag. After a couple of months, when it got settled, we paved it with bricks. The slag came from a steel mill only three miles from Kultham, where about three dozen people were employed manufacturing fodder cutters and sugar-cane expellers – both ox-driven and motor-driven. The mill owner kindly let us have it for free because it was a good cause, and we used tractor trolleys to haul it.

We improved the gurdwara buildings and the landscaping in the courtyard, and we reformed the religious service. On special commemorative days, like the martyrdom of Guru Arjun and the birthdays of Guru Nanak and Guru Gobind Singh, we had big processions through the village. Each time it took six or seven hours to complete, starting and ending at the gurdwara and stopping six or seven times for preaching. Giani Mahinder Singh, the secretary of the SGPC, would send us very realistic preachers – particularly Giani Bakhshish Singh Khakh, who used to stay with us whenever he came.

He was an old man but a real Sikh. On the first occasion he was late, and I told my wife I was going to the bus stop on the main road to meet him. I had to walk two kilometres, and on the way I passed a majestic personality and greeted him. I didn't know that this was the person I was looking for. He reached my residence none the less, and I arrived an hour later, after going to the bus stop and back. On his way from Amritsar, riding on a horse-drawn tonga, he had an accident, and his clothes were smeared in a surface drain. He had to take a bath in a nearby home, and he changed and wrapped his dirty clothes in a bundle. He told my wife about it and explained that was why he was late. We had an artesian well, and my wife pumped a couple of pails of water for him. He said, "No, Bibi Ji, you can't do that. I have to do my own." Then he asked for washing soap. No matter how much she asked to do it, he said no. "It is a Sikh's duty to do his own chores. No one has done it for me but my wife, and since she died, I have done it for myself."

One time he took pretty near an hour preaching on the Ramdasia (leatherworker) side of the village, and there wasn't a sound from the audience. This kind of preaching had its impact, and later on some of the people became baptized and the character of the youth changed dramatically. There were two opium smugglers living in the village, and everyone left them alone; people thought that they might be paying the police not to bother them. Towards the end of my stay, on one of these processions, I said, "I am going to talk about it openly. We are not going to tolerate this sort of thing." I said it in a nice manner, but those two opium smugglers were very scared. If I had done it earlier, it might have had an adverse effect. You have to establish yourself first before you can say these things.

When I took over the gurdwara presidency, we had a granthi (priest) who wouldn't keep the gurdwara clean. Even the sacred room of Guru Granth Sahib wasn't so clean. I showed the village elders that the pages of Guru Granth Sahib contained some sand. Wind will blow the dirt, and if you are not careful, it will catch the pages. I suggested what should be done and began to do it myself. That started a feud with the granthi, and gradually it grew. Finally we had to push him out and bring in a new granthi. Of course we had a committee headed by me.

The old granthi had always been at loggerheads with a sant (holy man) named Mann Singh, and when we pushed the granthi out, the sant was very happy. Mann Singh was a classfellow of my younger brother and a wayfellow of mine – a high-school gradu- ate. But he happened to be one of many sants prevailing in Punjab and India, and now abroad, who actually misinterpret and mis- guide the naïve, innocent-minded Sikhs away from the real, straightforward discipline prescribed by the Gurus. A real sant, according to gurbani (scriptures), is a personality who has reached a blissful stage of communion and surrender to Almighty. In this world that is a rare case. A good Sikh or a good person can be called a bhagat (devotee), but a bhagat is not a sant. A student, whether in grade one or at degree level, is still a student. Too many so-called sants are not earning their righteous living but are living on the donations of others. They do not practice what they preach. Their preaching is all from the Sikh tradition, but they cre- ate personality cults and attract large followings. They drive around in station wagons like princes and use innocent people for their own pumped-up esteem.

This fellow Mann Singh had his headquarters at Nangal Khurd, between my birthplace village and Mahalpur, but he had quite an influence on people in Kultham. Every so often he would sponsor a pilgrimage and take a bus for two or three weeks to visit gur- dwaras all over India. My wife and I, along with a dozen other vil- lagers from Kultham, and in all about fifty people, happened to be part of one of these pilgrimages. We went as far south as Hazur Sahib in Nander in Maharashtra state, where Guru Gobind Singh died, and Nanak Jhira, the spring visited by Nanak at Buder, which is close to Hyderabad in Andhra Pradesh. Then we went east to Juggennath Puri on the Bay of Bengal in Orissa and Patna Sahib in Bihar, where Guru Gobind Singh was born. We came back from there through Benares and Nanak Mata in Uttar Pradesh and through Delhi and Haryana state. It took twenty-two days, and in that time we found out what kind of a sant Mann Singh was.

A Sikh is supposed to earn his own living and serve others. This fellow brought three men from his own settlement as attendants, and he had some of the ladies from among the pilgrims also serving him. At the historical gurdwaras that we visited he received preferential treatment and attention – better food from the Guru's kitchen and special saropa (robes). When we were travelling south to Nander, he was anxious to make time. We thought he must be trying to meet someone at some prearranged place to be in such a hurry. He had prepared food with him, and he had the front seat behind the driver fixed up so he could stretch out lengthwise. So he did not suffer as much as we did when the bus made long runs with no stops. We carried food too, but needed to get down from the bus to prepare it. On the way to Nander, starting one day at 10:00 a.m., we went for fourteen hours without a break. When it was dark, people began to ask for a chance to get down. Eventually he said, "There is a city nine miles ahead. We can stop there." But the bus carried through. We were so hungry, our stomachs were jumping like rats. On the far side of the city the driver pulled over by a dhaba (eating-house). "You can do what you want," he said to the sant. "But I am going to eat." "What is going on?" I asked. "Why have we not stopped in the city where we could have stayed at the gurdwara?" When we understood that it was the driver who had made the stop, we all got off and bought food. After that the bus carried on until 4:00 the next morning. The sant always did what he wanted without seeking our consent, and during the rest of the pilgrimage we had to hassle with him a few times for journey breaks and proper timing for food and rest.

At the shrine of Hazoor Sahib in Nander, on the second floor, the management had sixteen akhand paths going on at the same time. Sixteen granthis in a line, with hardly any space between one and another, were all reciting at once. In the Takht, where Guru Gobind Singh's weaponry is kept, they had four more akhand paths. This was in a small area, with pilgrims coming and going eighteen or twenty hours a day and kirtan (spiritual singing) being performed. Everything was intermingled. All these akhand paths were for Sikhs who had paid for them. I don't remember how much it was at the time – perhaps 251 rupees.

I couldn't tolerate it, so I wrote a petition to the manager. How could the granthis keep their concentration with so many of them reciting in the same place? The human mind is the fastest thing in the world, and it does not stop, even in sleep. It is only after a prolonged disciplined life as a khalsa (disciple of the Guru) or in the real stage of a sant, where no irritations can happen, that the mind stays at one level all blissful. I have seen a line of granthis reciting from Guru Granth Sahib, and one was off and about his thoughts for a few moments. When he came to his real thought, he was two pages behind, and he had to turn his pages quickly. With ordinary granthis, their concentration goes off, and then they catch up, and they are of no benefit to anyone.

The practice at Hazoor Sahib was a great disrespect to Guru Granth Sahib, which is the spirit of the living Guru in perpetuity. Would Sikhs have dared to ask Guru Nanak to multiply himself three or four times so they could increase their income? Sant Mann Singh heard about my petition, and he said he agreed and signed it. That was hypocritical because, in his own institution, he has two or three multiple akhand paths going on. When I brought the petition to the manager, he said that the shrine was controlled by South Indian Sikhs. "We have protested the practice quite a bit, but we can't do much." But the manager had his appointment from the SGPC in Amritsar, and the same thing was done in their shrines in Punjab. At Takht Patna in Bihar in the east, there was no such thing, but at Amritsar the management have been selling akhand paths at a fixed rate. They have only one recited in one place, but to multiply their income they have found various locations so they can have eight or ten going on at once.

In Rajasthan or Madya Pradesh, when we were on our way to Nander, we stopped to see someone that Sant Mann Singh knew, and that person showed us a small, handwritten gutka (prayerbook) in a traditional Punjabi script, which is a little different from today. This fellow said that it was the gutka that Guru Gobind Singh used to keep in his loincloth. I didn't believe it. If such a relic really existed, historians and researchers would have brought it to light. Guru Gobind Singh dictated the present version of Guru Granth Sahib at Damdama Sahib, the Fifth Takht (spiritual throne) of the Sikhs, over a six-month period. Every day, in the congregation, he recited so much gurbani (scripture) from memory or out of his spiritual being, and he would also explain the meaning. I asked the question, "If the Guru did not make a single mistake in reciting the whole volume of Guru Granth Sahib from memory, which is a fact, would he need a written booklet for his daily prayer?" I put the question directly to the sant, and he just sidetracked it. "It doesn't mean that," he said. "He just used to keep that."

At Juggennath Puri on the Bay of Bengal we visited a shrine where Guru Nanak stayed during his travels to the east. In that place there wasn't any Sikh population, but one Sikh was looking after the shrine as caretaker and granthi. In Benares we visited the shrines of Bhagat Ravdas, the shoemaker, and Bhagat Kabir, the weaver. After Banaris, at Nanak Mata in Pili Bhit district in Uttar Pradesh, we came to the place where Guru Nanak faced the sidhas (master yogis). They were trying to defeat him in debate, and with their occult powers they uprooted the pipal tree under which they were sitting and it started to fly straight upwards. Guru Nanak stopped it after it had gone up about ten feet. The tree is still there with its roots coming out of the ground and a raised platform built around it. When we were driving through that district, every third or fourth mile we would see a big flag-pole flying the khanda (the Sikh flag), which is the sign of a gur-dwara. The Sikhs in this district were all refugees from Pakistan at the time of partition, and they had worked hard to turn bush area into rich, productive land.

We spent two days in Delhi, where there are about a dozen his-torical gurdwaras, including Sisganj gurdwara, associated with Guru Tegh Bahadur, and Bangla Sahib, associated with Guru Har Krishan. The Delhi Gurdwara Prabandhak Committee, which manages these gurdwaras, is a big institution among the Sikhs, second only to the SGPC in Amritsar. The Sikhs are very good at establishing educational institutions. They have at present more than one hundred Sikh national degree colleges, and Khalsa Col-lege in Amritsar is the largest in India. But they are not achieving their goal with all this effort because the majority of the youth from these higher institutions are turning towards materialism and socialism and away from Sikh discipline. An institution like the Delhi Gurdwara Prabadhak Committe could do a lot to con-vince the Sikh youth of the value of the Sikh way of life by encour-aging scientific research on the benefits of human hair. It wouldn't take too much money to establish a research laboratory, but it would pay dividends enormously.

With this view in mind, and with the Guru's grace, I dared to go to the Delhi Gurdwara Prabandhak Committee office at Sisganj gurdwara in Chandni Chawk early in the morning, after my prayers and presence at the Guru's house. Generally, in India I am dressed in simple traditional dress, with a blue turban and a simple pyjama and shirt, which gives the impression of an ordinary Akali jathedar (Sikh party group leader) or an ordinary Sikh. I went up to the secretary's office, which was in a room about sixteen feet square, and there I saw three Sikh gentlemen. One was doing some writing work in ledgers, in a volume on a table in one corner. The others weren't doing anything at the time. I greeted them with "Wahiguru Ji ka Khalsa. Wahiguru Ji ki fateh." The answer they gave was very weak. A Sikh must greet with full force because it is not his greeting but Almighty's.

There were two chesterfields, so they requested me to sit on one of them. I waited for a couple of minutes, thinking that they would ask me why I had come. Then I started. I said, "I have come here for some purpose." They said, "Yes, kindly, what is your purpose?" Of course, their language was complimentary, but their approach wasn't humble. I said, "We have organized and built so many educational institutions, yet the youth coming out of these institutions are hardly adopting the Sikh way of life."

The one who was writing in the ledger seemed like he wasn't paying any attention. But he looked up, and he was a little emotional. "Do you mean that we shouldn't have these institutions? Is it your purpose that we should stop opening these schools?"

When he lifted his face, I saw that he appeared like a well-educated sort of person. I said, "Sardar Ji, you didn't let me complete my explanation, and you have reacted with an untimely question, because I never said that."

He was a little pushed back. Then I said, "We have only two big religious establishments that have the monetary capacity to establish a research laboratory to find out the physical, spiritual, and human benefits of human hair to human life." My language was very simple Punjabi, but it had to be learned Punjabi to mention those things, so they came to know that I was somewhat educated.

One of these fellows said, "What will be the benefit of the laboratory research?"

I said, "Once it is proven that the human body and mind benefit from the hair very positively, then the educated Sikh youth will gladly and realistically accept the Sikh form and way of life."

To my surprise, one of them said, "What about, if it is proven negatively?"

Then I turned to him and clasped my hands and said, "Very nice, Sardar Ji. If a Sikh leader's faith is that raw, then I should say, "Wahiguru Ji ka Khalsa. Wahiguru Ji ki fateh, and go from here."

Quickly, that educated fellow came to his rescue. He said, "Sure, you have a good point, and we appreciate that, but you should write it in the form of an application."

I said, "Sardar Ji, if some friend of yours has a marriage ceremony at home and sends invitation cards to others, whereas he comes in person to invite you, which will be the preferred invitation?"

He understood it, and he said, "The personal one."

So I said, "I am here in person. And you seem to be either the secretary or the treasurer of this administrative body. Hence you are a big leader. You have accepted my point. That is all I needed. So I want you to show this into a result."

He said, "Well, I think I might request you to write it too."

He was very polite then because he had no way to surmount me. I pointed to his wastepaper basket with my finger and said, "Sardar Ji. You know if my personal approach is not sufficient to move you people into action, then that application will also end up in that paper basket. Hence I don't want to waste my time writing that kind of thing."

So many fake rituals go on. Outside these headquarters at Sisganj at Chandni Chawk, a contractor has a little stand selling flowers for garlands that people take inside. They keep a picture of Guru Tegh Bahadur in a cell, and people go to it after they enter the gurdwara. I did it many times, visiting that gurdwara, before I realized that it was wrong because it was picture worship. In Kultham, Sant Mann Singh had a lot of control with this kind of mythological approach. But when he was faced with a realistic lay person like myself, he had a hard time. The educated youth of the village were impressed by the big processions we organized, and that loosened the grip of the sant a lot.

The secretary of the sgpc, Giani Mahinder Singh, could visual-ize what kind of righteous work we were doing. He had been on that North American tour in 1974 when we had so many confron-tations with the barehead Sikhs, and when I was in Kultham, he complied with every reasonable request we made for preachers and sacred musicians and religious film shows, and he really se-lected good people. In 1978 the sgpc sponsored a great celebra-tion for the four hundredth anniversary of the founding of Am-ritsar. About 150 gora Sikhs (white Sikhs) came from North Amer-ica to attend. There was a story about them in the newspapers, and I saw them at the celebrations. They were sitting there during kirtan (spiritual singing), really keeping still like statues for a cou-ple of hours. With the help of Giani Mahinder Singh, I was able to meet them at Guru Nanak Niwas, the residential building in the Golden Temple complex where they were staying.

I wanted these white American Sikhs to come to Kultham to perform kirtan in the village. They were willing to do it, but they said it should be for more than one performance. So I arranged for them to go to Phagwara as well. Altogether they organized a mixed troop of twelve ladies and men, who travelled by taxis so they could return to their headquarters in Amritsar the same night. They came with two armed guards because they were go-ing to be driving back in the dark. We gave their performance good publicity, and although it was in the evening, villagers from five and ten miles away came to listen to them. Between four thousand and five thousand gathered in the large courtyard at the Shahidan gurdwara. This was at the tail end of summer, after the rainy season, so the weather was pretty good.

This troop of American Sikhs had trouble with their transport from Amritsar. One of their taxis developed some defect, and they were two hours late. In India you don't have that many garages on the highway where you can get repairs. We had food all ready for them, and we were waiting for them at the road. When they drove up, we immediately sent a bike to the gurdwara to let the people know they had arrived. As soon as they got out of their taxis, they felt the need to water out. I requested them to come with me. "We have a flush system at home." But one of the ladies said, "This mother earth – all these people are living on it – it is fine for us. We can go a little distance into the field." That really impressed me. When we got to the village, it was real dusk time, and we requested them to take food. Again, the answer was so excellent. "How about those people who are waiting?" they said. "Is it not a shame that they are waiting. The Guru would not like that." So they would not take anything.

They performed a very melodious kirtan. Midway through, the power went off, but that did not interrupt their melody. During the performance two messengers came from Phagwara to find out what was going on. It was so late. We sent a message back, and the people at Phagwara kept announcing that the gora Sikhs would be coming and nobody left. When the performance at Kultham was over, we again requested them to take food. They said no because it was late; it was not because they weren't hungry. At Phagwara they have a very large courtyard surrounded by three- and four-storey buildings. At least twelve thousand or thirteen thousand people were waiting there in the courtyard and on the buildings. From the stage you could see that the buildings were all loaded. The people at Phagwara asked me to introduce the kirtani jatha (musical troop) of gora Sikhs, and I did so in English and Punjabi. My way of dressing was so simple that people wouldn't think I was a Canadian retired person. But that performance by the gora Sikhs made me so well known to the gentry at Phagwara. Whenever I went there after that, people would see me and just walk up to me and ask me about it, and I could see that it had a big impact on the reasonable people there as well as at Kultham. It was past midnight when the performance finished. The people at Phagwara had prepared boiled milk and fruit. They asked the gora Sikhs about food, and finally they took it.

During those years in India, first Tarsem, the middle son, came to visit with his wife and daughter and father-in-law. Then, the next year, Surinder Singh, the elder son, visited for a couple of months with his wife, and father-in-law came with him too. I was able to improve the house at Kultham by adding on to it, and we had to spend money to keep out the flies because they were more of a problem than ever before. And I improved the farm land at Kultham. I could see the wonders of the new strains of wheat and rice and yellow corn (maize) prepared by Ludhiana Agricultural University. At that time my younger brother Chatter Singh was constructing a very good farmhouse and connecting buildings at our birthplace village of Sirhala Khurd to replace the existing buildings, which were getting old. Our youngest brother, Santok

Singh, had left the army to work on the farm, and we wanted to help him. Chatter Singh, Piara Singh, and I had discussed it in Canada. Our plan was to spend thirty thousand rupees, but with Chatter Singh's generosity the cost went up to eighty thousand, and he did a good job. Because I was unemployed, he did not ask me for more than my ten thousand-rupee share. So I said, "I will give another five thousand," and he appreciated that.

My middle son, Tarsem, wanted us back in Canada. Of course the other children also wanted us to return, but Tarsem particularly asked because my health had improved. So we booked our flight from Delhi airport in early May 1979. Before we left I received a few letters from Tarsem and from others about developments at the Ross Street gurdwara in Vancouver. The traditional Sikhs had won a majority on the gurdwara management committee. In a real nail-biting election seven or eight traditional Sikhs and only three or four modern Sikhs had got on to the committee. Both sides made big efforts to bring in supporters, and the difference between winners and losers was only a few votes. When I got back to Canada I learned that the vote by secret ballot was recounted perhaps three times, and the counting carried on to the next day. The traditional Sikhs ran a mixed slate, some clean-shaven and some turbaned. So did the modern Sikhs. But the traditional Sikhs elected the president, the secretary, and the treasurer, and they had control.

Daljit Singh Sandhu was the new secretary. He found out from Tarsem that I was coming back, so he wrote me a very nice personal letter mentioning the election results. He said that the believers in the barehead tradition were becoming fewer in number. There were several things that he wanted me to do before I returned, but I didn't have enough time. If he had written earlier, I could have done a lot, because I had good contacts with the SGPC His number-one priority was a new granthi. The workload at Ross Street had increased manifold, and the head granthi, Giani Balbir Singh, had lost his credibility with the traditional Sikhs. Some of them had taken a case to court to bar clean-shaven Sikhs from gurdwara management. It is written that a Sikh should keep uncut hair and tie a turban: "Na pak pak kar hadoor hadisa sabat soorat dastar sira." (Let your Hadith – holy books of the Muslims – be a purified mind, in the presence of God, with complete form the turban on your head). Giani Balbir Singh testified under oath in court that this edict was addressed to a Muslim and not to Sikhs. He was a preacher, but what he said was a total violation of faith. This stanza comes from a shabad (hymn) by Guru Arjun in Guru Granth Sahib. Even though the whole shabad refers to what a true Muslim should be, you can't say that it pertains to Muslims only. Each and every word is a teaching. For a Sikh, all is to be observed, whether a single stanza, a part, or the whole of Guru Granth Sahib.

In his letter Daljit Singh Sandhu said that the Vancouver Sikhs were preparing for the quincentenary of the Third Sikh Guru, Guru Amar Das, in June. He wanted some literature about Guru Amar Das or a documentary film from the SGPC He said they needed four groups of kirtani jathas (sacred musicians) to tour North America in rotation. And he mentioned imprints of photographs of the Golden Temple and other takhts or shrines for a religious calendar for distribution in 1980. But most important, he said, was to find a good replacement granthi who had competence in English as well as Punjabi. He said that as soon as I gave them the name, they would sponsor that granthi on a visitor's visa, and they would get his immigration status confirmed later on. His letter was written on 23 April, and I was leaving Kultham for Delhi on 4 May, so I got it just in the nick of time, and didn't have any chance to discuss it with anyone. With my experience, I didn't take it that seriously. When people have some success for the first time – in gurdwara elections or in other things – they are a little overenthusiastic. When they face the realities, their enthusiasm shrinks. Even if I had time to arrange for a granthi, I didn't know if I would be successful in getting that person over. So I left it for later, to survey the situation in Canada and then do it.

We took our flight from Delhi airport on 8 May 1979 and stayed for a week in England visiting relatives from my wife's side. On 15 May we reached Vancouver. During our time in India we had watched big political changes. In the election of 1977, following Indira Gandhi's emergency rule, the Janata Party came to power at the centre, with the help of the Sikhs. In Punjab we got a majority Akali Sikh government headed by Prakash Singh Badal. At one big election gathering in Amritsar there must have been a million people listening to the Janata leaders and their political propaganda speeches. They made good promises but didn't do much later on. While they were in power, they never passed the all-India gurdwara act that the Sikhs wanted. And they did nothing about the capital region of Chandigargh, which the Sikhs said should be returned to Punjab. In 1978 the so-called Nirankaris planned to take out a procession on Baisakhi Day in Amritsar, right in the heart of Sikhism. The procession was very derogatory to Sikhs and Sikhism, but the government did nothing. Sant Bhindranwale and some educated youths had the courage to go right to the Nirankari headquarters to tell them not to do it. Right in front of the police, the Nirankaris fired with automatic weapons, killing quite a few of those Sikhs. That was when the campaign against the Nirankaris started. From then on, Bhindranwale's religious impact roused the feelings of the youth and many grown-ups.

15 Trouble in Punjab

I was in India when the head granthi for the Ross Street gurdwara in Vancouver gave a wrong interpretation of Sikh scriptures in a court case about who could be on the gurdwara committee. This was Giani Balbir Singh, and the testimony he gave under oath had a big impact because the court had no one else to consult. When he said that the Guru was just addressing a Muslim in the verse that says you must not cut your hair and you must have a turban, the court had to listen. If the religious Sikhs fighting the case had been more knowledgeable, they might have asked the court for an opportunity to bring in a higher authority from Punjab. But they weren't, and the court dismissed their case with costs, which amounted to nine thousand dollars. The bearded Sikhs then won a hard-fought election in the gurdwara under a manifesto demanding Giani Balbir Singh's replacement. They were controlling the Khalsa Diwan Society and the Ross Street gurdwara when I returned to Canada in May 1979, and they took me on to their advisory committee. At that time I told Giani Balbir Singh that he had done a great sin and that if he wanted to save his place in the community, he must renounce that testimony. "You are handcuffing the religious future of the Sikh spirit in Canada." Later on I reminded him of that again, but then I didn't say anything more.

The same group who were going to replace the granthi also said that they would eliminate membership dues in the Khalsa Diwan Society. These were their top priorities. But within that group

there was a faction that thought we should keep a minimum donation of five dollars as a fee. And there were people who were
purposely trying to evade action about Giani Balbir Singh. After a
few committee meetings, an overwhelming majority did agree to
remove the membership fee. We would still issue membership
cards, but they would be freely available. Four of us were given
the task of drafting the amendment to the constitution and printing it prior to a general meeting.

All of a sudden, the idea of a five-dollars fee came in again from
the back door. At a special emergency meeting a core group of
seven or eight leading people took up this item as if it wasn't already decided. I was there, and when I saw what was going on, I
told the others, "I am not fit for this kind of politics, and I won't be
too long with you people." They tried, very nicely, to induce me to
stay on, so I said, "All right, we will see." That night I could not
sleep. In the early morning I prayed to the Guru to give me a direction whether I should pull out or stay, and the atma within me
said I should withdraw.

It so happened that the owner of the northern India agency for
British Airways, Mr Bansi Lal Nijhawan, was visiting Canada
then. He had come to promote British Airways travel among the
East Indians in British Columbia, and he wanted my assistance on
Vancouver Island. I have known him since I first travelled to Canada, when he had a little office for BOAC in Delhi. I always appreciated him. He is a man of integrity, very truthful and sincere. So I
readily agreed to go with him. Before we left for the island, I received notice of a general meeting of the Khalsa Diwan Society
that Sunday. That meant that we were able to make a tour of only
two or three places as far as Port Alberni before I had to come
back. I left Port Alberni on Sunday morning so that I could attend
the meeting in the evening.

I had already written a few lines as a letter of resignation, just
giving personal reasons and making no complaint. I thought, "Let
them pull their two-faced horse whichever way they want. Why
should I protest?" At the meeting the executive brought up the
five-dollar membership, and when I could not agree with the discussion of it, I made my point. Towards the end of the meeting I
handed over a sealed envelope with my resignation to the president, Bikar Singh Dhillon. He is a straightforward person, but uneducated and he was unaware of all the intricacies in the situation.

The real man behind the five-dollar membership was my younger brother Piara Singh. He liked to control things, although he generally kept quiet, and he would never come to the stage. Bikar Singh Dhillon was upset with my resignation, and we had quite a verbal tussle. But I told him, "Piara Singh and I are two brothers. One takes one side and one the other. So I have made a decision, and I don't want to turn around."

At that meeting the society adopted the five-dollar membership. But later in the year the good people on the opposition side – the modern Sikhs – came to the conclusion that it should be dropped because it had become a real point of feud. So the pendulum swung very heavily, and with the grace of God and the Guru, the management accepted a petition to eliminate membership dues and fees. After that we had no more feuds on that subject. But it wasn't long before elections were being fought on a very large scale. The two sides were bringing in people by bus from all over the province, and elections became very expensive. We had a lot of factionalism, prejudice, and disagreement among families. People would want to know why you didn't vote this way or that.

In the gurdwara election for 1980 (held in November 1979) I went on the Punjabi-language radio program for eight or nine minutes to strengthen support for the traditional group. The Shiromani Akali Dal Society paid for that time. This society had the active support of about twenty-five families, and the directors were all amritdhari (bapized) Sikhs with full form. Their goal was reform of all the gurdwaras. They had filed the case trying to ban clean-shaven people from gurdwara management committees and they had opposed gurdwara membership fees on the grounds that membership should not be a matter of money but one of belief and practice. When the new gurdwara management committee was elected in 1979 and then did not take a strong stand on these issues, the Shiromani Akali Dal Association did their best to point it out to the public.

In the summer of 1979 Dr Mohinder Singh Dhillon of Patiala came from Punjab to Vancouver to visit his daughter. He had written many books on Sikh religion and history and on medical subjects, and he expressed a keen desire to write a history of the Sikhs in North America. Everyone who heard about it was happy, and the directors of the Shiromani Akali Dal Association induced the gurdwara management committee to sponsor the project. We had a meeting at my residence in August and formed a subcommittee. The gurdwara society (the Khalsa Diwan Society) agreed to pay for Dr Dhillon's travel to eastern Canada and the United States, and he carried on his research over a period of ten months. When he completed his manuscript, he was supposed to send it to the gurdwara management committee, which was going to provide the money for printing. Somehow, Dr Dhillon became doubtful about individuals on the committee and did not want them to have the manuscript without a witness. So he sent it to Mr Paviter Singh Sumbol, president of the Shiromani Akali Dal. That created further problems, and it looked like the project might not go ahead. Dr Dhillon asked the Shiromani Akali Dal to take it on financially, and twenty-four members contributed over fourteen thousand dollars. My contribution was one thousand dollars. In 1981 Dr Dillon arranged for the book to be printed in Patiala – five hundred copies in Punjabi and five hundred in English. Some universities and some libraries bought it, but the disagreements and frustrations that had gone on beforehand hindered its distribution and sale.

Many times, in 1979, in 1980, and in 1981, the leading hands from both sides of the fence tried to convince me to fight the election for president of the Khalsa Diwan Society. I reminded them of only one thing – that I had taken a solemn pledge before the Guru not to run for any office in the society. (The advisory committee was different because it was not elected.) The faction that got a majority on the gurdwara management committee in 1979 won the election the next year and every year after that. But the difference between their ideology and the teachings of the Guru was very wide. We made two attempts to reach a compromise between this group and dissidents like myself, but we could not resolve all the issues. A few projects, like the history of the Sikhs, kept us linked for a while. But the gap kept on widening. So I became really dormant in gurdwara activity.

At the same time I was involved with the Pacific Interfaith Association. Because I had been on the Interfaith executive before I went to India, I automatically went back on it when I returned. The Ross Street gurdwara gave me a letter of support so that I could represent the Sikh faith. The Interfaith Association would have functions at the temples of various faiths, and in October 1979 we had the Thanksgiving function at the Ross Street gurdwara. Between 1979 and 1983 there were at least half a dozen conferences in Vancouver like the World Conference on Religion and Peace and the Disarmament Conference in which the Interfaith Association participated. That was quite a time. We also conducted educational seminars on various faiths at Langara College in south Vancouver.

In January 1983 I resigned from Interfaith. The cause was a basic disagreement between the president, Mr Aziz Khaki, and myself. One big reason was the importance that Mr Khaki gave to an interfaith prayer for the schools. When we discussed it at the subcommittee level, we agreed that an interfaith prayer was a very touchy question. Non-believers didn't want any kind of prayer: already there were objections being raised to the Christian prayer in the schools. So we feared that the opposition to an interfaith prayer would be so strong that our educational program would suffer. In my view it was more important to disseminate knowledge about religions in the schools than to have an interfaith prayer. Mr Sid Bentley, who was teaching in Surrey, had a project called "Religions in our Neighbourhood," which carried a lot of knowledge and explanation. A subject like that could smooth out ignorance and prejudice in a multiracial society without imposing anything on students. We didn't want to see his effort hurt by the interfaith prayer question, which didn't have an educational dimension.

The World Christian Council was going to be meeting in Vancouver. In Interfaith we thought it an opportune time to prepare a book giving a brief account of each of our member religions. For the Sikh faith I gave the address of the Federation of Sikh Societies in Ottawa as the umbrella organization. I contacted some competent people among the Sikhs to write the chapter, but they didn't have the time. So finally I took it upon myself to do it. Chuck Anderson, a clergyman at the University of British Columbia, was one of the editors. On completion of my script I gave it to him, and he was very happy with it. Then – I don't know how it happened – Mr Khaki got the Khalsa Diwan Society to write a chapter and mine was rejected. When I discovered that, I was very upset. The Khalsa Diwan Society has a glorious past, and I hope that it will continue as such. But it is just one society and not an umbrella organization for the Sikhs. At the general meeting of the Interfaith Association in January 1982 I requested the floor for a few minutes, and I am thankful that Mr Khaki gave it to me. In my talk I summed up my reasons for withdrawing and gave my resignation. A lot of associates were so sorry to lose me. But God has given me a clear conscience that, whenever my contribution is causing frustration, then I withdraw. I do not want to be the cause of disruption.

With the programing of Almighty, I was put into a community service again within a few days. The religious Sikhs in the Shiromani Akali Dal Society had started a community paper in Punjabi. In the beginning we had a new immigrant, an educated lawyer named Subeg Singh, as editor. There were other community papers for Punjabis and other East Indians, but they were run on a business basis and did not represent a fundamental line of policy. In other words, they exploited the people on some issues and did not always channel thinking in a proper and useful direction. We purchased a typesetting machine with a bank loan, and Subeg Singh started putting out a paper every fortnight. It was called *Qaumi Samachar* (News of the Nation). Subeg Singh was a nice fellow, and he did pretty good work, but towards the end of 1982 he wasn't getting along too well with the directors of the Shiromani Akali Dal. There was some strain in the relationship. About the time I resigned from Interfaith, they really pressed hard on me to take it over. I told them, "If you really push me into it, then I can't run it on a fortnightly basis." So I made it a monthly, and I wanted it to be bilingual – English and Punjabi – which they accepted. It wasn't difficult because I had experience from publishing *Punjab Weekly. Qaumi Samachar* was twenty-four pages, and my own contribution was at least one-third; and I was cutting and pasting as well as doing the editorial work and writing. I included articles from other sources, but even the rewriting of that material took a lot of effort. When the enthusiasm was there, I had help, but not that much later on. We had some circulation, but most of the papers went for free distribution, and we sent them all over the world. With the help of Shiromani Akali Dal, I kept this paper going regularly until February 1986. Then we had to shut it down on account of my ill health and lack of money.

The Sikh population in Canada had really increased in the 1970s. In 1974, when I was on the Khalsa Diwan Society executive, there were only around a dozen Sikh gurdwaras in the province of British Columbia, and hardly any in the rest of the country. By

1980 there were forty to fifty registered Sikh societies in Canada, and most of them either had gurdwaras or were planning to build them. So there was a real need for a central organization to co-ordinate their efforts over the extensive span of the whole country. In 1980 some Sikhs in the Ottawa and Toronto area issued invitations to all the societies to send delegates to a Sikh convention in Ottawa at Carleton University. In Vancouver we had a meeting of the lower-mainland Sikh gurdwaras to select a delegation. There was no question about staying away. We felt the need to go, although people were saying that the Sikhs in Ottawa should not dictate the course of events. After a couple of meetings we selected a delegation of nine or ten. Victoria also sent a couple of people, and there were one or two delegates from the interior of the province.

The convention was a great success. At the end of it we agreed on a draft proposal for a Federation of Sikh Societies and a committee to work on it. In August 1981, the Calgary Sikh Society hosted the second Sikh convention. This time there were a few rough occasions. The Calgary society had sponsored Khushwant Singh, the well-known writer from India, and BC county court judge Wally Oppal, who had grown up as a Sikh in Canada, and most of the delegates opposed the choice of these speakers. Khushwant Singh had made some discouraging remarks in one of his books about the future of the Sikhs; Mr Oppal was a smoker, and his smoking was an infringement on his belief in the practice of the Sikh faith. These two speakers did not fit into the structure of a convention that had been organized for the promotion of the Sikh religion. So people had a point to make, but I did not approve of the way that some of them went about it. At Calgary the delegates passed the federation constitution, but not without disagreements. The Vancouver Sikhs asked for the next convention, and the rest of the delegates gave it to them very happily. But somehow, later on, individual prejudices got in the way. There were differences over speakers and over the location of the federation headquarters – whether it should be in Ottawa or in Vancouver – and that convention never materialized.

One important thing that the Federation of Sikh Societies did do in 1982 was to present the Sikh case on Punjab to the United Nations Commission on Human Rights. About twelve of us went from BC. We drove down to Seattle and took an overnight flight to

New York. Someone picked us up at the airport and drove us straight to the UN building. Sikhs had arrived there from all across Canada and the United States, and at first we were told that only five or six delegates could go in. Then people started thinking in their own way that if A and B went, C shouldn't be left behind. After some discussion, the federation president, Gurcharan Singh from the Ottawa society, intelligently convinced the commission to receive the whole bunch. We were taken into a big boardroom, where we presented our brief on human rights violations in Punjab to the deputy chairperson, who was a lady. She was impressed with the cohesion of our delegation representing Sikhs from all sections of North America. And she promised that our case would be presented during the next annual session of the Human Rights Commission. We flew back to Seattle that night, so we spent the night going and the night coming back in the airplane. I really think that if the Sikhs had shed their differences and followed up that case, we would have had some result, or at least a better result than we have had from the world body.

We didn't have another Sikh convention until July 1983, and it was in Ottawa again. Everything went fine until we had to choose the incoming executive. We discussed the need for a world-level organization for the Sikhs and passed a resolution. We discussed the establishment of a chair in Sikh studies at the University of British Columbia, and we agreed to make it a priority. And we discussed a project to make an informative film about Sikh religion and Sikh people. But when we came to the selection of the executive, personal egos started creeping in. Because there wasn't any unanimity, we had to adopt an election process, and I was chosen election chairman by show of hands. Even then, some people from Toronto became very frustrated when they were not successful.

I was living with my middle son, Tarsem, at the time. By nature he is business-minded. His technology training has not been any use to him. In 1976, when I was in India, he put some money into an Indian cuisine restaurant as a partner. I sent him a telegram, with letter following, telling him to pull out immediately. In the letter I explained that a restaurant was not good for family life. It would mean continuous hours. The location would have to be in town. And liquor would be involved. On my return we discussed buying a farm, and we saw a few places. Finally we bought a blueberry patch in Richmond on No. 6 Road, about a kilometre from where we were then living. It had five acres with a house and a good garage, and it cost about $225,000. I knew it would be a secure place, away from the misfits of society, climatically better than the city, and a better place for Tarsem's children to develop good work habits and good communication within the extended-family system. We sold the house on Amethyst Avenue for $97,000 and moved on to the farm in June 1980. The previous owner had liked the place because it had a big front yard where he could park his trucks, which he used to haul chips and sawdust for the sawmills. He wasn't a farmer, and the blueberry patch was in a very poor condition, with weeds and grass taking over and a lot of dead blueberry plants. If we counted all the hours we put into it to bring it back into shape, it was a heavy loss. But a farmer who does not count his time in terms of money is not a loser.

In 1983 my youngest daughter, Parkash, finished two years in accounting at Kwantlen College. She wanted to go on for a degree, but I told her that I couldn't manage it very easily. "I am very disabled and I don't want to stay too long in this country because of the weather. It hurts my back." She agreed. Coincidentally, that April I was invited to speak in English at the first Baisakhi Day celebration in Toronto. In 1980 the Vancouver Sikhs had started having a big procession on Baisakhi Day (15 April), and because of the publicity the Toronto Sikhs organized one too. In Toronto, I stayed for four days with a Sikh family, and they had a very nice boy – physically, educationally, age-wise, and in manners. I felt, God willing, this boy might make a match for my daughter. At departure time I passed on my thought to the father and suggested, if he was willing, that he could think further. In July, I received a letter from one of his relatives with an affirmation. Because they were mature and educated, it was my feeling that the boy and girl should meet at least once. Although the father of the boy didn't want that, I really pushed him into it. So it was accepted. The father and son flew to Richmond, where the boy and my daughter were able to discuss their future, and we set a date for the engagement. My brother Chatter Singh, myself, and my wife went to Toronto for the engagement ceremony, and the marriage was fixed for October.

After the marriage my wife and I decided to return to India as soon as the next blueberry season was over. Unluckily, in June 1984, after Operation Bluestar, when the Indian Army attacked the Golden Temple in Amritsar, the situation in Punjab became so bad that we had to drop our plans. That situation didn't improve, but got worse. The executive of the Federation of Sikh Societies of Canada started to work right away on the formation of a world organization of the Sikhs. They held two regional conventions, one in the west at Kamloops and the other in the east at Toronto. I was at the Kamloops convention. By then General Bhullar had arrived from India, and he came to that convention. He had been with Sant Jarnail Singh Bhindranwale just before Operation Bluestar, and in a few speeches in various gurdwaras he had given the impression that Sant Bhindranwale had sent him to lead the Sikhs in foreign lands. The federation executive put up a proposal for a world Sikh organization, which was approved unanimously. A second resolution called on the Sikhs to push our case on human rights violations and to carry on the struggle for a Sikh homeland. Some people wanted the word Khalistan, while the executive and their supporters, including myself, wanted "Sikh homeland," and by that we meant Punjab. We reasoned that no foreign government that was friendly to the government of India would sympathize with the Sikhs on the issue of an independent Khalistan. But the issue of human rights and a Sikh homeland would have mustered quite a bit of support.

In August 1984 I went to the one-day founding convention of the World Sikh Organization in New York, We stayed overnight in a gurdwara this time, and I spoke at that gurdwara the next morning. Nearly five thousand Sikhs attended the convention, and the organizers booked Madison Square Gardens up to 6:00 p.m. What I saw and heard was an opportunity wasted by fanatical so-called Sikhs who demonstrated total indiscipline and no respect for the time and expenses of so many people who had travelled there from far and wide. One such youth leader was supposed to speak for only a few minutes prior to lunchtime, yet he deliberately took pretty near two hours. He couldn't give a reasonable lecture. He had no presentation, but just kept creating slogans to raise emotions, and it is easy to ride that wave when people are upset. The organizers had to extend the business of the convention past 6:00 because he had misused their complacency. That cost another seventeen thousand dollars, and they had to appeal to the audience to fill the gap.

The government of India has treated Punjab with more prejudice than a stepmother. We could have made a clear-cut case to convince any genuine foreigner about the situation there, and we could have provided proof for the leaders of foreign governments. Had we followed that path, then the massacre of innocent Sikh people after the shooting of Mrs Indira Gandhi could have created a lot of international pressure on the government of India. For three days the international TV showed so much brutality directed towards the Sikhs. If that had won the hearts of foreigners, then it could have prompted the solution of the mess in Punjab. But we didn't have the calibre of leadership to take the right approach.

With all the trouble in Punjab, my wife and I gave up our plan to go back there that fall. Then, in 1985, the marriage of my youngest daughter, Parkash, ended in a separation, which led to a divorce. When she was living in Toronto with the family of the boy she had married, there were differences, particularly in cultural adjustment. The father was too critical of any acceptance of Western culture, like birthday ceremonies, Christmas, or Halloween. I brought up my family in a different manner, and let them into the mainstream while I kept a quiet scrutiny and advised them, face to face, what was good and what was bad. He wanted Parkash to go to work in Indian clothing, which was very tough for her to do. She was working and going to college too. Her plan was to start a family after she got her degree, but her in-laws expected the young couple to start a family right away. Within two years they reached a friction point, because Parkash did not want to lose her chances for education. One evening I got a phone call from the father-in-law. He said he didn't know what had happened, but Parkash was going to leave. I spoke on the phone to the boy and then to Parkash, and I asked her to wait for me to come to Toronto so that I could talk to everyone and work it out. But she said she couldn't wait, and she moved out right away.

Three or four months after Parkash came back to us, the family got together to take a final decision about the marriage. She is a good person, and she knew I was a good father. I am a disciplinarian, but God has given me the judgment to see that you must practise discipline before asking others to do likewise. It is a suggestive game, not an enforced matter. If you enforce discipline, even though your children or subordinates may not protest, it will cause frustration and gradually turn into hatred. I said, "That is the end of it, because the other side is adamant in their view, so let us accept it as a dissolution of the marriage." I told Parkash, "I have failed once in my choice, so now it is your choice to decide your mate. If your mate is up to my liking, I will be there with all my wishes. If not, I won't be an obstruction."

This marriage breakdown of Parkash had an adverse effect on my wife. After a while she developed a stomach ulcer. We tried all kinds of remedies, but she kept on losing appetite, losing weight, and having stomach upsets. We put her into Shaughnessy Hospital in Vancouver for lengthy treatment, but I could see that she needed herbal medicine. Western doctors know about minerals and vitamins, but they don't understand the nature of each food material and which food combinations are useful and which are not. The research in Western allopathic medicine lacks depth. I knew that the Indian ayurvedic system would be the best for her. But there was difficulty in going back because of the situation in Punjab. So we waited quite a few months.

My youngest son, Manjit, was married in September 1985. He got his degree from Michigan after we came back from India in 1979. Because he was away from home, he indulged himself in Western culture – parties and dancing – without judging what he was adopting. He never came before me with a bare head, and he was too scared of me to come home without a beard, but he always had it trimmed. A couple of times I gave him very admonishing lectures. At the time he got his degree, I gave him advice: "It will be your degree that gets you your first job. From then on, it will be your performance on previous jobs. Make sure that you do obey the management. It doesn't matter if they put you as a sweeper, as long as they pay you as an engineer. That will create better work habits in your mind and better discipline. When you rise in the ranks, you will know the feelings of your subordinates, and you will be reasonable. If you don't know how to obey, you won't know how to command."

He got a good job with de Havilland Aircraft in Toronto and stayed there for a year or so. Then he shifted places. At one time he was in Calgary. Whenever he visited home, I gave him good advice: "Get married and get settled." He wanted me to be involved in the marriage, and I told him clearly, "I will only join in your marriage if you are married into a Sikh family with outer form. This is my private principle as an individual. Otherwise you are free to marry into a clean-shaven family and there won't be any objection from me." Behind the scenes, he tried in many ways to find a suitable match with a Punjabi girl. He put ads in the matrimonial sections of the Punjabi papers, and when he was in Calgary, he found someone. His elder brother, Surinder, and sister-in-law, Gurdarshan, visited him, and he showed them the pictures of the girls whose families had responded, and he tried to get their approval. But his choice was the one his brother put at the bottom of the list.

He soon discovered his mistake. That girl really took advantage of him, and he ran away from Calgary and took refuge at home. His health wasn't very good then either, and he came home and said, "I am a defeated person, if you can accept me." We put him to work on the blueberry farm and paid him by the hour, and gave him technical jobs and paid him for that. I told him, "This is the greatest flaw in your mind – that you don't know how to handle your income." I didn't manage his money for him because I wanted to show him that I wasn't going to dominate him, although he could have had his expenses from me if I had done it. When he was healthy, even though his brothers wanted him to settle in Vancouver, he managed to communicate with someone in Los Angeles and get a job there.

He was close to thirty, and I told him, "Punjabi families marry their daughters by age twenty-five. Those daughters that don't marry by that age are either exceptionally strong personalities, or the opposite. As you are only an average person, a strong female will not accept you at all. And if you don't settle now, you will become a drifter, and at a later stage you will come to grief." Step by step, I loosened my approach. At first I wasn't going to have anything to do with his marriage. Then I said that the family could take part, but I would stay away. Then I said that the family could take part and I would give money, but I still wouldn't come.

Finally, a very respectable Sikh family responded to one of his ads. The father was Mr Narinder Singh, the editor of *Ranjit*, a Punjabi paper in Vancouver. They were searching for a match for their daughter, who was in her mid-twenties. Like any good Punjabi parents, they asked about the family of the proposed spouse. So Manjit had to disclose his identity. Once they learned that he was my son, they were very happy. And they met my complete criteria. I never expected that he would marry into such a good family. So I joined in, and Manjit agreed to have complete hair. We carried out all the formalities and had the betrothal ceremony, and we set the date for the marriage at the end of the blueberry season. I asked Narinder Singh to print our wedding cards as well as theirs at their print shop.

When Manjit came up from California to visit us before the marriage, he wasn't completing his form, and I questioned him. He said that it would be completed by the time of the marriage. I didn't think it was going to happen, and I told him that I would phone the *Ranjit* establishment to hold the printing of the wedding cards. His older brother, Surinder, suggested that Manjit take an oath. So we went in front of Guru Granth Sahib, and he took a solemn oath to complete his form and not to cut his hair. He kept his promise up to the time of the wedding. But he went back to Los Angeles a few days after the wedding, and he trimmed his hair and beard the moment he got there.

16 Retirement

My wife's stomach ulcer was getting worse, so I sent her back to India for ayurvedic treatment in December 1985. She didn't need a visa because she was an Indian citizen, and was able to go right away. In January 1986 I sent our youngest daughter, Parkash, for six months. Then, when the blueberry season was over in September, I applied for a visa from the Indian consulate in Vancouver. The consulate were aware of my community activities and my role as senior editor of *Qaumi Samachar*, and they did their duty to ascertain that I wouldn't be causing any irritation in the already volatile situation in Punjab. That took a lot of investigation, explanation, and discussion; and I had to get good recommendations from the gentry of the Sikh community. Finally, after three and a half months, they were satisfied about my reasonable and peaceful approach, and I was able to go to India in January 1987.

As soon as I reached my wife's village of Kultham, I set about her treatment. She had changed doctors quite a few times. In India some allopathic doctors know ayurvedic doctors, and she was going from one to another. In a lengthy ailment, constant caretaking is important for analysis and treatment. That is why I decided I should be there. Another factor was Harjinder Singh Kang, my wife's nephew and the caretaker of our land and house and all our affairs in India. He is the vice-principal of a high school and a highly educated and a very good human being. Any parent could wish to have a son like him. He happened to have a slight whiplash in the neck from carrying green feed for the milk buffalo. Because he didn't know anything about human physiology and wanted a quick cure, his minor ailment became a major one. Although he had X-rays and sleeping pills and other medicines, he became very sick. So I went back to India partly for his treatment too.

I took my wife and Harjinder Singh Kang to Tarn Taran, which is sixty or seventy miles from my wife's village, for ayurvedic treatment from Bhai Mohan Singh Vaid and Sons. That is the name, although Mohan Singh is dead and his elder son is retired. Nowadays, his younger son, Sukhbir Singh, sits for the morning and his grandson, Harcharan Singh, for the afternoon. They are very humble people with just a small billboard to show their establishment, although they have one shop in Delhi and one in Amritsar just for selling medicines. Mohan Singh was a commissioner for Tarn Taran and a great author, with over three hundred books and short booklets on many subjects. He wrote high-calibre novels on family and social affairs and ran a magazine by the name of *Dukh Nivaran* (Healing of Suffering), and he was the first author to translate Guru Granth Sahib into Hindi. His biography is about five hundred or six hundred pages, and I got it from Victoria when I first had difficulties with my health in Canada. That is when I became impressed with his approach. I sent money from Canada to his sons twice for free treatment of the poor, but they put that money into my account. When I went back in 1960, I discussed it with them, and they said that it had been their father's practice never to ask anyone for payment, and they had continued the same way. Customers had to ask how much they owed, and then they told them. While I was there, I could see that one-third of the customers never paid anything. In one case the fellow wanted to pay and the vaid (doctor) wouldn't let him. That is how they looked after the poor. So I said, "Well, although it is being done, the money I sent could have added to it." The vaid's answer was, "Yes, but you know that it would have caused a deficiency in our contribution."

What my wife's nephew, Harjinder Singh Kang, needed was a slow, prolonged treatment, but he wanted a quick return to normal health. From his viewpoint the treatment that he got from Bhai Mohan Singh Vaid and Sons wasn't very good. Because he was serving us as if we were his parents, it was our duty to do what we could for him. We tried to bring him over to Canada for his summer vacation to let him have a change in environment and climate, but the immigration office in Delhi would not give him a visitor's visa. They told him that he didn't have enough money. To me, that wasn't reasonable. As a vice-principal, his pay was around 2,500 rupees a month. He had land and he had 30,000 rupees (about $3,000) in the bank. They said that 30,000 rupees was not enough for himself, his wife, and two sons for the two months they would be away. I was sitting outside in the lobby, and he told them, "My uncle is here. He can discuss." But they said, "No. No. We don't want to discuss with him."

When we came out of there that evening we talked to some of the other applicants. An elderly fellow told us that his Canadian relatives had sent him a return ticket and a sponsorship affidavit so that he could go for a wedding, but the visa officer told him, "We are afraid that you might try to stay there." Perhaps it had become a government policy to hunt for excuses to refuse visa applicants. We were disappointed, but I felt that it was the will of God, and it turned out that way. After my wife and I left India, Harjinder Singh Kang was changing buses at Jullunder station when he met a relative who told him about another vaid and said that he should try him. So Harjinder Singh went to that vaid and in just two or three months responded completely to his treatment. Later on we got the news that his health was very good.

Our house in Kultham had developed termite problems, and the brick foundation had to be sealed off. I did those repairs while I was there in 1987, and I spent money on gauze walls and shutters for the outdoor kitchen and dining area to keep away the flies. All these repairs took about six weeks and cost thirty thousand or forty thousand rupees, which is quite a bit of money. The village panchayat took advantage of my presence in Kultham to involve me in a few of their projects. Kultham is a big village, but it did not have a panchayat ghar (a council meeting-house). When I attended a meeting about it, I was pleased to find out that the panchayat had acquired a real slum corner in a busy traffic area of the village. In that place there was an old well with a hundred-year-old banyan tree growing out of it and a one-room building on a spot that had formerly been used as a refuse dump. (There are now laws against dumping inside the village perimeter, but with nowhere to go, people still throw animal and household wastes wherever they can.) I said, "If you construct another room right away, I'll donate five thousand rupees. Sometimes villagers can't agree where their panchayat ghar should be located; some want it on one side of the village and some on the other. We were lucky because the forty or fifty people who were at the meeting were unanimous, so we went ahead and built two good rooms and fenced in the courtyard.

One day not long before we left for Canada, a high-school teacher approached me when I was at the railway station. He knew that I had been involved with the school in the past, and he wanted me to give a lecture to the children. I expressed my concern that an invitation should come from the headmaster. After that I got an official letter, and the time was set in the morning. With the grace of Almighty, my subject was education. I spoke for three-quarters of an hour to grades six to ten, and I could see that the talk had an effect. Those children had been just passing by when they met me in the village. Afterwards they greeted me with respect. After the lecture the headmaster took me to his room. The schoolyard had been landscaped with flowers and eucalyptus trees, but it had been a waste of time because there was a tube well but no power room to house a motor and no motor to pump the water. The headmaster mentioned this, so I told him, "All right, when I return to Canada, I will discuss with my sons, and most positively the money will be sent." We got a bill from the headmaster for over eight thousand rupees, and my sons and I paid it. Now they can plant eucalyptus all around the playground.

When we returned to Vancouver on 29 June 1987, we were surprised to see that the early crop of blueberries was ready and the pickers were in the field. That was the earliest commercial picking we had had. I had been so busy in India, and when I reached Canada we were right into our blueberry season with no relaxation. My weight had already run down to 110 pounds, but when you enjoy your work, it doesn't hurt you. As soon as I got back, I applied for my Canada Pension and old-age security. I had a strong desire to spend my old age in my wife's village of Kultham to do service for the needy because I could do more there. The buying power of the Canadian dollar increases five- or six-fold in India, and our simple way of living does not involve too much expense. I could not serve physically any longer due to my disabilities, and in Canada I could no longer serve from the stage. I would assure the gurdwara management that I had no motivation to take advantage of any situation and no intent to form any following, but whenever I tried to find an opportunity to take the stage in the gurdwara, somehow they would push my name to the bottom of the list. With my back, I could not sit too long for my turn, and if I did wait, by the time the last speaker was called, most of the audience had generally gone. The feeling came to me, "Why bother going there even. For my religious needs, God and the Guru have been so kind to me that the Guru has come to my residence and is guarding the whole family and has given us the chance to serve him and learn from him in our own home."

About the end of the blueberry season Professor Johnston phoned to ask if he could meet me a few times. During those meetings he gradually released his real intention, which was to write an account of my life. It is the Creator who directs, operates, and inspires individuals to do what he wants. An individual is nothing at all. Throughout my life Almighty has provided the situations and the means to get things done. I feel his existence within me. The thought came to me when I was in Port Alberni in the 1950s that I should write at least a booklet about my experience of the divine guidance and provisions of Almighty. But I didn't have the time. My family and community duties came first. Then, when I quit my job in 1973, I had some call from within to write something, but my disabilities handicapped me so much that I could not do it. I could not sit for an extended time without pain, and my right hand could not write properly. So I bowed to His will and gave up the idea very contentedly. It was a surprise when Mr Johnston expressed a desire to do it. I told him, "I can only accept your project if its intent is to show the working of Almighty through individuals and to glorify His name, and not to build up the life of a lowly individual like myself." He assured me that his goal was the one I had expressed, so we started on this book.

About that time I had a dream in which I went into a congregation. In that congregation I saw a lot of people moving around. In an instant, I saw Guru Nanak as a young man wearing an Arabic-type turban as he is shown in the picture of him with Mardona, the minstrel from Talwandi who was his companion. He was walking as he preached. I didn't come close enough for a direct encounter, but I took in that scene for quite a while. A dream like that is a gift. In my experience, dreams are reflections of your own character and thoughtfulness, although they may be bewildering or intermingled. All of your thoughts are stored in the seat of the mind, on the tape that never stops. The only mirror of its continued activity when you are awake comes during prayer or meditation on spirituality. Then you know how many violations occur. My mind runs away like a goat to chew on everything around. But through the practice of discipline, you can change your mind, and this evolution changes the reflection of your dreams as well. I now have dreams of a spiritual nature more often than I used to do.

My next younger brother, Piara Singh, died in December 1987. When he immigrated to Canada in 1971, he settled in Cloverdale, where my sister and brother-in-law have their farm. Later on, because he didn't have a good environment for his children in Cloverdale (his son was the only Sikh in the school there), he wanted to come to Richmond, where I was living. So I opened my door to his family, and after a few months he rented a place close by. Some time later he and his wife bought a house on Garden City Road, and he got into gurdwara politics (which he hated when he first came to Canada). Then he started his own printing outfit on Fraser Street in Vancouver, with a press that was equipped to do both English and Punjabi. Within a few months, in 1981, he had a heart attack. Then he had an operation from which he never recovered his health. His heart condition became very complex, and his death came after seven years of physical suffering.

My Canada Pension and old-age security began in February 1988, so my wife and I started making plans to go back to Kultham at the end of the year. On 2 January 1989 we left Vancouver on Singapore Airlines. Going by way of Singapore, we lost a day crossing the International Dateline, so we arrived at Palam International Airport on the outskirts of New Delhi around midnight on the fourth. Our nephew Harjinder Singh Kang came to meet us. In the morning we took a deluxe Punjab Roadways bus from the central bus terminal in New Delhi. After an eight-hour journey we reached home a little before sunset.

For five or six weeks we visited with relatives and friends. They all came to see us in Kultham, and then we reciprocated by going by taxi to their homes in the surrounding towns and villages. Then I began putting in new floors because the old cement floors in our house in Kultham were not moisture-proof. The water-table in Punjab is much higher now than it used to be because there is so much rice grown and rice needs a lot of water saturation. Earlier, Punjabi farmers did not grow much rice. Rice growing came in during the late 1960s and early 1970s with the introduction of electricity and the tube-well irrigation system. The water-table is now so high that the moisture not only comes up through the floor but it gets up into the walls and keeps the house and its contents damp. Our house was worse because it had been closed most of the time we were away. All that time the rooms were opened up and cleaned only twice a month. The moisture would carry the soil salts through the floor and into the walls, and you could sweep it up with a broom. Repairing the floor, sinking a tube well, and putting in a two-hundred gallon tank for the household water kept me busy until June.

During that time I became acquainted with some of the good youth in the village, and we had a good mixing-in period. Gradually people learned that we were going to stay – that it wasn't just a visit. Some of the village elders were asking if I could be the head of the village panchayat, and in private talks I told them one by one that I had no intention of taking that on. Of course, when we discussed it, they wanted to know why. I told them that it would interfere with my main objective in life, which was prayer. I needed prayer time. And I had a second reason. "The police people are pretty corrupt these days," I said, "and they are the immediate authorities with whom you come in contact as a village head. I won't be able to feed them free meals and give them free time, particularly when they want it, and that will create conflict."

When you live in a situation, you find out what it is really like. There was corruption in Punjab before, but it multiplied furiously under the regime of Rajiv Gandhi. When I was there in 1976–79, there was no bribery for recruitment into the army or the police force, although there was bribery in higher education. To get into medicine cost thirty thousand rupees. Since then it has risen to one hundred thousand. Now you have to pay five thousand to ten thousand rupees to get into the army, and that much or more to become a corporal or private in the police force. The irony is that you still have to possess the physical and educational qualifications. It takes that and a bribe too. Everyone knows about it and talks about it, but to make ends meet, they are forced into it.

The governor and his administration in Punjab announced that they were going to fill three thousand government vacancies with people from scheduled castes (untouchables). Two scheduled-caste fellows from my village tried to get clerical jobs paying eight hundred rupees a month, and they were told that they would have to hand over bribes of three thousand rupees. I lent the money to one and gave it to the other (he also called it a loan). He was a bright kid. They were both BAs, and if I were selecting for the government, I would select both. They had interviews at the district level, and they had to go to Chandigarh to get some recommendations. Altogether it cost them two or three dozen trips, and after nearly a year one of them was still waiting. The other was told that he would have to pay five thousand rupees. Then he was told that the bidding had gone to ten thousand, so he dropped out. He was lucky enough to get the money back because he had a relative who could mediate for him.

In Canada, when you need help and the policeman arrives, you generally feel relief. In Punjab now, when the policeman arrives, you feel tension. You feel he is going to ask for money, and if you don't pay, he is going to frame a case against you. When I was in Kultham in 1987, I was told about an incident in the village of Domeli. Robbers broke into a house during the middle of the night. A strong, determined lady in that house grabbed one of the robbers and bit his arm deeply right through his shirt. Luckily, the villagers heard the commotion and got together and raised a hue and cry. But the robbers made away with a few things before the villagers arrived. The next day the people of that house reported the robbery to the police. A police team came to investigate, and a lot of the village gentry gathered around. When the police asked the householders to name a suspect, that strong lady pointed at the head constable and said, "That is one of them." He denied it and tried to admonish her. She said, "All right, show your arm. What is this? This is where I bit you last night!" The press didn't get this story, because the authorities did not want to publicize it, but it was on everybody's lips for twenty or thirty miles around.

In Punjab these days people fear officialdom. The terrorism that started in the early 1980s is a kind of forced state terrorism. When a youth is caught by the police, he can expect to be handcuffed, taken to the police station, and beaten. He doesn't expect any justice. That is why so many of the educated youth have become fugitives and live in danger, with a life expectancy of only three years or so. The police provoke encounters, and in many cases the victims are innocent youth. That is what people talk about every day. And agents of the political leadership, disguised as separatists and terrorists, have infiltrated the so-called terrorist lines. The situation is more tense in the districts bordering on Pakistan – Gurdaspur, Amritsar, Ferozepur, and Bathinda. In my area people are living peacefully. Their God-conscious culture is holding them together. There are rotating checkpoints on the highways, but in my regular routine I do not have to go through those checkpoints all that frequently. But nobody dares to speak against an authority for fear of being prosecuted or victimized.

When the village elders asked me if I could be head of the village panchayat and I told them that I wouldn't do it, they accepted my reasoning. So I gave service in other ways. At Sirhala Khurd, my birthplace village, they had a very good soccer team, and I encouraged them by donating 8,000 rupees for a roadside wall for the village stadium. I was invited to a college at Sukhchain-Ana, where there is a historical gurdwara, so I donated 5,500 rupees there. The neighbourhood gurdwara near our house, gurdwara Kang Patti, needed repairs, so I contributed 9,000 rupees for that, and I contributed about 1,500 for the Ramdas gurdwara attended by the leatherworkers. The committee handling the affairs of gurdwara Shahidan, a common gurdwara, invited me to a couple of general meetings when they were selecting a new granthi. They asked me to take over as president, and I said, "Well, if you are unanimous on that, you can call a meeting and I will be glad to do it." That was in July 1989. We started some new construction and did a lot of renovation and cleaned up the courtyard, which involved work on and off over a period of four months. With the Guru's grace, we were able to organize processions with floats on tractor trailers going down the main street, which is pretty near circular and wide enough for the floats to pass. The first of these processions, lasting six hours, was on Guru Nanak's birthday in November. The second was on Guru Gobind Singh's birthday in December.

My wife needed an extension on her Canadian visa because she was staying in India for more than six months. According to Canadian immigration rules, a landed immigrant can stay abroad for six months but has to get permission to stay longer. We applied a couple of months ahead of the expiry date and then waited for five and a half months. I wrote two double-registered reminders, but we didn't receive any answer. So the two of us, with a helper, travelled down to Delhi by rail. At the entrance gate to the Canadian immigration office we found a big line-up. We waited outside for a long time, and then we were taken inside the gates and given chairs. But our turn did not come up, so we had to stay overnight in Delhi. The next day we got to talk to the interviewing officer through the glass. He questioned me very strongly like a lawyer for five minutes, trying to put me off my track. "Why does she have to overstay? You have property here. Why are you keeping your property here? Why aren't you selling it? You say she needs medical treatment in India. Why can't she take her medication in Canada?" All these questions were unnecessary because he could have looked in my file. When I had my chance, I took him to task: "Your office efficiency isn't very good. There wasn't any reply to our letters for so long, and we disabled people had to travel to Delhi." "Well," he said, "that shouldn't be a problem. Your wife can go to Canada on a visitor's visa." His solution was for her to give up her landed-immigrant status.

I told him, "It is our right to keep that immigrant status. The way you are handling it, you are actually forcing people into giving wrong statements." Then he went inside and studied his rules, and after that he was quite co-operative. He said, "Well, you don't have to apply here for an extension, up to the summer of 1990." And he put that in our file. "If you are going back before then, just write us and give your travel details, and we will mail the re-entry permit to your wife."

In the spring of 1990 our grandson Iqbal was going to be married in Vancouver. So I made our travel arrangements, and towards the end of March I wrote to the immigration office at the Canadian embassy in New Delhi by double-registered mail. That letter reached the embassy on 2 April, but we waited and waited and got no reply. Our flight was on the morning of the thirtieth. On the twenty-eight we went to Delhi, and on the twenty-ninth we lined up outside the immigration office before 7:00 a.m. We were not in the usual line but in a special line for those who had some correspondence. We had to wait for several hours, but our turn did come at 11:00 a.m. – before lunch.

The interviewing officer had my file in front of him. I gave him my copies of our letters and our airline tickets. He found our case quite unpleasant, and he said, "Why did you not come earlier?

You need to give us a few days to process this." I said, "Look here, you have my letter, which gives departure time, and it reached you on 2 April. How much time do you need?" At that point he took his pen in his teeth. He read the file, thought a few seconds, and said, "You can pick up your wife's entry permit tomorrow."

"Didn't you read the departure time of our flight?" I said. "It is 9:00 a.m., and you don't open your gate before then!" So he had no escape, and he said, "You can pick it up in the afternoon." "Do we both have to come?" "No. Not the both of you." I asked the time. He said 3:30 p.m. So I had to shuttle through the streets of New Delhi until then. I came back to the embassy at 3:00 and they gave me the permit at 4:00.

I have been back to India a few times since I first immigrated to Canada. In the past the treatment that I got in the immigration wing at the Canadian embassy in New Delhi was very nice and fair. The immigration officers were so co-operative. This recent behaviour is different, and I have a hunch that it isn't the officials themselves who are responsible but the policy of the government of Canada. Why else do we have repeated problems? I spent the prime of my life as a dedicated Canadian and raised five children. But I have found the sunny climate of Punjab gives me less pain and better health, and I can be of better service. And my wife has better health when she is there. That is why we have kept our house and property in Punjab. But we made our children good citizens of Canada. They are all well settled. Even my third generation is doing fine.

PART THREE

A Sikh

17 Following Sikh Discipline

As soon as I get out of bed or even while I am in bed, prayer begins. My way of prayer is recital of gurbani (scriptures) from memory and simaran, which is the recital of His name. The Guru says you should give a tithe of your earnings and a tithe of your time. A tithe of your time means at least two and a half hours out of twenty-four in service as well as prayer. It could mean two and a half hours in prayer and then service. But in your intense worldly life, when you have children and work and society, you can't do that much. Now, Almighty has been so kind, I get more time.

In the morning, prayer begins with simaran. That is just repeating a couple of words, "Sat Nam, Wahiguru" or "Wahiguru, Wahiguru" or "Ram." This simaran continues while I do my bathing, and it takes two to two and a half hours. Then I recite gurbani for an hour and a half. During the day, whenever possible – during eating time and so on – simaran continues at heart without enunciation. In the evening, rahiras sahib (the evening prayer) takes about thirty minutes. Then my daily schedule ends at bed with another ten minutes of kirtan-sohila (singing the bedtime prayer), mixed with some simaran.

Prayer is the vehicle for travel on the path of spirituality to the destination that is Almighty. When we apply ourselves to prayer, whether in recital of scripture or concentration on God consciousness, then we find out how nimble the mind is. It keeps running around on worldly things. Mind is constant thought. We don't detect all its activity during the day when we are not in prayer, but when we are in prayer, it will try to perform, to think about things that have to be done. One should not get disheartened with these disruptions or deviations. We have to goad the mind into prayer. Sooner or later – and that depends on Almighty – there will be some enjoyable lapses or moments in prayer. Meeting the source which is Almighty is the ultimate goal of life, and it can't be acquired that easily. The evolution is slow and sometimes unfelt, but if we continue, the reward will be there. Once we attune ourselves to Him in prayer, we will see ourselves with our inner eye, just as we can see the spots on our face with our physical eyes by using a mirror. We must use the mirror of prayer to see what we are and to understand the flaws that we have. Then, through the process of introspection and effort, we can weed out the vice within. It is that vice or ego in which our individuality is wrapped or muffled, and it is that masking that keeps us away from absorption into the universality of Almighty. When I feel the warmth of it and the pleasure within, I run into tears of thankfulness.

But prayer can only be sweetening when we also carry on unselfish service to His creation. As long as we have selfishness, we won't achieve absorption easily. And if we don't love His creation, we can't serve Him. Most people do serve Him to some extent, but very few without some thought of reward. When we serve Him without thought of reward, then we have the chance of getting closer to Him. Prayer is not complicated, but at the same time it is tough. It is a continued process throughout life. There is no special time or area of life for prayer.

An individual, from birth, is gifted with some virtues and some vices and an environment of family, society, belief, faith, and material. Sensitivity, which is God-given, expands or advances only under His will. If He doesn't provide the chances, then the situation may get worse. A person should be thankful to Him for any attainment or progress. That is the key to evolution. Worship is two-pronged – internal and external. Internally, we should always try to be at the Master's feet. Externally, the first and foremost thing is to serve His creation. Naturally, He gets pleased, and that pleasure enlightens us and increases the desire within to carry on. If we help a needy person, the return is happiness within. But it is very elusive. If we feel we did it, then we fall prey to individuality and get disconnected from universality. If I help someone monetarily or materially, then I am so thankful to Almighty because He provided me with that money or material and gave me the situation and the desire to do it. The more fruit a tree bears, the lower its branches bend to the ground. To me they are just bowing to Almighty. Those bare trees without fruit, they just shoot up. That, to me, is pride. As long as I have stayed in the plane of surrender to Him, I have been free from fear and full of hope. But whenever I obeyed my own individuality, I felt stress and fear and aggravation.

Each individual is created differently. There are no two people who are equal at all levels – physically, mentally, or in their destinies. Some will advance quicker than others. It is up to Him. Those who progress won't be concealed. Their thoughts and deeds will always benefit the society and environment around them, and they will attract like-minded people who want to have more of their company. According to Sikh teachings, there are four stages of spiritual evolution. The final stage is called sahija. This is the stage of sainthood, of true sants (saints), not these self-appointed sants whom we have nowadays. At that stage you are at the same plane as Almighty, assimilated with Him, totally under His will, with no desire left.

I haven't reached any advanced stages, so I can't describe them from experience. I am at the first stage. With prayer, I am able to watch myself within, just like looking at material laid out on a table. This brings in impartiality, which accumulates virtues and eradicates vices. In my earlier age I had confusions and some illusions when I prayed, but I have no confusion now. I once met a Sikh who had reached the second stage of spiritual evolution. That was Foreman Khidmat Singh, who came to our house when I was waiting to go to Canada for the first time and who talked to me about his spiritual experiences. At the second stage your thought does not run around that much, and your concentration becomes very focused. It magnifies your inner enlightenment one hundredfold. But according to gurbani (scriptures), some vice, particularly hau-main (self-pride), remains. At the second stage occult powers can come, but they are an illusion, and if you accept them, you are lost. Such powers can earn you fame, but in the court of Almighty, it is all shame. Use of those powers goes against the renunciation of your individuality and your will. But occult powers are very strong.

It happened to Khidmat Singh that once he had those powers for three days. He told me that he had added Guru Gobind Singh's composition Chand ki Var – a battle prayer – to his daily prayer routine, and he had been reciting it in the morning, along with the morning prayer and simaran. After almost a year, when he was on his annual leave in his village of Sansarpur, he had a very strange experience. He got up around 2:00 a.m. and went into the fields for a motion and to bathe at a Persian wheel. It was a moonlit night. There were so many Persian irrigation wheels running, as well as some farmers ploughing their fields by moonlight, taking advantage of the cool of the night. Surprisingly, while he was walking, he felt his body getting tense. The muscles were pulling and stretching – overenergized. He knew what was happening, and he figured that, through the recital of Chand ki Var every day for nearly a year, some occult power had got into his system. So he tried, by speaking, to release it into the wooden plough nearby, and all of a sudden, with a crack, the farmer's plough broke. The next morning the same thing happened. This time he released the power into the wooden yoke of a Persian wheel, and that yoke broke. On the third day he broke something else. Then he clearly understood that the occult power had come. He went home, and after his nit nem (his regular recital of scripture), he prayed to Almighty that he had simply added Chand ki Var to gain a little more depth in his spiritual ablutions, and not to acquire any occult powers. "I don't want them. I just want to be at your feet. Kindly relieve me of them." On the fourth day they were gone, and after that he stopped reciting Chand ki Var.

The only time that I understand the scatteredness of my inner individuality is when I get into prayer or recital. Repeatedly, I try to bring my individuality back to concentration. The frequency depends on my worldly situation. I have more communion and more lasting communion in a congregation. Then I forget about my individuality and become totally absorbed in prayer. Anything that enters through the outer doors of the physical self – the eyes, nose, mouth, ears, skin, and genitals – will have an impact. When we see something beautiful, we have a reaction of appreciation. When we smell good food, we have a desire to eat it. What we hear and what we touch also create feelings. If we have good pictures to view in our house and good scenery around it, that will affect us. If we have inspirational pictures, of Guru Nanak or of Christ, then we will feel as if we are in the same context. And when we read or hear something about what is beyond the material world, that will always reach the inner individuality.

The food that enters our mouths is the total fuel of energy – physical, moral, and spiritual. We should not waste food. If we waste such an important ingredient, how can we expect to better ourselves in other spheres of life? We should only have as much at the table as we are able to consume to the last. We don't know how to eat. All we know is the taste, the smell, the look of food, not the real ingredients. Every kind of food has a nature, and some natures do not combine with others. In the auyurvedic system, dairy products never go with meat. Sweet and sour, when they are taken at the same time, create health problems sooner or later. Similarly, hot and cold do not go together. Our digestive system can take only so much variation, and it can withstand excesses for only so much time. Cold drinks from the fridge are hard on the body. A banana is a product of a hot climate and should be eaten there. It has a cool nature and fits with the diet of a hot country. Vinegar and pickles are useful at the right time, when the digestion is cooling. Otherwise they create so much acidity and cause so much gastric trouble. The creator has given everything a useful purpose, and it is only our ignorance and selfish indulgence that makes it otherwise.

It is the spirit that enlivens the physical structure. So the physical structure goes the way that the inner person goes. If an individual has an uncontrolled desire or some bad habit, it will tell on the physical self sooner or later, and end in disease. First the morality is diseased, and then the physique. But what is outside the body will also reach within to impress upon your goodness. If you have twisted imagery, or art that breaks the imagery of nature, it will have an impact on the inner individuality. You cannot go on unimpeded. Crime shows on TV will alienate your goodness. People watching crime shows will not do community work. Children watching crime shows will end up in crime. I will not have a picture of even a partially nude body of a woman in my house. It is a weakness to have such a picture there. If you keep around you good music, good actions, good objects, that will strengthen the inner individual, which is the real individual. When you choose your company, whether it is the company of people or of literature or of objects, you should choose well.

Our suffering is due to our thinking and actions. For the most part, we create it in our present lives, although we do face some miseries that appear to have been predestined. God is nothing but love and truth. He will never pull his hand back from the most evil person. He doesn't try to retaliate in any phase of our evil acts or crimes. He has given us a kind of equation: if we do wrong, then a time will come when we should suffer, just as – if we put a hand on a stove, it will burn. He lets us suffer to correct our thought, which is where every action originates. In the same way, a tutor or parent punishes a delinquent student or offspring. There is no Satan in all existence. Our vices are the expression of human mentality. The Gurus have enumerated them under five headings: sexual lust, anger, greed, attachment, and pride or ego. Lust is the strongest and most vicious; it can cause so many problems, and that is why it is mentioned everywhere in Guru Granth Sahib as the number-one vice. All our evil thinking can be brought under these headings.

It is only in human life that we have the chance to earn salvation and end the cycle of rebirth. In the guru's teachings and in Hindu belief, there are 84 lakh (8,400,000) of species on this planet. The Guru has put them into four classifications: life from egg, from placenta, from heat (mosquitoes and flies who come with the warm weather), and from seed or soil. An individual may go through life as each of those 8,400,000 species before ending a full cycle with a human life. All the other categories of life have only one phase of performance, and that is bhugta (the receiver – following what is predestined). Human beings have two: karta (the doer) as well as bhugta. Other species lead the lives they are designed to lead. For example, in sex they only perform when the need for regeneration comes. Human beings have been given an interval of thirty days, yet they indulge in extracurricular sex. That is karta, going beyond the order of nature, designing a new thing for which there will have to be an answer.

According to the Guru, if you don't earn salvation in your human life, then after death you have to go back through the cycle of rebirth in some or all of the other categories. How many lives and for how long depends on your performance in your human life. The angels who record your deeds are Chitra and Gupta. Chitra means picture: it is what you create. Gupta means within yourself: it is your inner essence. Chitragupta, as one word, means enacted thought. Every action has two phases, first the thought within, and then the thought put into practice and made physical. If you think about a crime, even if you don't perform it, you have still committed yourself, and the recording angels will have it in their accounts.

At Goindwal on the Beas River where the Third Guru had his headquarters for a long time, there is a famous tirath (place of pilgrimage). At that tirath there are eighty-four steps, just as there are eighty-four lakh of lives in one cycle of rebirth. These steps go down to the River Beas under the cover of a curved roof of bricks. We visited that tirath at Goindwal with our youngest daughter, Parkash, in the summer of 1976. A Sikh can reach salvation at Goindwal by completing ablutions and praying at every one of the eighty-four steps. First you perform an ardas (prayer) before Guru Granth Sahib. Then you take a bath in the Beas. You don't have to massage your body too much: just take a dip. Then you sit down at the first step and recite, with full concentration, the entire Japji Sahib (the morning prayer of Guru Nanak). You repeat that process eighty-four times right up to the top step. It takes twenty-four hours, and all that time you don't eat anything and don't have any motions. It is tough, and you have to prepare yourself. How many can do it, God only knows. How many have done it, I don't know. I have heard that some have done it.

The mind is constantly active. This activity has to be harnessed, and I don't know any other harness than religious discipline. For the Sikhs, the Guru has streamlined a discipline. If a Sikh follows that discipline internally, then gradually doors of universal wisdom will open. Mankind has been given leadership over everything else in creation. As the masters we must own a sense of protection, sharing, and compassion for the other categories of life. And our performance must not be worse than animal behaviour. Animals have no religious or educational institutions. Their behaviour comes from two sources. Some they have from birth; it is God-given. Some, like hunting and refuge-building, is acquired from parental coaching. With mankind as well, the gifts of nature are there from birth, and the mother and father have a big role in shaping the development of the child. But human beings acquire unnatural behaviour that isn't there among animals.

The family is the most important institution in society. The second most important is religion, and the third is the school. The family impact on a child is very deep in the first seven or so years, and, with some exceptions, it is life-lasting. Later on the child learns from the discipline of the school and the character of the teachers in the school as well as the teachings of the religious institution. But the family influence is the one that does more than any other to formulate the future life. Without the family our society will be totally haywire. How can a child develop into a good human being without the breasting of a mother or the hugging and direction of a father or without tasting or understanding the relationship of a brother or a sister? In the West the family is in a big decline. But it is only the family that can mould a child into a caring personality for brotherhood, sisterhood, and parenthood. Such a child will respect the school, the teacher, and the church, and feel like a part of creation for a useful purpose.

Whatever you have done in a previous life carries through in the cycle of birth and death and is there when you are given another chance as a human being. All children have different mental characteristics. Some are hot-minded. Some are cool. Some are this way, and some are that. They are affected by their astral sense – by their sense of what has gone before. We have a term for it in Punjabi – purble karma da asar (a previous life's effect on character). In some children the negative effect is so extreme that, no matter what correction you give them, they will end up as society's dropouts. In others the positive effect is so strong that, no matter how bad their family situation, they will become real assets to society. The astral sense can be developed and strengthened. It stays up to the seventh year. In those years you can promote desirable characteristics and correct bad ones more easily than later on. After that a child can be bent, but not too far and not for too long. The character is formed, and when the time comes, it will get loose again.

Of the two parents, the mother is the more effective and has the greater impact. If both are present, that is a boon. I didn't happen to be that lucky, because I was absent from 1953 to 1960 and again after 1966. When I returned from Canada the first time, Manjit, our fourth child, was close to seven. But Parkash, our last child, was born in 1961, and I was with her up to her sixth year. That was long enough. This child is far more spiritual and more courteous and responsible than the others. This does not mean that the others are not good. But I was not able to be with them during those important years.

When I was in India with my children, I gave them three don'ts – don't call names, don't tell falsehoods, and don't steal. Anything else – damaging something or quarrelling – would be excused, although we would discuss it, and I would advise them about it. If we punished them, most often it would be a ban on their sports time. Only rarely, and only after a very repeated thing, would we use a slap. In those years I had a few open courts with my children. I learned it in the army, where they have open durbar or open court with all ranks present. In those sessions the men are treated as equals with the officers, and that is the only chance that they have to make open complaints against their seniors and have those complaints discussed and get a decision.

In one of our family durbars my elder son, Surinder, said, "Father, how come you told a lie one day?" I was so happy and I encouraged him and said, "Let me know what it was, and I will apologize if I did it, and I won't do it again." He reminded me that a fellow asked to borrow my kehi, which is a spade-like hoe with a short handle, for digging and filling. Surinder told me, "You said that somebody had borrowed it, but it was there." I patted him and said, "You are right, but there was a serious reason for it. That man is very unreliable, and there was a big chance that I wouldn't get that tool back. So I had to tell a lie." Still, it was a lie, and I had to explain and elaborate for the children quite a bit.

In 1988, when we were living on No. 6 Road in Richmond, we started a Satsang congregation in the family, alternating households each time. We would begin with kirtan (spiritual singing). The grandchildren were taking lessons, so they could sing. Parkash knew it very well, and Surinder could do it. My wife would lead sometimes, and Kuldip Kaur, our eldest daughter, and her husband would do it. Another family would join us, and that young fellow sang too. After kirtan I would generally give an explanation of a shabad (a verse from Guru Granth Sahib) or a historical event, particularly in the history of the Gurus. Towards the end we would have an open session, with all ages present. It was up to the youth to ask any kind of question if they had any difficulties or doubts, and we would discuss it frankly, with no repercussions later on.

In my family, when two people meet, they greet each other. That is a part of the family discipline. At the first meeting in the morning a greeting is a must. When a person goes away for a day or two, and when they come back, they greet everyone else. When I come in from outside, I greet those who are inside. Sometimes the little ones forget when they come home from school, so I offer them a greeting first, and then they remember. If two people have a disagreement in the evening, then the first greeting in the morning takes away the hard feeling quite a bit, and it opens the way for further communication. Everyone in the family knows that the practice is very useful.

People from Eastern societies who are living in the West are trying to cling to their extended-family systems and to social codes that have been chalked out and streamlined for millenniums. Even in India people are holding on to old values in the face of adversity created by foreign impact and a corrupt political set-up. In the extended-family system the grandparents, with all their experience, are caretakers, coaches, and even teachers, and they give a young couple a better chance for earning money. The extended-family system was in vogue in Western society not too long ago, but the era of modernization and the attitude of change have created the nuclear family, individuality-prone people, sexual greed, and so many unnatural approaches. When mothers and fathers nurse their offspring according to their own individuality, and when each couple hold to their own way, then human beings are in a kind of whirlpool mess.

At puberty, sex is a very dominant instinct among males. When the youth cannot get involved openly in physical sex, that leaves them with no other avenue but marriage, and it gives them a deep desire to meet the opposite sex through marriage. If the youth are allowed to indulge in a pre-marital extravaganza of sex, then their expectations from married life become very frail, and they try to slip away from the responsibilities that rest on the shoulders of a married couple. In the so-called love marriage it is not love that is involved in the first instance but the sexual instinct. It is the sexual instinct that creates the closeness between two individuals, and pre-marital physical sex takes away the sweetness and satisfaction that otherwise would be experienced. In the guided-marriage system, parents and grandparents make the selection because, with their several decades of experience of married life, they are better equipped to do it. After the marriage they give guidance, and they provide sympathetic consultation in the times of indifference that come to most new couples. Marriage, for the most part, is companionship, and it creates a feeling of take and give. In many cases love marriages break down, but in guided marriages the divorce rate is very low.

Materialism has created so many doorways to attract human thinking towards luxury, enjoyment, and selfishness, and in Western society, in the past three or four decades, the guidance of the family, the school, and the church have fallen away. Good and evil have always been present nearly everywhere, but evil let loose through social indiscipline does result in many maladies. Most diseases are self-inflicted. How much suffering comes from tobacco smoking? Drugs, liquor, and bad eating habits are the cause of so many abdominal and other physical disabilities. Sex has become too explicit in Western society. God never intended it for total pleasure. Semen in the human male is the top essence in the body. It is not an ordinary thing. Indulgence into sexual extravaganza has caused depletion of physical energy and resulted in the bombshell AIDS.

Today Western society considers sex a gift from God mostly for enjoyment. Some Christian churches are falling in line with that attitude. When they conform to modern opinion like that, they take away the great virtue of responsible behaviour and discipline. We need religion for the realization of life and its source, the Creator. If we have freedom without discipline, we are put into an unguided wilderness of society. A religion that does not observe the basics of spiritually oriented thinking will just fade away.

If we evaluate the world religions that have flourished, and if we do it from a neutral perspective, then, with some allowances, we will find that the basics are the same. The first thought that we receive is that Almighty is the force that creates and destroys, and we are his creation. He is the father and the mother, and we are the sons and daughters. The second thought is that all of mankind are equal, regardless of religion, colour, race, or sex. These are the two tiers of faith. From time to time God has created individuals, whom we call prophets, to bring the message. With our wisdom as individuals we cannot measure the calibre of these supreme beings. There is some variation in their teachings, and we can guess that God equipped them for the needs of the time and for the needs of the region at that time. There may be some fundamental reason why, in the Islamic belief, a man can have more wives than one. But that is not a doctrine; it is an option. In the same way, I never thought that Christ would ever have said that only those who believe in him will stand to meet God. I have had the pleasure of living and working with people of faiths other than mine. As I see it, Sikhs, Hindus, Muslims, Christians, Buddhists, and others can all coexist and live as friendly neighbours or brothers and sisters without conflict if they observe and practice the basics of their religions.

I feel very lucky to have been born a Sikh because the originality of the teaching of the Sikh Gurus has not been twisted too far. The Sikhs are the only religious community with an ongoing Guru in the word and embodiment of their holy book, Sri Guru Granth Sahib. The enlightenment of Guru Nanak, the founder of Sikhism, carried through ten lives until it was enshrined in the Pothi Sahib (the Sikh scriptures) as the Eleventh Guru, Guru Granth Sahib. When Guru Nanak passed on the guruship to the individual named Lahina, he bowed at his feet and called him Guru Angad. In the same way Guru Gobind Singh bowed before the Pothi Sahib and called it Guru. When I pray, I give regard to the Guru, but my prayer is a direct prayer to God. A Sikh cannot ignore the Guru, because it is the wisdom that comes through the Guru that brings help. But the Guru cannot do anything for us if we do nothing for ourselves. The Guru is the teacher, but it is our performance that will carry the credits.

I have read about well-educated Sikhs who have experienced the spiritual phenomenon through Guru Granth Sahib. In one instance an executive engineer heard kirtan (spiritual singing) at approximately 1:00 a.m., although his usual time for prayer was 4:00 a.m. At first he thought it was a dream. Then all of a sudden the room was lit by a divine light. It was so blissful that it couldn't be measured by worldly gauges. That celestial music of kirtan continued, and he saw Guru Nanak as the singer. His concentration became 100 per cent focused within, and he felt weightlessness, as if he was above his body. He enjoyed it for three hours, and when that samadhi (transcendent state of contemplation) broke, it was past 4:00 a.m. He wrote about it for the enjoyment of others.

The Gurus have given Sikhs a code of conduct that includes five physical symbols that a Sikh must wear. You cannot question it. If you question, you doubt, and if you doubt, you don't have complete surrender. And these five symbols have their significances. The first is kachchara (underwear), which is very comfortable –

snug and loose and easy at the same time, so you can be very active and comfortable. The kachchara will not open or expose you outside the proper place, which is a sexual performance in wedlock. It is the Guru's seal on the control of your sexual instinct. The second symbol, the kirpan (sword), hangs next to the hip. The Guru named it from two words, kirpa (kindness) and an (honour), to remind Sikhs that they are not given power to take or usurp, but only to serve in the name of goodness. The kara (bracelet) is worn on the right hand because most of the world is right-handed, and it also reminds Sikhs how and when they should use their strength. The kara must be made of steel or iron. Some Sikhs wear gold, but that is just ornamentation, and it is a violation of the code. The kangha (comb) is the fourth symbol. The Guru says it must be wooden, and that shows the Guru's genius because wood does not conduct electricity. Like so many modern-day materials, plastic is a hidden danger, and the constant daily use of plastic combs upsets the balance of electricity in the body. The brain is at the centre of the whole machine, and it is affected positively with kangha and negatively with a plastic comb. In times of stress from emotion or from work, when I comb my hair with kangha, that stress is removed.

According to the SGPC (the management committee for Sikh shrines in Punjab), the five symbols include the keshas (hair) and not the keski (small turban). But the first four symbols – kachchara, kirpan, kara, and kangha – are foreign to the body, and that leads me to believe that the turban or keski is the fifth K. The keshas (hair) are far above these symbols. They are a part of the body, and the Guru has forbidden interference with them. Bhai Nand Lal, who was the topmost poet in the court of Guru Gobind Singh, has written a Persian quatrain in which he says, "Without the hair, all the symbols are nothing."

When I was in India in 1977–78, the Sikhs had a majority government in Punjab. Before that the Congress Party had been in control, but in 1977 the Akali Party, which is a Sikh party, won the election. Even at that time I could not find many youths in the village who had uncut beards. Some would trim their beards. Quite a few were cutting the hair of the head, although they would wear turbans. Many wouldn't even wear turbans and they were becoming clean-shaven. One factor in this deterioration of tradition has been the practice of rolling up beards. In the British Army, Sikh soldiers had to roll up their beards, although they kept the rest of the traditional religious discipline. I experienced this personally during my army service. During the First World War the Sikh leadership officially accepted the practice, and to me it was a very innocent mistake that came in because people thought that tying a beard made a soldier look more active and more beautiful. After independence the attitude in the army became more lax, and some lazy fellows started to trim their beards. Under British rule they would have been punished. Later on, when some resolute Sikhs in military service tried to keep flowing beards, they were expelled. So the Indian government were creating their own interpretation of the Sikh code. When I was in the army, you could get hair fixers in the market to improve the look of the beard, and people were using them – not just Sikh soldiers but Sikh civilians as well. So the sense of allegiance to the code became very loose.

If we do not interfere with the beard, it keeps its form, strength, and length in a majestic and dignified shape. When it is cut, the hair of the head grows an eighth of an inch a week, which is miles in total hair length. This hair is all protein, and protein is the major ingredient in our food. By shaving or trimming, we are using protein from the body and wasting it. At the root of each hair is a factory that manufactures vitamin A. If we go to the hair of the body, we find it under the armpits and around the genitals. These are major centres of our lymphatic system, which controls disease. Interfering with that hair will hurt that system and weaken its function. We have hair over the whole body. Each pore is an exit for the filtration of refuse material, and the hair standing right in the middle keeps that door open. When ladies follow the fashion to shave the legs, they get a few days of beauty and pleasure for a lot of suffering later on. And the hair has spiritual impact. All the great beings – the prophets or spiritually elevated sants – had complete hair. If we believe that Almighty's creation is perfect, then why not maintain it?

The symbols, including the keski, are for male and female equally. I appreciate the North American Sikh ladies – the white converts to Sikhism – who wear the turban like traditional Sikhs and then put the dupatta (shawl) over the turban to please the modern Sikhs. Up to the early 1930s Sikh women wore the turban for the amrit (baptism) ceremony. It was Giani Gurmukh Singh Musafir, the jathedar (chief priest) of the Akal Takht in Amritsar (one of five seats of religious authority for the Sikhs), who began to baptize women without the turban. People protested strongly, but gradually fashion took over, and it has become customary. The Sikh code of conduct, which was drawn up in the 1920s, does not direct amritdhari (baptized) women to wear the turban. Perhaps because the Sikh renaissance was so strong in those days, and the religious standard of the Sikhs was so good, the leadership did not think that Sikhs would dare to interfere with the hair as excessively as they have. But the present leadership also allows artists to draw historical pictures showing women with the dupattas (shawls) only.

The organizational body that should give directives for keeping Sikh traditions is the SGPC. But the first priority of the old established brass of the SGPC, the jathedars (chief priests), pranbandhaks (administrators), kirtanis (singers), and dhadis and sarangais (musicians), is collecting donations and remunerations for religious performances. Sikhs have taken to making money from the sale of their Guru, Guru Granth Sahib. Even the SGPC sells Guru Granth Sahib at cost price. And the publishers, including the SGPC, wrap the volumes with cheap cloth – pretty near the cheapest in the market – and pack them in a cheap wooden box, and they let the buyer carry the Guru away whatever way they can. This is the respect they show the Guru – the living Guru in word! No wonder the discipline, morality, and courage of the Sikhs has deteriorated and they find themselves in a humiliating position, unprecedented in their history.

Some innocent Sikhs bow their heads before pictures of the Sikh Gurus. These pictures are imaginary, because the Gurus didn't allow artists to draw them. They forbade picture worship. So these pictures only represent the calibre of the artist, not the calibre of the Gurus. For example, we find the Gurus in these pictures with a rosary in the right hand, or garlands of pearls or diamonds. Some pictures show Guru Gobind Singh or Guru Hargobind with their beards and moustaches fashioned like modern Sikhs with hair fixers. Some people decorate these pictures and adorn them with garlands of flowers. During the past two decades people have started putting pictures of the Gurus on the walls of the congregation halls in the presence of Guru Granth Sahib. And some people are going a step further and making small clay statues of the Gurus – no more than a foot high. So idol worship is creeping in. I blame the leadership. All these things are sold around the major shrines, like Harmandar Sahib (the Golden Temple) in Amritsar. At one time I spoke to the secretary of the SGPC and he said, "What can I do when all the leadership are themselves haywire?"

The SGPC takes bookings ten years in advance for akhand path ceremonies at Harmandar Sahib, and they have six or seven akhand paths going on simultaneously, with one fellow reading aloud and the others reading silently. Sikhs living abroad send money, and these ceremonies are done in their name, even though hardly anyone is present. It makes a mockery of the teachings of the Ten Gurus and Guru Granth Sahib. In 1980 the jathedar of the Akal Takht in Amritsar visited Canada. We sat with him and discussed this practice. He agreed that it was wrong, but he didn't do anything after that to stop it. Under the modern administration of Sikh shrines, the akhand path has become a ritual only, performed for money, without respect and without benefit. There should be no fixed charges for akhand paths. There should be no multiple performances. Would anyone have asked Guru Nanak to multiply himself when he was preaching before a congregation? Once the recital has started with the first line on the first page of Guru Granth Sahib, it should continue to the end, carrying on day and night without a break. It doesn't matter if there isn't any audience present. Even if there is no audience, the recital should be given aloud because, when it is spoken, it gets into the environment. A silent recital doesn't cast the waves of sound that enrich the environment, spiritually and intellectually.

A big part of the problem with the administration of Sikh shrines in Punjab is the voting system. When the Sikh leadership accepted the Gurdwara Act of 1925, given to them by the British, they accepted a voting system for choosing the management committee. That voting system has given the political process total domination in Sikh gurdwaras and Sikh administrative bodies. It created the same kind of electioneering as in any other election, with misappropriation of the Guru's golak (money-box) to win elections. In the past couple of decades the SGPC has become no more than a very good nursery for political advancement.

The amrit ceremony, which is the baptismal ceremony for the Sikhs, has also become a ritual instead of a reality. Too many people have been persuaded to take amrit when they were not ready. Or they have been affected by some event, such as the Indian

Army attack on the Golden Temple, and they want to become amritdhari Sikhs. The Guru never administered amrit to those who
were undisciplined in the faith. A person should practice the internal moral and spiritual teachings for some time, a year or two,
before entering the fold of the brotherhood of the Khalsa as amritdhari Sikhs. The Gurus didn't want numbers; they wanted quality.
Now we have people who take amrit and are called Khalsa and
then commit serious violations of the disciple the next day or
within a few days.

What is a Khalsa? During the Mogul empire the Persian word
for the property of the monarch was khalsa. That was the monarch's personal property; it wasn't the property of the state. When
Guru Gobind Singh used the word for his baptized Sikhs, he
meant "God's own property." At the first baptism at Anandpur
Sahib, with every sprinkling of the prepared amrit, the Guru
asked the recipient to pronounce the words that are used at every
amrit ceremony today. The Guru said, "Bol: Wahiguru Ji ka
Khalsa, Wahiguru Ji ki fateh." And the recipient said, "Wahiguru
Ji ka Khalsa, Wahiguru Ji ki fateh," omitting "Bol," which means
"Say." The words mean that the Khalsa belongs to Almighty and
that victory belongs to Almighty. Nothing belongs to the Khalsa.

If we look into the Khalsa raj – the rule of Maharaja Ranjit Singh
– we have an empire with full representation from all communities, belonging to any philosophy or thought, all equally treated. If
the present movement for Khalistan should end up with the same
set-up as the Gurus designed for the Khalsa, then I am all for it.
But I am not for any Khalistan that is just a parallel political set-up
ruled by Sikhs who are not themselves practising Khalsas. During
the raj of Maharaja Ranjit Singh, when the capital was in Lahore,
some Khalsa Sikhs brought a complaint against the loud recital of
namaz by Muslims in their mosque. They complained that it interfered with their concentration in their early morning ablutions.
Maharaja Ranjit Singh brought both sides into the open court. The
Muslims said that, according to their prophet, when they pray to
Almighty, they are supposed to pronounce it at a very deep pitch
of their voice, just like calling someone at a very distant place. The
Maharaja said, "Dear Sikhs, you are doing the prayer to the same
Almighty, which Guru Granth Sahib clearly explains. So it is only
fair that all people should be free to have their prayers in their
prescribed way."

That is the nature of Khalsa raj. Khalsa raj is not rule by people of the Sikh faith and Sikh form who are motivated politically first and who use religion to meet their own ends. A Sikh is anyone who believes in the teachings of the Ten Gurus and Guru Granth Sahib. But a true Khalsa is a Sikh who has reached a stage of self-lessness through years of practice and dedication. A careless person cannot be a Khalsa, yet we see so many so-called Khalsas wasting food from the Guru's langar. A true Khalsa does everything in the name of Almighty, even in maintaining the physical body, because the mind cannot function without the body in this physical world. When people of that kind are at the helm of a family, or a neighbourhood, or a community, or a country, the actions that originate with them will create an environment of equality without prejudice. That, to me, is Khalistan.

How does one get back to the truth? Very easily. Find it in your individual self. Forget what the religious leadership says. Faith is the rock-bottom foundation from which you cannot run away. Practice the basics and follow what is inside you. The objective of worship is to bring your thought to a total attunement with His presence. When that happens, then the guidance from within starts to dominate the thought of individuality. The mind is part of universality created as individuality. The Guru says:

Man toon jot saroop hain. Apna mool pachhan.
Man Har Ji terai nal hai. Gurmati rang maan.

Mind, you are a spark of light divine. Recognize your source.
Mind, the Lord is with you. The Guru's wisdom leads to bliss.

The seat of the human mind is in the forehead, right above the nose. All the thoughts that come from my individuality originate right there in the pituitary gland, the life gland. Atma or universality guides me from the seat of my heart, right underneath the sternum. Goodness or positivity always comes from that source, and anything wrong or negative within me is right above the nose. Whenever I have followed the guidance of atma from my heart, I have been very successful. But it has been a lengthy process for me. I have learned that an individual should not be dissatisfied if realization does not come for some time.

In my birthplace village of Sirhala Khurd, a nice Bengali gentleman stayed as the caretaker in our orchard for years and years. He was a man of character in many respects, except for food. That is how he used to lose his money – satisfying the big taste of his tongue. When I was there in the early 1960s, I used to sell him the crop of the different varieties of fruit that kept producing all around the year, and I often used to subsidize him and help him out. One day I was working in our vegetable patch when four collegiate students came along the pathway on the route to Khalsa College in Mahalpur, five miles away. The Bengali caretaker had gone to the sugar-cane field for his physical need of excretion, and those students took advantage of that and started picking guava fruit. They could see me, but they probably thought that I was just a worker working around there. When they took that fruit, it upset me, and I gave them an impressive lecture laced with annoyance. "You are students and future leaders of the nation. If your character and honesty are such that you have no respect for the labour of the poor, what can we expect?"

They walked away as the caretaker came back. That pinched me further, and I hurled another remark after them. "Aha! Truth is hurting you," I said. "You have eaten so much of his fruit and now you are slipping away without buying anything."

One of them looked back over his shoulder and replied respectfully, "Yes, Sardar Ji, truth does hurt that is hurled like a cane blow." I stood there for the next five to ten minutes and pondered within, and I could see the affirmation coming from the heart seat, not the seat of the mind. "This boy is totally right in the essence of his remark. That is where you are not successful with people when you try to make them understand about truth or right and wrong." I had an understanding that truth was valued. But in practice, perhaps, my presentation of truth created reaction and tension. A lot of time has lapsed since that incident, and I have experienced positive development. Those flaws of mine are reducing, gradually, with the guidance of universality at heart. But I am not a victor yet. They still come over me, although not as strong as before.

Postscript by the Amanuensis

In the spring of 1991 I visited Tara Singh's home in Punjab for the first time. He was not there because he had flown to Canada on the very day that I left for India. My own schedule was tight, and I arrived unannounced in the village of Kultham late in the afternoon, along with my Punjabi guide Jitrendra Verma and a hired car and driver. It took only seconds to establish who I was – Tara Singh Bains' friend from Canada – and to gain entry to his house. Gian Singh, the caretaker, threw the keys down from the terraced roof, and I entered through the gate to the compound at the rear. Someone sent for Tara Singh's nephew, Harjinder Singh Kang, the school vice-principal, and he put aside the pile of papers he was grading to entertain us with true Punjabi hospitality. That night we slept in Tara Singh's compound, and Harjinder Singh Kang, as a good host, joined us. Gian Singh had offered us a bedroom and he would have turned on the air conditioner, but the summer air was inviting, and we bedded down outside on charpois under the breeze from an electric fan, which was enough to discourage the insects.

Early the next morning we set off for Sirhala Khurd with rough directions from Harjinder Singh Kang. We had no printed map to locate the small villages and secondary roads on our route, so we used the road map of Punjab, which is to say we stopped every two or three kilometres to ask. All we had to do was roll down the window because there was always someone in the crowd alongside the road who would reply, with a waggle of the head, "one more kilometre," or "straight ahead," or "to the left." Our excursion that morning impressed on me more forcibly than ever how compact the homeland was for the Punjabis who have gone overseas. Between Kultham and Sirhala Khurd we covered about thirty kilometres, and in that short distance we traversed a good part of the tiny corner of Punjab in which emigration has been concentrated. "The saying is," my driver told me, "potatoes and Punjabis are to be found everywhere." He might have added that the Punjabis that one encountered in Canada, the United States, or Great Britain were most likely to be Sikhs and very likely to be from one of the villages we passed. Our road took us through parts of three tahsils or subdistricts, Phillaur, Nawanshahr, and Gharshankar. These three tahsils cover less than 6 per cent of the area of Punjab, which itself is only 1.5 per cent of the area of India. Yet the people from these tahsils have a large presence in Indian populations abroad.

There are twelve districts in the modern Indian state of Punjab, each with several tahsils. Hoshiarpur and Jullundur, the districts to which Tara Singh and his wife belong, occupy a triangle bordered by the Sutlej and Beas rivers on two sides and the Shivalak Hills on the third. Punjabis call this area Doaba, just as they refer to the area south of the Sutlej as Malwa and the area between the Beas and Ravi rivers as Majha. Tourist maps do not show Doaba, Malwa, or Majha because their boundaries are not recognized in any formal sense, only in popular consciousness. They have real meaning none the less. In past generations Punjabis would not marry across these boundaries: the Malwais considered themselves superior to the Majhails and the Majhails, to the Doabias. In Tara Singh's lifetime this has changed, as the economic success of Doabias has eroded old distinctions. Emigration has been a factor. But emigration has not affected the whole of the Doaba area equally. As the Sutlej River breaks away from the Shivalik Hills and broadens as it flows westward towards the Indus, it describes a loop with a radius of twenty-five or thirty kilometres. Within this loop lie the eastern tahsils of the Jullundur and Hoshiarpur districts. This is the corner of Punjab that gave birth to Tara Singh. Everywhere you stop here you find people with relatives in Canada, the United States, or Great Britain. It would be hard to find another part of India where the connection with these countries is so evident.

Why is this so? One factor has been the relative prosperity of the farming people in this small part of the country; another has been the way in which the receiving countries have regulated immigration over the course of the past eighty or ninety years. One might assume that military service made a difference by taking men from Punjabi villages and giving them experience in the world beyond. But military service appears to have been more an alternative to emigration than a cause of it. The Malwa area south of the Sutlej River has been a prime source for army recruits but not for emigrants. Because most of the emigrants were Sikhs, one is tempted to look for a religious explanation, and it is true that the pragmatic outlook of the Sikhs has allowed them to dismiss the taboos that prevented orthodox Hindus from visiting foreign countries. Sikhs did not have to worry about losing caste if they crossed the sea. But the point should be qualified. The Hindus and Sikhs of Punjab shared a regional culture within which caste and caste rules were less important than elsewhere in India, and among the early immigrants to North America were a number of Hindus from the Doaba area and elsewhere in Punjab who did not recognize much difference between themselves and Sikhs.

Tara Singh's small part of the Punjab has done better than other areas partly because it has sent out more emigrants and received more in remittances. Emigration has been an investment that promised a good return for an entire family, not just those who left but those who stayed behind. But emigration was not available to everyone. Tara Singh was fortunate to have a sister in Canada who could advance the money for his fare. Without that advance, he could not have gone. For those who could not borrow or raise money, emigration was impossible. Forty or fifty years earlier the emigrants of his father's generation had managed without help from overseas because they belonged to a land-owning peasantry in a productive area with rising land values. They could obtain money through mortgages. Their families were better off than most of the surrounding population and better able to pay for travel to distant places. Advantage spawned advantage. In the neighbouring province of Uttar Pradesh, where the terrain looks much the same as on the plains of Punjab, emigration has been uncommon. The population here is Hindu, but that may not be the critical reason. In this province large zamindars (landlords) dominated until after Indian independence, and a subordinate tenantry did not have the means to go abroad.

The concentration of emigration in the eastern parts of the Doaba area of Punjab still demands explanation. Men from these tahsils may have emigrated because they could not get into the army as easily as Malwai Sikhs. Or they may have responded to an excess of males over females, which was more acute in their tahsils then elsewhere: the competition for marriage matches prompted men to improve their position by earning money abroad. Or the explanation may lie simply in the fact that the farming population of this area was better off than in the rest of Punjab and better able to finance a large emigration. Whatever the reasons, in the early years of the twentieth century Doabias became the largest group in the Sikh settlements of British Columbia and California. In the next stage, as the idea of working in North America became more popular and more feasible, more Malwais and Majhails might have joined them, but by the eve of the First World War migration had stopped. By then exclusion was the rule in Canada and the United States. After the war Canada permitted the men who had already immigrated to bring out spouses and children, and that enabled the existing Doaba-based community to survive. But from the 1914 era onward, for nearly half a century, there were no openings for other immigrants from other parts of Punjab or India. In the 1950s, after the Canadian government introduced its immigration quota of 150 individuals a year from India (in addition to the spouses and children of Canadian residents), the Sikhs of British Columbia monopolized more than half the places for their relatives. And in the 1960s, when the government abandoned the quota and made it easier for people from India to immigrate, the long-established Sikh families attracted a large influx from the Doaba area. In this way the particular connection between the Doaba area and Canada continued over several generations.

On the day that we arrived in Kultham we came from Chandigarh, the capital of Punjab, by way of Rupnagar, and crossed the Sutlej River to follow the Bist Doab Canal for an hour, driving slowly by North American standards but fast enough, considering the hazards of bicycle traffic and bullock carts. At one point a vehicle backfired. It sounded like a rifle shot. Our driver pulled to the side of the road and shut off his motor. Ahead we could see a grove of trees and, to the left and right, open fields. In most of India it was election day, but not in Punjab, where elections had been postponed. During the previous weeks, every day had brought the report of the assassination of yet another political candidate in Punjab, and the news had become so commonplace that it had been relegated to the back pages of the Delhi newspapers. Jitendra's friend in Chandigarh had said, "I don't want you to stay in the villages after dark." He thought that the trip we were undertaking was risky. Along the road we encountered several police checkpoints, where we slowed up but did not have to stop. The police seemed bored and did not look in our direction. Aside from the moment when our driver reacted to the report of a vehicle backfiring, we saw or heard nothing that would suggest, to a casual visitor like myself, any underlying tension; the countryside and its people appeared wonderfully peaceful. Our driver was from Delhi, and perhaps he was more nervous than a local driver would have been.

Punjab was green, in striking contrast to the parched districts of Uttar Pradesh and Haryana that we had come through on the Grand Trunk Road from Delhi. It had rained briefly a few days before, but this was still the dry season. Annual rainfall in this part of India is modest, and most of it comes in one short season, from the end of June through to late September. In the autumn and winter one cloudless day follows another for weeks in succession, and there is so much dust in the upper atmosphere that the sky is a pale blue. Irrigation, however, keeps Punjab in crop all year, with harvests spring and fall. Half of it is by well and half by canal. In the proportion of land under irrigation, Punjab exceeds all Indian states. The development of year-round canals began in the middle of the nineteenth century, following the British annexation of Punjab. The Upper Bari Doaba and Sirhind canal systems were built, phase by phase, during the seventy years before Tara Singh was born, and by the 1920s these canals brought water from the foothills of the Himalayas to over eleven thousand square kilometres of arable land in the region that constitutes the modern state of Punjab. Since then the area under canal irrigation has been expanded by another 30 per cent, but this has not affected much of Tara Singh's own Jullundur-Hoshiarpur area, which depends mainly on wells and has long had the best well cultivation in Punjab. In his youth the Jullundur district had more pakka wells, with masonry walls and worked by Persian water-wheels, than any other district. More recently these wells have been superseded by tube wells operated by electric pumps, and some of the money for tube wells has come from emigrants, as has happened in Tara Singh's family.

Rural Punjab changed remarkably between 1966, when Tara Singh left for the second time, and 1976, when he came back after an absence of ten years. These were the years of the Green Revolution, when Punjabi farmers managed to increase their yields per acre dramatically with the use of chemical fertilizers, improved strains of wheat, and tube-well irrigation. Land consolidation (which Tara Singh describes), the extension of electrification following the completion of the Bhakra-Nangal Dam on the Sutlej, and the research advances of agricultural scientists, particularly at the Ludhiana Agricultural University, were essential pre-conditions. And a price-support system for farmers, introduced by the government of India in the early 1960s, gave them incentive. In the mid-1960s India experienced its last severe food shortage, with famine in several states. Since then Indian farmers have given the country a secure food supply. In the 1990s we no longer associate famine with India. In bringing about this change, the farmers of Punjab have led the way. The bricked streets of Kultham, as well as the tarred road from the village to the highway, provide immediate evidence of the affluence that has come as a result.

When we arrived at Sirhala Khurd, we found Tara Singh's youngest brother, Santokh Singh, at the farmhouse, and he took us for a walking tour. Just inside the gateway to the village (erected in 1976 to commemorate Sirhala Khurd's most influential son, Air Vice-Marshal Harjinder Singh) we passed the entrance to Havaldar Khem Singh School, where the children sat in class on wooden pallets under the shade of leafy trees, within a courtyard bordered by flowering plants in a scene that had not changed much from Tara Singh's boyhood. I wanted to see the old family home, and Santokh Singh led me along the curving main street to a set of blue wooden doors framed by elaborate masonry columns with the name S. Basant Singh, Canadian, painted prominently on the wall above. When Santokh Singh opened the door, there was no house inside, only weeds and neat piles of bricks. The pakka house that Basant Singh had built after his return from North America in 1919 had been taken down in 1989 because it required repair. The family wasn't using it and did not want to spend the money. In this case, progress meant demolition.

The sight of weeds inside the doors of Basant Singh's house was one of the surprises of my visit. Another was the tomb and mosque that Master Harjinder Singh Kang showed us while we were at Kultham. He had taken us to four different gurdwaras within the village perimeter, and then we had gone to the west side to Tara Singh's tube well. Across the fields, beside the narrow, tarred road that runs from Kultham to Mandhali and no more than four or five hundred metres from either village, we could see a large Muslim shrine. Up close we found the main building in perfect repair, with graceful minarets and a well-proportioned dome and finished with intricate tile-work, all within a walled compound of about an acre. It was by far the most impressive structure in or around Kultham. Inside, after we had taken off our shoes, Harjinder Singh introduced us to the saint of the shrine, Pir Bhajan Shah, a good-looking man in his forties with a bare head and trimmed beard, wearing an elaborately embroidered, full-length black and gold kaftan. This man, I learned, was the most recent in a succession of Muslim saints going back to the days before partition. A yellow sign at the flag-stop alongside the railway tracks, some distance from the village, displays the name of the first of these saints, Kultham Abdulla Shah.

In all the time that I spent with him, Tara Singh had not mentioned either the shrine or the saint. The failure was mine. If I had asked the right question, he would have told me. And the omission was significant because the shrine illustrates a continuing flexibility in the life of Kultham and Punjab. More than that, Tara Singh had a story about Abdullah Shah that he wanted to include. When I sent an earlier version of this postscript to him, he was surprised by my reference to this gap in our account. He thought it had been covered. Later he wrote to say that he had checked the manuscript very carefully and I was right. For me it was a revealing assessment. It showed that, despite his acute understanding of what was involved in writing a book like this and his appreciation of the role I had played, to say nothing of the changes he had seen in the successive drafts, he was beginning to view the manuscript as a complete and authoritative transcript of our interviews. If it wasn't in the manuscript, then he was satisfied that he had not talked about it.

Subsequently, Tara Singh gave me his Abdullah Shah story in a letter he sent from Kultham. The cramped and uneven writing showed how much effort was required of him, with his injured back and shoulder, to compose his recollections on paper. When he was a boy, there was a Muslim population in his birthplace village of Sirhala Khurd, but those families were all gone by the end of September 1947, the victims of the terror that swept the countryside in the days and weeks before and after partition. For nearly fifteen years their houses stood empty, until, as Tara Singh tells us, they were taken down so that the bricks with which they had been built could be used to pave the village streets. Six bloody weeks had transformed Punjab in 1947, and when they were over, there were only a few tahsils on the Indian side with a remnant of a Muslim population, while millions of Sikhs and Hindus had fled from the Pakistan side, leaving almost none of their people behind. When Tara Singh took up residence in Kultham in 1950, following his medical discharge from the army, there were no Muslims in any of the adjoining villages to look after the beautiful shrine of Abdullah Shah. The only visitors to the tomb were pigeons, and the building was smeared with their droppings. In the mosque, which was part of the complex surrouding the tomb, a Sikh priest had installed the Sikh holy book, and he was using the premises as a gurdwara. Tara Singh began to visit this gurdwara and, noting the filthy condition of the tomb, took on the responsibility of cleaning it up.

He was then suffering from a severe infection. Medical treatment had not helped much, and he was following a scrupulous daily routine of prayer. Every morning he would sweep the tomb of Abdullah Shah and take a bath there before saying prayers in the gurdwara in the mosque. This he did for over a year until a Muslim caretaker was appointed to look after the shrine. "In doing so," Tara Singh wrote to me, "I only did my duty in pursuance of teachings of the Sikh Gurus." During this period he talked to some of the elders of Kultam who had been contemporaries of Abdullah Shah. "I learned from them that spiritually he was quite rich and advanced."

The opportunity to emigrate to Canada kept Tara Singh away from Kultham for most of the next decade, but in 1960, within a couple of months of his return to Punjab, he had an experience that he took to be a visitation from Abdullah Shah himself. He was having breakfast along with his family, and they had been joined by a Sikh priest, when unexpectedly a very simple person of about seventy years of age, with the garb and style of a Muslim, stood before them. "I humbly requested him to partake the food," Tara Singh told me, "which he agreed to and had a satisfying full meal." The moment that this individual left, it occurred to Tara Singh that this was some spiritual being whom he had not treated with full respect. He immediately got up to apologize, but the man had disappeared, and, hastening to ask all his neighbours, Tara Singh discovered that no one had seen him either coming or going. Within seconds he had vanished without trace. "Right away," Tara Singh said, "I was imbued with the thought that he was Abdullah Shah, and he had come to affirm my service done to his tomb years before."

Moving on another thirty years to the 1990s, the presence of Abdullah Shah's shrine at Kultham might not seem remarkable, because beautiful buildings survive when people do not. Still, I was mystified by the evidence that it was a living part of the community and not simply an artifact from the past until my guide, Harjinder Singh Kang, gave me some explanation. This shrine in the heart of Sikh country is supported not only by Muslim pilgrims but also by local Sikh villagers who come to the present saint for healings and give their donations. And it has been partially absorbed by the Sikhs. The exterior is decorated in Arabic lettering, but over the pump, where all who enter the compound must wash, the words of Nanak, the First Sikh Guru, are neatly painted in Gurmukhi, the sacred script of the Sikhs. The people who come and go from this mosque display a natural respect for sacred places, forms of worship, and holy men, whether Hindu, Sikh, or Muslim. In Tara Singh's youth Punjab was a pluralistic society, and despite partition, vestiges of that pluralism remain.

The Sikhs were a minority in the old, pre-partition population of Punjab, in which half the people were Muslims, more than a third were Hindus, and about an eighth Sikhs. The modern Indian state of Punjab is just a fraction of the old province: two Indian states, Himachal Pradesh and Haryana, with large Hindu majorities, have been cut away, as well as all of the Pakistan portion. In this reduced Punjab live about twelve million Sikhs and eight million Hindus. The twelve million are a majority with a minority complex. They make up 80 per cent of the total Sikh population in India, with most of the remaining 20 per cent in adjoining states (Haryana, Rajasthan, Uttar Pradesh, Himachel Pradesh, and Jummu & Kashmir) as well as in the Delhi capital region. In no state in India outside Punjab do Sikhs amount to much more than 6 per cent of the population. In the whole country they are less than 2 per cent, while Hindus are nearly 85 per cent. Even within the major cities of Punjab – Amritsar, Chandigarh, Jullundur, Ludhiana, and Patiala – Sikhs are a minority. In the countryside Sikhs predominate, but when they go to Chandigarh, the capital, or to their sacred city of Amritsar, they are outnumbered by Hindus.

It is natural for Sikhs to be proud of their identity and, at the same time, familiar with the Hindu and Islamic cultures that surround them. When the First Sikh Guru, Guru Nanak, began to teach nearly five hundred years ago, the world of reference for his followers was Hinduism and Islam. His own poems addressed Hindus and Muslims in terms they understood, using their symbols and concepts. And while he dismissed the rituals of both faiths, he did not attempt a clean sweep of the old imagery but used it to convey his message that beyond formal religion there was a greater truth. In his narrative Tara Singh mentions a verse from a hymn of Guru Amar Das that is addressed to a Muslim. The hymn begins, "Oh man of God, Oh creature of the Unfathomable Allah," and continues with a series of metaphors with special meaning to Muslims – "offer the prayer of truth on the prayer-mat of faith," "make thy body thy mosque and the mind the Mullah," "look upon compassion as pilgrimage to Mecca," and "deem the practice of the Prophet's word as Heaven." Allusions to Islam appear throughout the Sikh scriptures, side by side with allusions to Hinduism. The Gurus spoke to two traditions with one message: "The Koran and the Purans praise the same Lord. They are all of one form. The One Lord made them all." Most of the hymns in the Sikh scriptures were written by the Sikh Gurus and their disciples, but the Guru Granth Sahib also contains the hymns of an Islamic saint of the late twelfth and early thirteenth centuries, and twelve Hindu saints, from several regions of India – Bengal, Benares, Rajputana, Maharashtra, and Sind – whose lives spanned more than three hundred years, from the twelfth to the sixteenth centuries. The truth, the Gurus showed, could be found in many times and places.

The shrine of Abdullah Shah – an unexpected find during my brief visit to Kultham – reminded me of the tolerance and respect that Sikhs have for other religious traditions. During my hurried tour of the village I had asked Harjinder Singh Kang to show me the gurdwaras, particularly because I was conscious that they illustrate another aspect of Sikhism – the persistence of caste divisions. Nanak, the First Sikh Guru, travelled throughout India and, according to traditional stories of his life, as far as Mecca, visiting Hindu and Muslim shrines, teaching everywhere and for everyone. The Sikh tradition that that he founded, however, took root in one small area, and notably with one endogamous group.

Tara Singh and his wife, like a majority of all Sikhs, are Jats. The Jats are a caste with a tribal rather than an occupational origin who belong to a region centred in Punjab but extending to other parts of northern India and Pakistan. In the old, pre-partition province they were by far the largest of more than fifteen landholding castes, and yet they formed only a fifth of the total (rural and urban) population. Some Jats are Hindus and some are Muslims, but in the districts that now form the Indian state of Punjab the Jats are typically Sikh. They dominate the Sikh community because they are the largest element in it and also because they have the status and influence that comes with land ownership. In the past Jat families enjoyed a master-client relationship with the other village families whom they retained as artisans and menials, with fixed payments of wheat and corn at harvest time and with gifts at weddings. The Ramgharias repaired their tools and implements; the Kumars made their pots; the Mehiras carried their water; and the untouchable Chuhras and Chamars swept their courtyards and lanes and cleaned their barns, or made shoes for all the members of their households. In recent generations these master-client relationships have lapsed or been eroded. Villagers buy and sell labour in a market economy, but the ranking of the old order remains, and the prestige of the Jats keeps them at the top of the rural hierarchy.

The Sikhs remain conscious of caste while professing a belief in the equality of all humankind. The ambiguity was evident in Kultham, where two outcaste groups, the Chamars and Julahas, maintain their own gurdwaras, separate from the Jats, although the village also supports a common gurdwara. I could see the Chamars' gurdwara – called Gurdwara Ravdas Bhagat after the cobbler saint whose hymns are in the Guru Granth Sahib – from the gate at the back of Tara Singh's house. The Kalidhar gurdwara of the Julahas was only a few paces from gurdwara Kang Patti, which belongs to the Jats. On the northeastern edge of the village stood the common gurdwara, gurdwara Shahidan (Martyrs' gurdwara), named for the Fifth and Ninth Gurus, who were martyred by the Moguls. This was the one that I knew Tara Singh attended and the one to which he gave his service. Sikh Chamars, like the Chamars of Kultham, are known as Ramdasias, after Ram Das, the Fourth Sikh Guru. As the followers of Ram Das they form a sect that is restricted to their own outcaste group. The Chamars, Julahas, and other Hindu outcastes have found some relief from the stigma of untouchability through conversion to Sikhism, which has given them membership in a community that is egalitarian in its ideals, if not always in practice. Tara Singh tells stories of the persistence of old attitudes among the Jats of Kultham against taking water or food that had been touched or handled by Chuhras and Julahas, but his stories suggest that these attitudes were on the wane by the time he was a young man. Intermarriage between caste and outcaste members, however, remains inconceivable within village society.

Tara Singh describes a renaissance of Sikhism during the early years of his life. This renaissance contributed both to the strengthening of Sikh nationalism and to an increased awareness of the teachings of the Gurus. Basant Singh, Tara Singh's father, was involved in the gurdwara reform movement of the 1920s and jailed for joining in marches against the proprietary priests of the major Sikh shrines of Punjab. These priests belonged to an ascetic sect, the Udasis, who followed Sri Chand, the eldest son of Guru Nanak (rather than the succession of Sikh Gurus from Nanak to Gobind Singh). The Udasis were clean-shaven and attended to Hindus as well as Sikhs. In their shrines they had installed the images of Rama and Krishna and other Hindu gods as well as the images of the Sikh Gurus and the Guru Granth Sahib. They also observed caste rules and refused to administer temple food to outcaste groups. In northern India there were a number of small sects besides the Udasis – Sahajdharis, Nirankaris, Nanakpanthis, Radha Swamis, and others – who took inspiration from the teachings of the Sikh Gurus but departed from mainstream Sikhs by giving greater attention to Hindu saints, or by following living

Gurus, or by developing their own rituals, or by cutting their hair, or by tolerating a variety of religious disciplines within their own communities. They contributed to a blurring of the boundaries between Hindu and Sikh. But it was not just in these sects that the boundaries were unclear or sometimes considered unimportant. In Basant Singh's generation many Khalsa Sikhs, who wore the turban and maintained uncut hair, thought of themselves as both Hindu and Sikh. For them Sikhism was a tradition within Hinduism. The most articulate and vigorous voices within the Sikh community, however, were insisting that Sikhs were not Hindus, that the Khalsas were the only Sikhs, and that the non-Khalsa Sikh traditions were deviant. Their assertiveness had an impact on the ranks of the small sects on the Hindu-Sikh boundary because they forced a choice between Hindu identity and the Khalsa Sikh form. The mass agitation in which Basant Singh participated carried the controversy to a new level and drove a sharper wedge between Hindu and Sikh than had existed before.

In 1974 Tara Singh accompanied four preachers from Amritsar on a memorable tour of the gurdwaras of British Columbia. The occasion was the centenary of the founding of the Singh Sabha of Amritsar. The Sikhs are a historically conscious people, and the Singh Sabha movement of the late nineteenth century has acquired an important place in their remembered past. Sabha means society. The Singh Sabhas were study and education societies that had a profound impact on Sikh consciousness at a time when some observers were predicting the disappearance of Sikhism altogether. By the end of the nineteenth century there were nearly one hundred such societies distributed across Punjab. The Amritsar Singh Sabha was the first and, along with the Lahore society, the most influential. It was organized a quarter of a century after the British annexation of Punjab and drew its membership from a Sikh elite who were alarmed by the success of Christian missionaries – American and British – in making converts not only among outcastes but also among families of the Sikh aristocracy. The response of the Singh Sabha was to meet proselytism with proselytism, to become propagandists for the Sikh faith, and to show that it contained a message that was every bit as appropriate for the modern world as Christianity. Within a few years of its inception the Singh Sabha of Amritsar faced a challenge from a Hindu reform movement, the Arya Samaj, which had a strong following among anglicized Hindus and had missionary ambitions among the Sikhs. Out of that confrontation came a Singh Sabha emphasis on the separate nature of Sikhism. Taking the scriptures as their authority, the Singh Sabha reformers defined a code of conduct for Sikhs with conformity to the Khalsa discipline as a central requirement. At the same time, they were active missionaries among outcaste groups, and their efforts contributed to a remarkable increase in the size of the Khalsa Sikh community.

By the time of Tara Singh's birth the Singh Sabhas had been eclipsed by a new movement, the Akali Dal, which had a broader base of support. It was the Akali leadership that organized the confrontational marches and protests in which Tara Singh's father took part. The Singh Sabha leadership, who had always sheltered under the patronage of the British regime, were trying to mediate between the government and the Sikh community, while the Akalis were sending bands of volunteers to occupy Sikh shrines and to eject the proprietary priests. Militancy produced martyrs; in 1921 a band of 130 Akalis were ambushed and murdered by the hired guards of the shrine priest at Nankana, the birthplace of Guru Nanak, and when the police intervened to try to stop marches, the Akalis defied their orders and there was more bloodshed. In this struggle Sikh opinion swung so solidly behind the Akalis that the government was obliged to recognize their influence and, in the end, to respond to their demands. Before Tara Singh's third birthday the agitation had reached a conclusion, and he grew up with the consequences, both negative and positive.

The gurdwara legislation of 1925, passed by the Punjab government under pressure from the Akalis, created a new political institution, the Shiromani Gurdwara Prabandhak Committee (SGPC), responsible for the management of Sikh shrines in Punjab. From the viewpoint of the Hindus, who had been accustomed to worshipping at these shrines, the legislation was a defeat. The campaign leading up to its passage had alienated Hindu and Sikh in a way not known in the past, and the subsequent history of Hindus and Sikhs in Punjab has been an unravelling of the consequences. For the Sikhs the SGPC gave them what they had not had before, a central political institution. The committee has had a large revenue from the shrines under its control. With this money it has been able to support missionary activity among the Sikhs, publishing books and pamphlets and sending preachers and musicians to villages across Punjab, and it has carried on this work from the time Tara Singh was a boy until the present. The Akalis who led the struggle for gurdwara reform subsequently dominated the SGPC, and, from that base, injected themselves into secular politics. They became the principal voice of Sikh nationalism, and after independence they provided the Congress Party with its main opposition in state and national elections in Punjab. In the 1950s the Akalis began an agitation for a new division of Punjab, to create a state in which their constituency was a majority rather than a perpetual minority. In the Akali marches of 1960 Tara Singh's father was again a volunteer, and again he was arrested, which meant that Tara Singh found himself in Sirhala Khurd, managing his father's affairs, instead of in Kultham, where he had planned to settle on his return from Canada that year. Five years later the government of Indira Gandhi gave the Akalis the Sikh majority state they were demanding, but that concession did not resolve much for them because they remained a minority party, opposed by some of the Sikhs and all of the Hindus. The politics of a continuing Akali–Congress Party confrontation have contributed to the disintegrating situation in Punjab today. The tensions have a history that reaches back more than a century. Sikh nationalists, from the Singh Sabha of the past to the Akalis of the present, have sought to sharpen the boundaries around their community while combating the caste divisions within it. The results, as Tara Singh's story tends to suggest, have been mixed.

Developments in Punjab have always caught up with the Sikhs in Canada sooner or later. When Tara Singh first came to Canada in April 1953, there were two gurdwara societies in Vancouver. The historic Khalsa Diwan Society managed the first gurdwara built in North America and exercised a titular authority over most of the other gurdwaras in the province. The schismatic Akali Singh Society had recently constituted itself and had just purchased a church building. The old society took its name from the Singh Sabha of Amritsar, an organization known as the Chief Khalsa Diwan. The new society assumed the name of the militant gurdwara-reform movement. In each case the names were chosen for their contemporary resonance. The split had been caused by a disagreement over the status of non-Khalsa Sikhs. The Khalsa Diwan Society had changed its constitution to permit clean-shaven Sikhs to participate on its management committee, and a group interpreting this as a backward step had broken away.

In its early years the Khlasa Diwan Society of Vancouver displayed considerable missionary zeal. Many immigrants of Basant Singh's generation became Khalsa Sikhs after they arrived in North America. They belonged to Hindu families or Hindu-Sikh families or Khalsa Sikh families but had lapsed in their religious discipline, and they landed in Vancouver or Victoria with names such as Munshi or Dalip, without the Singh that identifies a Khalsa. These men discovered their Sikhism as expatriates. Many were initiated at amrit ceremonies organized during the missionary tours of Sant Teja Singh, who spent five years in North America from 1908 to 1913, completing an AM degree at Harvard while ministering to Sikh mill-workers on the Pacific coast. Sant Teja Singh was a former vice-principal of Khalsa College, Amritsar, a Singh Sabha institution. He had been studying in Britain when he decided to take a summer course at Columbia University in New York. There he attracted the attention of a professor who asked him to deliver a public lecture on Sikhism. The lecture was reported in the press, and the Sikhs in Vancouver read about it and asked him to visit them. His missionary work among them began then. He appears briefly in Tara Singh's narrative because he visited British Columbia as an elderly man while Tara Singh was working in Port Alberni. Tara Singh went to hear him speak at the Khalsa Diwan Society gurdwara in Victoria (where one could see the foundation stone the sant had laid in May 1912).

Tara Singh tells us that, after an absence of more than four decades, Sant Teja Singh was shocked by what he saw of Sikhism as it had evolved in Canada. A great many Sikhs had abandoned the Khalsa discipline and were cutting their hair, and it had become their custom to enter gurdwaras without covering their heads. Tara Singh observes that they were imitating the behaviour of Christian congregations. Sikhs were adapting to their North American environment, even though they were not integrating with the host community. They were also resurrecting the old traditions of the Sahajdhari, or clean-shaven sects, and they had articulated a distinction between Sikh and Singh. In their construction a Sikh was a follower of Guru Nanak and potentially a convert to the Khalsa discipline, while a Singh was an actual convert. The form of one's worship, they argued, was a matter of personal conscience, and no one should impose a form on anyone else, even if it was simply a matter of covering the head in a gurdwara.

This development of a kind of Sahajdhari tradition in Canada ran counter to the increased adherence to the Khalsa discipline that characterized twentieth-century Punjab. When immigration from Punjab to Canada rose in the late 1960s and early 1970s, the established Canadian Sikh families faced a challenge from newcomers who questioned their religious practices. Tara Singh found himself at the centre of controversy as a member of the gurdwara executive, and the immensely contentious issues that he coped with affected relationships within his own family and divided generations of immigrants within his community.

The old Sikh community in British Columbia was small and insular. Although its members lived and worked in many different localities, they knew each other or had friends and relatives in common, and as Tara Singh recalls, on the great festival days of the Sikh calendar they would gather at one gurdwara or another to celebrate. Like Basant Singh, nearly every one of the early pioneers who immigrated before the First World War came without family. They formed an all-male cohort, and very few ever brought out wives. Instead they would go back to India for several years at a time (a pattern that Tara Singh still followed in the 1950s and 1960s). When their sons were old enough to work, they sponsored them, and many of these sons brought out wives, so family life in Canada began with the second generation. Even so, in 1953, when Tara Singh immigrated, there were scarcely three thousand Sikhs in the country, with most of them in British Columbia and a majority working in the lumber industry. During the next fifteen years a few professionals arrived, and the population grew by as much as 400 per cent. But the old families continued to control the gurdwaras and the community. They were the sponsors of immigrants who sponsored more immigrants, and the sense of obligation felt at each stage created a hierarchy with a small number of families at the top. After 1967, however, the community expanded so rapidly that it proved impossible to hold it together in the same way.

One of the incidents that Tara Singh relates from the 1960s was an exchange he had with two young men from the executive of the Khalsa Diwan Society on the subject of what women should wear. The two were younger than he, and clean-shaven, and they objected to women coming to the gurdwara in traditional Punjabi outfits. They wanted them to wear dresses, which was what Sikh women had been doing up till then. Pictures of early community gatherings show the women with dupattas loosely draped over their heads and falling over their shoulders but otherwise in Western clothes – skirts and dresses, blouses and cardigans. In many cases it was the men who had dictated the style. One of the women who arrived as a bride in the 1920s told me that her husband's eldest brother had burned all her Punjabi suits in the stove, one by one, because she persisted in wearing them. He had bought her two dresses on the morning of her first day in Canada and wanted her to put them on immediately. In the 1960s Sikh women began to attend community events in traditional costumes, and today many find it difficult to understand why earlier generations were not more assertive. The older people, however, remember that it was not as easy when there were fewer of them and other Canadians were less open-minded.

Tara Singh arrived in Canada in 1953 unprepared for the objections of his sister's family to his beard and turban. He was never affected by the clash of cultures more deeply than in those first few months with his Canadian relatives. In the background lay the attitudes of white society, but the emotional confrontation was with his sister and nephews. They lived within a community that was just beginning to gain acceptance in Canada, and they took nothing for granted. The Khalsa Diwan Society had secured the vote for Indo-Canadians only six years earlier, after lobbying federal and provincial politicians for more than a decade. Indo-Canadians had been the targets of discriminatory immigration regulations for forty-five years, and they still were, although they had won a concession with the quota system that made Tara Singh's entry possible. The men of their community were farmers, or labourers in sawmills, or fuel merchants delivering firewood and sawdust to homes in Vancouver and Victoria, or labour contractors, or, in the notable instances of Kapur Singh at Barnet and Mayo Singh at Paldi, sawmill owners. Outside farming and the lumber industry they found few opportunities. A handful of Sikhs were attending classes at the University of British Columbia, preparing for careers in engineering, law, and education, but they were venturing into new territory. In the recent past Asians had not been able to get into professional schools in British Columbia, and they had been barred from many lines of work, either by provincial legislation or by trade-union objections. They had been working around the prejudices of the host society, accepting that in many towns they could not go to the local barbershop for a haircut or to the movie theatre to see a film, and that it was pointless for them to apply for most jobs. Their approach had been pragmatic, and old-timers describe those days with gentle irony rather than anger. Tara Singh, however, experienced the difficulty that ran through their lives.

In 1962 the Canadian immigration department stopped enforcing its quota on immigration from India, and in 1967 it expanded the categories of relatives that Indo-Canadians could sponsor. By the mid-1970s immigration from India was averaging ten thousand a year. After that the immigration department took steps to slow it down by making it more difficult for independent immigrants to come, while allowing the sponsorship of close relatives to continue as before. During the years of easy entry Tara Singh brought out his eldest son and his wife, then his other two sons, and after that his own wife, youngest daughter, and father-in-law and finally his eldest daughter and her husband, as well as helping his sister to sponsor three brothers and two sisters and their families and assisting more distant relatives. He was doing what other Sikhs were also doing, and this brief period of greater immigration has given the Canadian Sikh community a distinctive age structure that, under present circumstances, will take some time to disappear. Most of the middle-aged are people who grew up in India and have spent their working lives in Canada. The young are Canadian-born or have grown up in Canada. Many of the elderly, like Tara Singh's father-in-law, Gurbachan Singh Kang, came out in retirement or old age to join their families. The dominant voices in the community are the middle-aged and elderly, who bridge North American and Punjabi cultures in a way that is not so natural for the youngest generation.

Much of Tara Singh's life in Canada has been focused within a five-mile radius of the north arm of the Fraser River, where there is a concentration of Sikhs. My home on the other side of the city is in quite a different world, climatically, topographically, and culturally. It would take me an hour to drive the twenty miles from North Vancouver to No. 6 Road in Richmond, where he was living with his son Tarsem and his family. Each time I made that drive – leaving the heavily wooded slopes of the North Shore mountains and heading for the open delta land of the Fraser – it struck me as remarkable that, in a province of mountains, he should have been attracted to an area as flat as the Punjab plain. He could see the mountains, but at a distance. In fact they were about as far from him in Richmond as the foothills of the Himalayas were from his paternal village in Punjab. On the last leg of my drive to Richmond I would cross the Knight Street Bridge. In the river I could see log booms, and the air wafting into my car carried the smell of lumber and sawdust from the mills on Mitchell Island under the bridge. Looking through the passenger-side window towards Vancouver, I could see the spare, angular form of the Erickson-designed gurdwara on Marine Drive and Ross Street. This had been the heart of Tara Singh's Canada, the mill sites where he had worked and the main gurdwara in which he had prayed and given service. By the time I began to interview him, however, he was drawing away from it.

In the early 1970s Tara Singh had been emmeshed in the struggle between old families and recent immigrants for control of the Marine Drive and Ross Street gurdwara. In the early eighties the old families finally abandoned the contest and built their own community centres or gurdwaras, where they could hold weddings and other ceremonies and events. Other divisions emerged as well. Sant Mihan Singh from Punjab developed a following among Sikhs in the Vancouver area, and his people built their gurdwara in Richmond in the early eighties. The Akali Singh Society in Vancouver continued as a separate gurdwara society, and a few groups organized worship in their own homes in place of regular attendance at any of the gurdwaras. Tara Singh himself became active in a group that was independent of any of the established gurdwara societies. Canadian Sikhs were creating a new diversity when their loyalties were tested in the aftermath of two traumatic events in 1984 – the attack on the Golden Temple of Amritsar by the Indian Army in June, and the mob violence directed against Sikhs in Delhi after the assassination of Indira Gandhi in October.

For two or three years Canadian Sikhs had been aware of a new militancy in Punjab. When Indira Gandhi returned to power in 1981, the Akali Party renewed demands for the settlement of Sikh grievances, both economic and political, and Akali representatives

who came to Canada in 1983 spoke of a growing crisis. The newspapers were reporting sporadic acts of violence, but from a distance the scale of this activity was hard for Canadian Sikhs to
judge. I attended a conference of Canadian Sikhs held in Ottawa
in July 1983 – when I first met Tara Singh – and it was evident that
the delegates were hungry for information about the situation. If
they felt any detachment, it disappeared the next year when Mrs
Gandhi ordered troops into the Golden Temple complex, where
the militant Sant Jarnail Singh Bhidranwale had taken refuge, and
those troops fought their way in, suffering and inflicting heavy
casualties and setting fire to the Golden Temple library, with its
sacred and historic manuscripts.

Feelings of outrage and injury seized the whole North American Sikh community. These feelings were not enough, however, to
paper over fundamental differences in outlook. In the immediate
aftermath of the attack on the Golden Temple there was general
support for a new umbrella organization to give expatriate Sikhs a
voice in the situation. Tara Singh went to New York with a contingent from British Columbia to attend the founding convention of
the World Sikh Organization in August 1984. When the executive
of the World Sikh Organization backed the Khalistan idea of an independent Sikh state, some Sikhs pulled out. Among them were
the members of the Akali Singh Society of Vancouver. Two other
societies in the Vancouver area kept clear of the World Sikh Organization from the beginning. One belonged to the followers of
Sant Mihan Singh, who insisted on a complete separation of politics and religion, and the other belonged to the older families, who
took the position that, as Canadians, they should not involve
themselves in Indian politics. These three societies, however, represented a minority of Sikhs in greater Vancouver. The Vancouver
Khalsa Diwan Society, with its large membership, along with the
gurdwara societies in the adjacent city of New Westminster and
the Surrey-Delta suburban area, stayed in the World Sikh Organization and aligned themselves with its objectives.

Tara Singh pulled away from the Khalsa Diwan Society long before it took up the banner of Khalistan. He continued for a little
longer to be active in other organizations, including the interfaith
committee on which he represented the Sikhs. (He has always
taken time to explain his faith to outsiders, not to convert them
but to promote understanding.) In 1986 he gave up all community

responsibilities in Vancouver, and since then his community work has been in Kultham. In the course of his life Tara Singh has withdrawn from many projects and associations because he wished neither to cater to the opinions of others nor to engage in futile disputes. This independence has been an authentic expression of his faith, and it reveals something of the nature of Sikhism. He has the scripture as his guide and his own inner understanding as his means of interpretation and verification.

In the Sikh tradition there is no hierarchy of priest and layman and no notion of an intermediary between an individual and God. The priest or granthi who officiates in the gurdwara does so as a servant of the community rather than as a spiritual authority, and while most gurdwaras have a professional granthi, any Sikh who can read the script can perform the function. Within this tradition the notion of a priest or temple functionary is quite separate from that of a spiritual teacher. One knows where to find the priest, while the spiritual teacher may well reside in the least expected place. The person who impressed Tara Singh most profoundly in his spiritual searchings was Foreman Khidmat Singh, a sergeant in the military workshops at Meerut. When they met for the first time on the road from Phagwara to Bahar Mazara, Tara Singh recognized Khidmat Singh's spirituality with a glance. He had not heard Khidmat Singh speak before he saw something extraordinary in him. The same trust in his heart's voice has given Tara Singh direction at many points in his life.

He and his wife have chosen to return to Kultham in retirement, although that is her village, and social convention would have them living in his village or with their children in Canada. I understood their decision better when I stood in the courtyard of the Shahidan gurdwara in Kultham. The gurdwara was not a big building, although enhanced by a large white dome and four minarets. The courtyard in front had been paved, and in the middle stood a pump and a shallow trough. To the right was a stand of flowering trees and to the right of that a small nursery school and library. Master Harjinder Singh Kang pointed all this out to me, emphasizing the role that Giani Ji had played in making all the improvements possible. At that moment I could see exactly what Tara Singh meant when he said that he could be of more service in Kultham.

Suggestions for Further Reading

As an informative introduction to the study of the Sikh faith, W. Owen Cole and Piara Singh Sambhi, *The Sikhs: Their Religious Belief and Practices* (London: Routledge & Kegan Paul 1978) manages to deal with controversial subjects without becoming con-troversial. A readable survey of Sikh history from a fairly traditional perspective can be found in Khushwant Singh, *A History of the Sikhs*, 2 vols. (Princeton: Princeton University Press 1963–66). A more recently published alternative is Harbans Singh, *Heritage of the Sikhs* (Delhi: Manohar 1983). For English translations of selections from the Sikh scriptures and other Sikh literature, consult W.H. McLeod, *Textual Sources for the Study of Sikhism* (Manchester: Manchester University Press 1984), or Trilochan Singh et al., *The Sacred Writings of the Sikhs* (New York: Samuel Weiser Inc. 1973), or Duncan Greenlees, *The Gospel of the Guru Granth Sahib* (Madras: Theosophical Publishing House 1975), or the six-volume classic Max Arthur Macauliffe, *The Sikh Religion: Its Gurus, Sacred Writings and Authors* (Oxford: Oxford University Press 1909).

W.H. McLeod has done more than any other scholar to apply critical methods of textual analysis to sources for Sikh history, and his work is essential for anyone undertaking a course of reading on the subject. Two collections of his essays sum up his views succinctly: *The Evolution of the Sikh Community: Five Essays* (Oxford: Clarendon Press 1976) and *The Sikhs: History, Religion and Society* (New York: Columbia University Press 1989). The ideas set out in these essays have generated a reaction from a number of Sikh scholars who insist that Sikhism can be understood and explained only by believers. This point of view is expressed in a collection of papers from a conference held in Los Angeles in 1988: Jasbir Singh Mann and Harbans Singh Saraon, *Advanced Studies in Sikhism* (Irving California: Sikh Community of North America 1989). The same scholars have raised similar objections to the work of Harjot Singh Oberoi and J.S. Grewal, and anyone entering fully into the subject should also consult the publications of these two historians, particularly Harjot Singh Oberoi, *Reinventing a Religious Tradition: Ritual Texts and Community among the Sikhs* (Delhi: Oxford University Press 1993), and J.S. Grewal, *The Sikhs of Punjab* (Cambridge: Cambridge University Press 1991).

The proceedings of a conference held at the University of Toronto in 1987 bring together a sampling of recent work in modern Sikh studies: Joseph T. O'Connell et al., eds. *Sikh History and Religion in the Twentieth Century* (Toronto: Centre for Asian Studies, University of Toronto 1988). For an account of the Singh Sabha movement and the agitiation for gurdwara reform, which emphasizes the growth of Sikh communal consciousness, refer to Rajiv Kapur, *Sikh Separatism: The Politics of Faith* (London: Allen & Unwin 1986). Richard G. Fox, *Lions of the Punjab: Culture in the Making* (Berkeley: University of California Press 1985) places the Akali movement within a larger framework of economic change. Mohinder Singh, *The Akali Movement* (Delhi: Macmillan 1978) stresses the links between the Akali movement and Gandhi's non-violent campaign for Indian self-rule. A compelling and popularly written narrative of the turbulent months leading up to and following the British withdrawal from India in 1947 is available in Larry Collins and Dominique Lapierre, *Freedom at Midnight* (New York: Avon Books 1975). For contrasting approaches to the study of politics of Punjab in the post-independence period, see B.R. Nayar, *Minority Politics in the Punjab* (Princeton: Princeton University Press 1966); Satya M. Rai, *Punjab since Partition* (Delhi: Durga 1986); Ajit Singh Sarhadi, *Punjabi Suba: The Story of the Struggle* (Delhi: K.C. Kapur 1970); Joyce Pettigrew, *Robber Noblemen: A Study of the Political System of the Jats* (Boston: Routlege and Kegan Paul 1975); and Paul R. Brass, *Language, Religion and Politics in North India* (London: Cambridge University Press 1974) The developments that led to the Indian Army's assault on the Golden

Temple and the subsequent assassination of Mrs Gandhi are described by the journalists Mark Tully and Satish Jacob in *Amritsar: Mrs Gandhi's Last Battle* (London: Jonathan Cape 1985) and M.J. Akbar in *India: The Siege Within: Challenges to a Nation's Unity* (New York: Viking Penguin 1985). Two collections of essays assemble a range of discerning opinion on contemporary events and issues: Amrik Singh, ed., *Punjab in Indian Politics: Issues and Trends* (Delhi: Ajanta Publications 1985); and Khushwant Singh and Kuldip Nayar, *Tragedy of Punjab: Operation Bluestar and After* (New Delhi: Vision 1984).

Tom Kissenger, *Vilayatpur* (Berkeley: University of California 1974), is an important study of changes in the society and economy of a Punjabi village from the colonial period until the 1960s. Murray J. Leaf, *Information and Behavior in a Sikh Village: Social Organization Reconsidered* (Berkeley: University of California Press 1972) does not have the same historical dimension but makes a useful companion with its description and analysis of the social structure and organization of the village of Shahidpur as it existed in the 1960s. To get a sense of Punjabi society under the British, at least from the perspective of the educated and urban Hindu Khatri elite, one can not find a more evocative book than Prakash Tandon's autobiographical family history, *Punjabi Century 1857–1947* (London: Chatto and Windus 1961). The unusual experience of a Western woman who spent two years with a Sikh villager in his village and on an ashram is told memorably in Sarah Lloyd, *An Indian Attachment* (London: Futura 1984).

A collection of conference papers edited by Gerald Barrier and Verne A. Dusenbery, *The Sikh Diaspora: Migration and the Experience beyond Punjab* (Columbia, Mo.: South Asia Books 1989), includes a short but suggestive discussion of early Sikh migration by W.H. McLeod, along with a good representation of new work on the Sikhs in Britain, Canada, and the United States. This collection also includes an article by Verne A. Dusenbery, "Of Singh Sabhas, Sri Singh Sahibs, and Sikh Scholars," which uses the 1974 North American tour by four representatives of the SGPC, as a starting-point for a well-informed examination of the relationship between white converts to Sikhism (the members of the 3HO) and orthodox Punjabi Sikhs. The same collection includes references to related work by Dusenbury. On the Sikhs in Britain, three titles stand out: A.W. Helweg, *Sikhs in England: The Development of a Migrant Com-*

munity (Delhi: Oxford University Press 1986), which offers an understanding of the ways in which the Punjabi homeland and the overseas community influence each other; Parminder Bachu, *Twice Migrants: East African Sikh Settlers in Britain* (New York: Tavistock Publications 1985), which looks at a group whose identity is no longer so closely tied to their place of origin; and Alan G. James, *Sikh Children in Britain* (London: Oxford University Press 1974), which gives a picture of the situation that Sikh families found themselves in fifteen or twenty years after the large influx of the 1950s.

Joan M. Jensen, *Passage from India: Asian Indian Immigrants in North America* (New Haven: Yale University Press 1988), follows the experience of the Sikhs in Canada and the United States through the first quarter of the twentieth century. Harish K. Puri, *Ghadar Movement: Ideology, Organization and Strategy* (Amritsar: Guru Nanak Dev University 1983); L.P. Mathur, *Indian Revolutionary Movement in the United States* (Delhi: Chand 1971); and Hugh Johnston, *The Voyage of the Komagata Maru: The Sikh Challenge to Canada's Colour Bar* (Vancouver: University of British Columbia Press 1989), all concern the political activities of Sikhs in North America in the years leading up to and through the First World War. The most comprehensive study of the Sikhs and other South Asian immigrants in Canada is Norman Buchignani and Doreen Indra, *Continuous Journey: A Social History of South Asians in Canada* (Toronto: McClelland and Stewart 1985). More specialized studies include B.W. LaBrack, *The Sikhs of Northern California: 1904–1986* (New York: American Migration Series 1988), and James G. Chadney, *The Sikhs of Vancouver* (New York: AMS Press 1984). Peter Ward, *White Canada Forever: Popular Attitudes and Public Policy towards Orientals in British Columbia* (Montreal: McGill-Queens University Press 1974), examines the roots of discrimination towards Sikhs and other Asians in British Columbia.

Sadhu Singh Dhami's autobiographical novel *Maluka*, first published in 1976 and reissued in a limited edition by the Punjabi writer's group Vancouver Sath in 1988, paints a warm portrait of the Punjabi workers' community that he knew in Vancouver in the 1920s and 1930s. The idea of attempting to record the story of Tara Singh Bains developed slowly but directly from a reading of *Guests Never Leave Hungry: The Autobiography of James Sewid, A Kwakiutl Indian*, ed. James P. Spradley (New Haven: Yale University Press 1969), which leaves one with a sense of the native Indian experience in British Columbia not so easily captured in other readings. A short list of comparable material for ethnic minorities in Canada might include Harry Assu, *Assu of Cape Mudge: Recollections of a Coastal Indian Chief,* with Joy Inglis (Vancouver: University of British Columbia Press 1989); Makeda Silvera, *Silenced: Talks with Working Class West Indian Women* (Toronto: Sister Vision 1989); James Walker and Pat Thorvalson, *Identity: The Black Experience in Canada* (Toronto: Gage 1979); and Murat Yagan, *I Come from behind Kuf Mountain,* ed. Patricia Johnston and Joan McIntyre (Putney, Vt: Threshold Books 1984).

H.J.

Glossary

The vocabulary in this glossary is Punjabi or common to Punjabi and Hindi unless noted specifically as Hindi. The glossary includes Punjabi names with their literal meanings.

Adhik r	power, privilege, potency
Aj t	invincible
Ak l	eternal, the Timeless One
Ak l	a devotee of Akal, a Sikh warrior, a supporter of the Akali movement or the Akali Party
Ak l Dal	"the army of the Ak l s," the political party of the Sikhs
Ak l Lahar	the Akali agitation of the 1920s for gurdwara reform
Ak l Takht	the throne or seat of the Guru's temporal authority at the Golden Temple of Amritsar
Akhand p th	a continuous reading of the Guru Granth Sahib
Am	honour
Amar	eternal, immortal
Amrit	the sweetened water used in the Sikh initiation ceremony
Amritdh r	an initiated Sikh, one who has taken amrit
An	see Am
pn	mine, yours, ours
Ard s	prayer, the formal Sikh prayer recited at the end of a Sikh ceremony

ry Samaj	a Hindu reform movement of the late ninetenth century
Asar	a sign, impression, effect
shram	the residence of a religious community
tm	the soul or spirit
Avt r	a divine incarnation
Aw z	a sound or voice
Ayurvedic	pertaining to traditional Indian medicine
B b	Father or Grandfather, a respectful title for a holy man
Bachint	without worry
Bais kh	the first day of Baisakh, the first month of the Indian calendar (13 April)
Bakhsh	forgiving
Bakhsh sh	a gift
Balb r	strength with courage
Baldev	the power of God
Bans	a descendent, one who belongs to a particular lineage or dynasty
Bar (Hindi)	turn, change, chance, rightful opportunity
Basant	the spring season
Batan	country
Bh g	fate, fortune, destiny
Bhagat	one who practices bhakti or loving devotion to a personal god
Bh	Brother, a respectful title for a man of learning and piety
Bhajan	prayer
Bhal	goodness, welfare, virtue
Bhath	a kiln or a large oven or furnace
Bhugta	a participant, receiver, enjoyer
Bikar	the name of an ancient Hindu king
Bind	a moment
Bol	speak, say
Br hman	the priestly caste, the highest caste among the Hindus
Cham r	the leatherworker caste
Chand ki Var	a poem from the Dasam Granth, a devotional collection attributed to Guru Gobind Singh

Chatter	wise, adept
Chawk d r	a watchman or guard
Chitra	one of the record-keepers in the court of Yama, the Lord of Death; picture, diagram, illustration
Chitragupta	the concious and unconscious parts of the mind
Chobd r	a gatekeeper
Ch hr	the sweeper caste
D	of
D d	one's paternal grandmother
Dal	a large army, a troop, a multitude or horde
D l	cooked lentils
Dalj t	the heart's victory
Dasam Granth	a collection of writings attributed to Guru Gobind Singh
Dast r	a turban
Desh	a country, region, place
Dh d	a musician, one who recites ballads
D w n	a congregation, tribunal, royal court
Do b	an area of central Punjab plains between the Beas and Sutlej rivers that contains the districts of Hoshiarpur and Jullundur
Doabi	a person from the Doaba area
Dupatt	a veil or scarf
Durb r	a royal court, audience hall
ek (Hindi)	one
Fateh	a conquest, victory, success
Ghadar	a mutiny or revolt
Ghadar Lahar	a revolutionary movement originating among the Sikhs in North America before 1914
Gi n	one possessing knowledge, a respected Sikh scholar or leader
Golak	a money-box or charity-box
Gor	a white person, a European
Granth	a book
Granth	a reader of the Guru Granth Sahib, a custodian of a gurdwara
Gu	wasted, lost, missed

Gund	a hooligan, hired goon
Gupta	one of the recordkeepers in the court of Yama, Lord of Death; subtle, secret, inner essence
Gurbachan	promised by the Guru
Gurb n	the Guru's testment, the Sikh scriptures
Gurcharan	at the Guru's feet
Gurdev	divine teacher
Gurdi l	the Guru's mercy
Gurdw r	"the door of the Guru," a Sikh temple or a place where the Sikh scriptures are kept
Gurmat	a resolution by an assembly of Sikhs
Gurmati	the Guru's wisdom (way), Sikhism
Gurmukh	the Guru's word
Gurmukh	the name of the alphabet used for the Punjabi language
Gurn m	the Guru in the Name
Gurpurab	an anniversary of the birth or death of one of the Ten Sikh Gurus
Gur	a spiritual teacher, enlightener
Gur Granth S hib	the sacred scripture of the Sikhs
Gutk	a manual or handbook
Hadisa	Hadith, the Muslim book of traditional sayings
Hadoor	the living presence
Hain	(you) are, (thou) art
Har (Har)	the Destroyer, God
Harbans	God's family
Harbhajan	Har (combined with) bhajan (prayer)
Harjinder	Indra, Lord of the gods
Hau-main	ego
Hav ld r	a sepoy sergeant in the Indian Army
Hukam	an order or command, God's will expressed in the universe
Hukam-n m	a decree issued by one of the Ten Sikh Gurus, or by panj piare from the Ak l Takht, or obtained from Guru Granth Sahib in a randomly selected passage
Ikbal/Iqbal	fortune
Jagat	the transient world

Jag r	a royal grant of land for meritorious service
Jagj t	world victory
Jamed r	a sepoy lieutenant in the Indian Army
J n	to go
Janat	the public, the masses
Janat Party	a coalition party – allied to the Akali Party in Punjab – which formed the government of India from 1977 to 1980
Japj	the morning prayer, composed by Guru Nanak
Jat	an agrarian caste
Jath	a corps, company, or band
Jathed r	a commander, the leader of a Sikh band
Jeewen (j wan)	life
Jhatt	moment
J	Sir, Madam (a term of endearment and respect)
J va	psyche, soul
Jogindr	devotee of Indra, Lord of the gods
Jot	the light (of the spirit), the essence
Jul h	the weaver caste
K / k (Hindi)	of
Kachchar	undershorts, one of the five Ks worn by Khalsa Sikhs
Kangh	hair comb, one of the five Ks worn by Khalsa Sikhs
Kar / karega	do / will do
Kar	steel bracelet worn on the right wrist, one of the five Ks worn by Khalsa Sikhs
Kar h	an iron bowl
Kar h parsh d	the Guru's food, made of flour, sugar, and butter in an iron bowl and dispensed in the gurdwara
Karam	fate, destiny, the law of cause and effect that binds the soul through successive lives
Karma	see Karam
Kart	Creator-Lord, Doer
Kart r	see Karta
Kaur	"Princess," the name taken by all female members of the Khalsa
Kesar	saffron
Kesha	hair, the uncut hair of the Sikhs, one of the five Ks worn by Khalsa Sikhs
Keshdh r	Sikhs who keep their hair uncut, Khalsa Sikhs

Kesk	a small turban
Khadar	coarse cotton cloth
Kh list n	the nation of the Khalsa, the name proposed for an independent Sikh state
Kh ls	"the Guru's own community," the Sikhs who follow the discipline established by Guru Gobind Singh
Kh lsa r j	the rule of Maharaja Ranjit Singh over Punjab, 1799–1839
Khand	the double-edged sword, a Sikh emblem
Khatr	a mercantile caste
Khem	happiness
Khidmat	service or duty
Khushwant	possessing happiness
Kirp	kindness, mercy, pity, grace
Kirp l	merciful, kind
Kirp n	the sword or dagger worn by Khalsa Sikhs as one of the five Ks
K rtan	the singing of hymns from the Guru Granth Sahib
K rtan jath	a troop of hymn-singing musicians
K rtan Soh l	a collection of five hymns sung before retiring at night
Kuld p	total light, the lamp of the family dynasty
Kulwant	esteemed family
Kurta pyj m	a loose-fitting shirt or jacket and trousers
Lakh	one hundred thousand
Lal	a beloved person, a ruby
Langar	the free kitchen of the gurdwara
Langdha	passing, going by, crossing, going over
Lath	a stick or club
Lok	people, folk
Mahinder	love of Indra, Lord of the gods
M jh	the area of Punjab between the Beas and Ravi rivers
M jhail	a person from the Majha area
Malk t	a property or landed estate
M lw	the area of Punjab south of the Sutlej River that includes the districts of Patiala, Ludhiana, and Ferozepur

M lw	a person from the Malwa area
Man	the mind, heart, intellect, or soul
Manj t	the victory of the soul
Manmohan	one who wins your heart
Mann	respect, prestige, pride
Mel	concord, unity, union
Mer	my
Mew	fruit or dried fruit, the fruit of service
Mohan	one who attracts you
Mohinder	*see* Mahinder
Moola	root, source, beginning
Mot	a large pearl
Mukht r	attorney, agent or deputy
Mukl v	the ceremony marking the consumation of a marriage
N	no
N l	with
N m	name; the Divine Name, the Immortal Creator
Nam z	the prayer of the Muslim
N m simaran	meditating on the divine name of God
N nakpanth	a follower of Guru Nanak
Nand	pleasure, joy, happiness
Nang	poor, penniless, naked
N n	one's maternal grandmother
Nark	hell
Nirank r	the Formless One
Nirank r	a sect, with origins in the nineteenth century, that emphasizes worship of God as "the Formless One"
Nirlep	disinterested, neutral, living in the world but not affected by it
Nish n	a sign, mark, flag, or standard
Nish n s hib	the Sikh flag, flown over a gurdwara
Nit nem	"daily rules," the set prayers recited as a daily routine
Or (Hindi)	again
Pachh n	identify, recognize, realize

Pahair	a period of three hours' duration, a quarter
Pahrei	periods of three hours' duration, quarters
P k	holy, pure, sacred
Pakka	solidly built, firm
Pakkainw l	one who lives in a brick house
Panch	a member of a village council
Panch yat	a village council or assembly
Pandit	a learned man or Brahman
Panj	five
Panj pi re	the "beloved five" who officiate at Sikh ceremonies and who represent the first five members of the Khalsa
Panth	the path, the way, the Sikh community
P r	across, over, beyond
Parega (Hindi)	(you) will have to
Park sh	light, light of day
Parm tm	God, the Supreme Being
Parsh d	a blessing, gift, sacred food
P th	a reader of scripture
Paviter	pure, sacred, holy
Pi r	dear, beloved
Poth	a book
Poth Sahib	Guru Granth Sahib, the sacred scripture of the Sikhs
Prabandhak	an administrator, manager, steward
Pr tam	beloved
Punj b S ba	the concept of a Punjabi-speaking state in which Sikhs would form a majority of the population
Purble	past
Purn	complete, full
Qaum	a people who stand together, a nation
Qaum	national
R d Sw m	a sect founded in the nineteenth century with many teachings similar to those of the Sikhs
R g	a melody
R g	a musician who sings in the gurdwara
R j	a kingdom, government or rule
R jwinder	rule of Indra, Lord of the gods
R m	God
R md si	Sikhs of the Chamar or leatherworkers' caste

R mghari	Sikhs from the Tarkhan or carpenters' caste but including other artisan castes as well
Rang	love (also colour)
Reha	keeping on (doing something)
Sabat	complete
Sabh	society
S dh	a holy man, a mendicant, one who renounces worldly possession
Sahaj	spontaneous, innate, natural
Sahajdh r	followers of Guru Nanak who do not adopt the Khalsa discipline
Sahaj p th	a complete reading of Guru Granth Sahib at a natural pace, with breaks for rest
S hib	Lord, Master, Sir (a title)
Sahiy (S h)	the fourth sage of emancipation, enjoying union with the creator
Samach r	news, tidings, information
Samadh	a deep trance, super-consciousness
Samundar	sea, ocean
Sangat	a religious assembly or congregation or fellowship
Sant	a spiritual person, a holy man, one whose nature has achieved a perfect balance
Santokh	contentment
Sans r	the world or universe
Sant sip h	one who combines spirituality with bravery
Sarang	a stringed instrument or the musician who plays it
Sard r	Commander, Chief (a form of address for all Sikh men)
Saroop	one's own true form or nature
Sarop	a robe of honour
Sarpanch	the headman of a village council or panchayat
Sat	truth
Satsang	spitual fellowship
Sev	dedicated communal service, particularly service in a gurdwara
SGPC	Shiromani Gurdwara Prabandhak Committee, administrative committee responsible for Sikh shrines in Punjab
Shabad	the Word of God expressed in a hymn in the Guru Granth Sahib

Shahid/ n	martyr/s
Shardai	a sweet cold drink with ground almonds
Shiromani Ak l Dal	"the army of the Akalis," the Akali Party
Sikh	a learner or disciple, one who follows the teachings of the Sikh Gurus
Sikh Gur s	the unbroken succession of ten Gurus, beginning with Guru Nanak and followed by nine successors, each appointed by his predecessor

Gur N nak	1469–1539
Gur Angad	1539–52
Gur Amard s	1552–74
Gur R md s	1574–81
Gur Arjan	1581–1606
Gur Har Gobind	1606–44
Gur Har Ra	1644–61
Gur Har Krishan	1661–64
Gur Teg Bah dur	1664–75
Gur Gobind Singh	1675–1708

Simaran	meditation; recollection, remembrance, recognition
Singh	"lion," the name taken by all male members of the Khalsa
Singh Sabh	a reform movement among the Sikhs, beginning in the late nineteenth century
Sip h	sepoy, a native Indian soldier
Sir	head
Sohan	I-am-He, beautiful
Somosa	pastry stuffed with potatoes and vegetables
Soorat	aspect, visage, shape, situation
Sr	a word used for respect
Sr R g	one of six major sections of Guru Granth Sahib
S b	a province
S bed r	a rank in the Indian army; the governor of a province
Surinder	song of Indra, Lord of the gods
Surj t	song of victory
Sw m	lord, master, one who has authority; a title given to religious teachers
Tahs l	subdistrict

Takht	"throne," one of five seats of temporal authority for the Sikhs (Amritsar, Patna, Nander, Anandpur, Damdama)
T n	then
T r	a star or planet
Tarsem	compassion
Teja	splendour, strength, lustre
Terai	thine, yours
T rath	a holy bathing spot, a place of pilgrimage
Toon	thou, you
Trauj	the third ceremony for a couple, following the marriage and muklava ceremonies
Udam	industry, effort
Ujjal	clear, sparkling, bright
Vaid	a physician who practices traditional Indian medicine
Visva	world, universe, cosmos
W h gur	God, Almighty
Yog	one who practices yoga